A Martyr for Sin

A Martyr for Sin

Rochester's Critique of Polity, Sexuality, and Society

Kirk Combe

DELAWARE

Newark: University of Delaware Press
London: Associated University Presses

Associated University Presses
440 Forsgate Drive
Cranbury, NJ 08512

Associated University Presses
16 Barter Street
London WC1A 2AH, England

Associated University Presses
P.O. Box 338, Port Credit
Mississauga, Ontario
Canada L5G 4L8

The paper used in this publication meets the requirements
of the American National Standard for Permanence of Paper
for Printed Library Materials Z39.48-1984.

Library of Congress Cataloging-in-Publication Data

Combe, Kirk.
  A martyr for sin : Rochester's critique of polity, sexuality, and society / Kirk Combe.
    p.   cm.
  Includes bibliographical references (p.   ) and index.
  ISBN 0-87413-647-4 (alk. paper)
  1. Rochester, John Wilmot, Earl of, 1647–1680—Political and social views.   2. Politics and literature—Great Britain—History—17th century.   3. Literature and society—England—History—17th century.   4. Political poetry, English—History and criticism.   5. Social problems in literature.   6. Sex in literature. I. Title.
PR3669.R2Z55   1998
821'.4—dc21   97-40382
                                                                            CIP

For Brenda,
who has put up with the most

In memory of Carter Kim Combe, 1953–1994;
gentleman, scholar, attorney, brother

Contents

Acknowledgments

PERSONAL debts of gratitude are, after all, the most important when acknowledging the many people who facilitate a book such as this. I will credit my family first. Brenda Boyle has been vitally involved with every stage of development for this work—from its inception, through its planning and drafting, to its final form. As her spouse, I am fortunate to benefit not only from her emotional and material support, but from her abilities as a keen critical reader and thinker. To our children, Clayton, Olivia, and Hannah, I also owe thanks for generously sharing their father—perforce—with so many hours of research time. Equally, immeasurable gratitude must be expressed to my parents, Bettie and Louis Combe, for their unending care and support as I pursue my personal and professional goals. Their generous backing of my early educational career is overshadowed only by their constantly urging me to do whatever it is I want to do. For this luxury, I thank them deeply. Finally, I want to acknowledge the implicit influence of my late brother, Carter Combe, on this book. Had he not turned to the practice of law, Carter assuredly would have been a far better scholar than myself. His intellectual standards are ones I always strive to achieve.

Because portions of this book trace their origins back to my doctoral work on late seventeenth-century British satire, several teachers and scholars at Oxford University must be recognized for their contributions. Dr. Roy Park of University College not only acted as a referee for my application to enter postgraduate study but suggested satire as an area of potential research. Dr. John Wilders, formerly of Worcester College, not only admitted me into that college, but he acted as an early guide and teacher in Restoration Studies and, I am fortunate to say, has become a continuing friend. To him and his wife, Benedikte, I owe many thanks for their support and encouragement both academic and personal. As my first supervisor, Dr. Glenn Black of Oriel College gave me sound advice, guidance, and criticism as he helped me find my academic path. He gen-

9

erously arranged both teaching and publishing opportunities for me as well during my graduate career. Prof. Emrys Jones of New College acted as my thesis supervisor for the bulk of its writing. He patiently endured many sessions with me while I struggled to formulate my ideas; he also meticulously read and rendered a critique of everything I wrote, allowing neither sloppy thinking nor writing to stand unchallenged. To all of these people, I offer my sincere thanks. Also, while at Oxford, I was lucky to become acquainted with, and to be included in, the commonwealth of letters of the late Dr. Harold Brooks. My work benefited greatly from his unrivaled knowledge and legendary magnanimity.

Thanks are due as well to several professional colleagues who have played a part in the development of my work on Rochester. To my fellow Oxford graduate student and continuing colleague and friend, Dr. Timothy Raylor of Carleton College, I owe special gratitude. Sharing an enthusiasm for the literature of the Commonwealth and the Restoration periods, we have had frequent discussions over the years that have sparked many useful insights for me. Similar appreciation must be extended to Dr. Christopher Wheatley of the Catholic University of America. As instructors at the University of Tennessee at Knoxville, Chris and I not only suffered through an unspeakably heavy course load together, but over beers discussed the finer points of Restoration drama and culture. In the same vein I would like to acknowledge the friendship and collegiality of Dr. Brian A. Connery of Oakland University. Our collaboration as coeditors of a book and as cochairs of scholarly panels on the subject of satire has helped refine many of my notions about the genre. With regard to more senior colleagues, at least two have offered me generous aid. Dr. Jack Armistead, formerly of the University of Tennessee at Knoxville and currently at Tennessee Technological University, helped secure my entrance into university teaching and has provided guidance in my early efforts at publication. Dr. J. Douglas Canfield of the University of Arizona read portions of my manuscript and offered invaluable counsel for some revisions. I very much welcomed the advice of these established scholars. Closer to home, two current colleagues with whom I teach at Denison University have been instrumental in revising and expanding my ideas about literary, critical, and social theory. I therefore offer thanks to Dr. Karl Sandin of the Art

History Department and to Dr. Richard Hood of the English Department.

Finally, I want to acknowledge the help of the many librarians who have made my work possible. These include the staffs of the Bodleian Library, the English Faculty Library, and the Worcester College Library, all in Oxford. I also want to thank the staffs of the British Library, the University of Tennessee at Knoxville Library, and the Denison University Library—particularly the interlibrary loan department. I also want to thank Denison University for its generous support of my scholarly efforts in the form of grants, travel support, and research sabbatical leave.

A Martyr for Sin

1
Current Theory

What more can be expected from a life spent in ostentatious
contempt of regularity?
> —Dr. Johnson, *Lives of the English Poets*

CERTAINLY the writings of John Wilmot, earl of Rochester, summon a variety of critical interpretation. No one should be sur-
prised by the statement that any satisfactory reading of his
works must involve a theoretical approach of some sophistication. I will not pretend to offer here *the* strategy by which to
respond to Rochester's poems and plays. Instead, I would like
to demonstrate one productive way we might read what we
attribute to his hand.[1] If I have an overriding theoretical concern for my inquiry, it is to address, using the case of Rochester, Edward Said's question, "Is there no way of dealing with
a text and its worldly circumstances fairly?"[2] It seems to me
that Rochester's verse affords us an unusually good opportunity to explore what has become, perhaps, our fundamental
critical dilemma as literary scholars at the end of the twentieth century.

Among specialists there is a relative paucity of comment
regarding the earl's politics—save perhaps among Rochester's
biographical critics early in this century, but even there the
commentary is not extensive. While Rochester is acknowledged as an influential poet, patron, courtier, and notorious
bon vivant about town for roughly a fifteen-year period before
his death in 1680, equally often he is viewed essentially as
apolitical.[3] In some odd way we regard him at a distance from
the considerable civil tensions at work in England during the
1660s and 1670s. Ostensibly, during his brief and madcap life,
Rochester was too busy imbibing and swiving to notice much
of the affairs of state going on around him. Yet in light of the

fact that Rochester was a gentleman of the bedchamber to the king, a peer in the House of Lords, and generally a member in good standing of the power elite of Restoration England, complete with all the trappings of pensions and appointments, it seems dangerous to accede to this level of disengagement from him. True, Rochester was no duke of Buckingham or Lord Shaftesbury; he expressed disdain for political strivers, intriguers, and "businesse" in general. But even if his role in that echelon of society were primarily one of a zany to Charles, to think his enmity constitutes apoliticality is oversimplification both of himself and of his poetry.[4] Rochester possessed a keen critical eye along with a satiric bent of mind. He neither lacked opinions nor was shy in expressing them; he also loved the art of dissimulation in his personal affairs as well as in his verse. Given the combination of such a personality within such a highly politicized environment, I doubt that we can safely dismiss the notion of Rochester's politics. That leaves us, however, with the admittedly perplexing task of trying to *identify* Rochester's politics. By and large, commentators who attempt to characterize Rochester's political beliefs proceed conventionally. Did he align himself with the Court or Country party, with the developing Tory or Whig faction? The consensus, of course, is Whiggish leanings for Rochester late in his life. One critic even goes so far as to stamp Rochester's as "savage republican verse."[5] For the majority of commentators who ignore Rochester's politics, concentration falls on analyses of his intellectual, ethical, and aesthetic beliefs. We have traced philosophical and poetical influences in Rochester. If consensus exists in this pursuit, it is only to acknowledge the intricacy of much of Rochester's writing, the apparent skepticism if not iconoclasm of his mind, along with, perhaps, a predilection to turn the world on its head.[6] It strikes me that we have been unimaginative in not combining better these two endeavors, that is, the recognition of the political in Rochester with the analysis of the intellectual and the textual.

I see Rochester's poems pursuing during the early modern period an agenda of exposing the relationship between *truth* and *power* in Michel Foucault's sense of those terms. In other words, these works display a level both of conceptual awareness and linguistic finesse capable of enmeshing the reader in what Foucault calls "the mechanics of power"; potentially, this might lead a reader to a realization of "historically how effects of truth are produced within discourses which in themselves are neither true nor false."[7] Most scholars are quite familiar by now with Foucault's idea that not only is "truth" a worldly, arbitrary, completely human construct, but that within a given society it becomes naturalized and institutionalized into an oppressive and self-serving "régime of truth"—in effect forming a politicized language system highly susceptible to semiotic scrutiny.[8] I believe many of Rochester's works perform such a localized semiotic investigation and attack: they debunk particular truth-producing mechanisms of Charles II's court; they unmask certain affectations of the luminaries of Whitehall; to employ a current usage that Rochester himself might have appreciated, they call bullshit a range of patrician social and literary practices. Obviously, these are political undertakings.

Foucault maintains that rules of right in society are implemented by the relations of power in the production of discourses of truth: "We are subjected to the production of truth through power and we cannot exercise power except through the production of truth."[9] Power functions in a netlike organization in which individuals "are always in the position of simultaneously undergoing and exercising this power." Foucault stresses that individuals are the "vehicles of power, not its points of application." Thus power holds good not so much as an oppressive force but as a productive network that runs through the whole social body, inducing pleasure, forming knowledge, and producing discourse.[10] At the same time, however, Foucault views the interplay of truth and power—that is, politics—as the continuation of war by other means. The seductive discourses of truth in fact mask mechanisms of authority and the hostile engagement of contending social forces.[11] In short, rights and laws *are* violence; they do not prevent violence *except* to the ruling class. I propose that Rochester in his writings is a participant in and, more important, a severe critic of this Foucauldian truth-and-power conflict. His verse, prose, and drama apprehend, expose, and censor the general politics of truth contrived by the ultimate privileged power broker of the day—the court of Charles.

Like Nietzsche (and, certainly, others), Rochester seems to think that human cognition leads to a terrible egoism, and that the chief power of the human intellect is that of duplicity. Nietzsche notes: "In man this art of dissimulation reaches its acme of perfection: in him deception, flattery, falsehood and fraud, slander, display, pretentiousness, disguise, cloaking convention, and acting to others and to himself in short, the continual fluttering to and fro around the *one* flame—Vanity."[12] These ideas aptly characterize what critics often point to as the strength and focus of Rochester's satires (e.g., *A Satire Against Mankind*)—that is, castigating purblind humanity.[13] Notably, Nietzsche also serves as the basis for both Foucault and Edward W. Said's combination of "a rigorous textual awareness with a practical involvement in the politics of reading."[14] Thus, as in the works of these three later thinkers, I see in Rochester's writings a deep unwillingness to accept spurious notions of objectivity, universality, and order over what manifestly is to be taken instead as subjective, individual, and chaotic reality.[15] Moreover, each of these thinkers, Rochester included, calls into question the nature of language and texts as well as implicates into the equation the powerful notion that language and text are *not* separate from the worldly circumstances of their production nor the political will-to-power. I think any sensitive reading of Rochester's works must take into account their simultaneous deconstructive (i.e., textual) and politicized (i.e., circumstantial) qualities.

I read Rochester, then, as an agent of chaos against order. In essence, his works create a truthless environment; perhaps we can regard their author as a truth-seeker who realizes that there *is* no truth—only fabrications of truth driven by various political agendas. As with Nietzsche and Foucault, Rochester will not abide system or truth that claims to be above rhetoric. Instead, Rochester engages in overt rhetoric not to assert a contending "truth" but to reduce all texts to the free play of *politicized* signification (to alter somewhat what perhaps has become a hackneyed phrase of postmodern theory). In other words, Rochester's discursive practice is to expose discursive practices. That intellectual and textual *act* is his political agenda in the world. Within a highly localized context, his most complicated textual structures demonstrate that everything is nonsense—to include his own texts. This is why in numerous works by Rochester so many viewpoints are voiced—often oddly privileged and disparaged at the same time as in the case of the narrator, Artemisa, in *A Letter from Artemisa to Chloe*—and why so many interpretations seem reasonably available to us. Furthermore, because of these unusual literary qualities, labels of "apolitical" and "restless" perfunctorily are applied to Rochester.[16]

Specifically, Rochester's works accomplish this political

agenda by exerting enormous textual pressure on their reader. If, as Paul De Man suggests, rhetoric "radically suspends logic and opens up vertiginous possibilities of referential aberration," and if a literary text "simultaneously asserts and denies the authority of its own rhetorical mode,"[17] then Rochester's poems push these textual circumstances to an extreme. It seems to me that Rochester does not want to be an *author* in the traditional sense of the term; rather, he seems to prefigure Barthes's notion of the *scriptor*.[18] In many of his works, Rochester does everything he can to obscure his authorial being— and by no means solely for the practical consideration of safety afforded by anonymity. Moreover, he also addles the nature of his narrators, making them sometimes maddeningly cryptic. Based on the writings, I believe Rochester carries out these stratagems intentionally in order to *promote* the possibility of *meanings*. Quite the opposite of John Dryden, say, in *Mac Flecknoe* or in *Absalom and Achitophel*, Rochester does not try to close a conversation; he does his damnedest to start one. When taken to an extreme, Rochester's writings seem *consciously* to refuse to assign, in Barthes's words, a "secret" to the text—that is, an ultimate meaning. According to Barthes, such indeterminacy in literature is truly liberatory, even anti-theological in its denial of God's infrastructure.[19] I would speculate that this textual activity is precisely Rochester's ambition as the scriptor of these works. I assert that Rochester's *writings* in fact perform, in Barthes's terms, such a *revolutionary function*.[20] I would go so far as to venture the idea that Rochester's works do *not* covertly function, as Said suggests, as colonizing agents in an oppressor (author)-oppressed (reader) relationship,[21] but in fact seek to explode that hidden agenda of textuality. And here we encounter the point where tremendous strain on the reader comes into play.

If, as Barthes claims, the notion of author is to be de-emphasized—that is, if as critics we restrain from contriving intellectual if not personal biographies for the authors whose works we scrutinize—then the real location of interpretation exists not with the diachronic (and ultimately mythical) author, but with the synchronic reader, the worldly conditions that gave rise to the text, and the text itself.[22] In other words, if Rochester's poems start a conversation, it is that conversation of the 1670s to which we must plug in and listen. Those texts by design speak to those readers.[23] Because of their extraordinary nature, Rochester's writings insist on (as opposed to conceal) the fact that their reader must play the part of what Charles Peirce calls the "interpretant"—a *reader* of the sign and so a forger of its signified.[24] By doing everything they can to minimize the dependability of the author and the narrator, and to maximize the role of the reader as an interpretant, Rochester's writings place the reader in an acute hermeneutical predicament—and, perhaps, trap. Since the works themselves offer no certainty, the reader is left, hopelessly, to look for certainty himself. Any he finds (and I use deliberately the masculine pronoun), upon reflection, will prove to be contrived. My project, therefore, is to investigate the exact nature of the textual impasse Rochester's writings posed to contemporary readers. This undertaking entails recapturing the rhetorical play Rochester's writings might have had for their original audience. Admittedly, the retrieval process cannot help but be imperfect. Warren Chernaik notes, quite correctly, that we still lack even a reliable biography of Rochester.[25] I am acutely aware as well that much in reception theory prohibits the very possibility of my undertaking. Still, if we are to deal fairly both with Rochester's texts *and* with the worldly circumstances that gave them rise, a thoughtful attempt to reconstruct his literary and social locality must be made. Said points out that "texts have ways of existing that even in their most rarefied form are always enmeshed in circumstance, time, place, and society—in short, they are in the world, and hence worldly."[26] Accordingly, I will proceed on the assumption that textual undecidability does not automatically—if really ever—bring with it absolute historical unknowability. Indeed, in the case of Rochester's works, it seems to be the key to better understanding their original place—and politicality—in the world.

Therefore the nature of my study is one of applied criticism that is theoretical in a particular way—that is to say, a theoretically informed close reading. Perhaps my theoretical orientation can be called *post-postmodern*, though I do not favor that convoluted term. Nonetheless, in trying to cope with a text and with its worldliness, as Said encourages, I have just asserted a way to read Rochester's writings that might at first appear to be a paradoxical if not a contradictory mixture of deconstructive indeterminability *and* historical fixedness. Frankly, I see little alternative when attempting to combine in a critical study of literature textuality *and* historicity. One must, I think, endeavor to place undecidability *within* a specific locale. Secondarily the effect of Rochester's texts may be to preclude all meaning and universality in, oddly, a kind of inversely meaningful and universalized way—that is, to borrow phrasing from Terry Eagleton, as only a celebration of serene linguistic nihilism practiced, for example, by the "mischievously radical" Yale school of deconstruction.[27] But such a generalized, diachronic reading of texts as *only* the free play of signification negates the very real and singular—and, I believe, critically primary—social conditions in which these texts originated and functioned in the world. I propose that Rochester seeks to create indeterminability and textual chaos *as a means* of disrupting the particular regime of truth in which he finds himself. Thus, we must recognize both Rochester's textual disruption and radical critique of language not unlike those of Nietzsche and Jacques Derrida (and with the welcomed theoretical help of a Yale schooler such as Paul De Man) *as well as* the ideological and materialist moment at which his works unleash their attack on the ruling class (by no means a huge critical stretch given that materialist and Marxist critics on the whole see language not as stable but rather as a field of ideological contention). In my view, the synchronic *forms* a part of the diachronic; in the particular *is* the general; Ferdinand de Saussure's notion of parole exists in *partnership* with his idea of langue. The reverse of each of these statements is accurate as well. As critics we can hardly afford to concentrate on one side of these things at the expense of the other.[28] To impose utter meaninglessness on texts is as artificial and limiting as saddling them with absolute meaning—and both approaches tend to nullify any localized significance for literary works. Moreover, recognition of the trickery of language should not—indeed cannot—freeze us into inaction either critically or politically. History may be a fabrication and a lie, but it is one that wants discussion and participation.[29] In this spirit I offer my necessarily imperfect and provisional discussion of Rochester's works as generalized linguistic chaos thrown at particularized political order. My hope is that the study will add some intelligent observation to a continuing conversation about an intriguing body of early modern literary expression. By applying mainly the social critique of Foucault to Rochester's writings, I argue that their obscured political nature can be appreciated more distinctly. This critical circumstance is perhaps similar to our not realizing that Newton's physics were flawed until, nearly two centuries after they were advanced, we developed instruments fine enough to measure their discrepancies. In kind, until Foucault and others analyzed and dissected the workings of the modern state in detail, Rochester's works were too finely political to gain our notice.[30]

To return then to the theories of Foucault, the core of my critical investigation will be to treat Rochester's writings as a particular event of "subjugated knowledge." Foucault defines this concept as blocs of historical knowledge hitherto obscured within the body of functionalist and systematizing theory.[31] Such is the condition, I believe, of Rochester's works when they routinely are stigmatized as apolitical productions. Subjugated knowledge, for Foucault, is "concerned with a *historical knowledge of struggles*" that exist in popular knowledge but that erudite scholarship tends to ignore; they are then "the memory of hostile encounters which even up to this day have been confined to the margins of knowledge." The reemergence of such knowledge requires genealogical research, characterized by Foucault as "a painstaking rediscovery of struggles together with the rude memory of their conflicts" that can occur only when "the tyranny of globalising discourses" is removed.[32] Thus, I will endeavor to practice what Foucault calls "effective" history, namely, that which breaks our faith in teleology, introduces discontinuity, and runs contrary to totalitarian theory. Foucault notes "that what this essentially local character of criticism indicates in reality is an autonomous, non-centralised kind of theoretical production, one that is to say whose validity is not dependent on the approval of the established régimes of thought."[33]

My repoliticizing of Rochester thus involves overturning considerable conventional wisdom about his writings combined with reestablishing the local power struggle in which he was engaged. As just outlined, the site of this hostile encounter—and so the form of Foucault's "popular knowledge (*le savoir des gens*)"[34] demanding retrieval—is the courtly libertine milieu in which Rochester lived and wrote. Especially amid the allusions of satire and the conventions of love lyric Rochester's writings seek to disrupt the entitled order of the Restoration elite. Moreover, my method will be to study the manifestations of truth and power not from the top downward but from the bottom upward. Foucault suggests: "What is needed is a study of power in its external visage, at the point where it is in direct and immediate relationship with that which we can provisionally call its object, its target, its field

of application, there—that is to say—where it installs itself
and produces its real effects." Rochester's literary clash with
courtly authority marks, in this instance, the localized battle-
ground where the mechanics of power unfold. In attempting
to "grasp subjection in its material instance as a constitution
of subjects,"[35] I hope to turn Rochester from historical object
into active subject as he resists forces intent on demarcating
his social being.

Importantly, at the heart of Rochester's critique of Restoration culture is the figure of Charles II. Foucault believes that
since medieval times royal power has provided the essential
focus around which Western legal thought has been formulated.[36] The essential role of the theory of right, therefore, has
been to fix the legitimacy of sovereign power—that is, both to
justify the rule of a monarch and to provide the legal obliga-
tion to obey that monarch. Concurrently, according to Foucault, such a "system of right" is "designed to eliminate the
fact of domination and its consequences." Foucault's historical
project, however, centers upon analysis that inverts this legal
paradigm in order "to give due weight . . . to the fact of domination, to expose both its latent nature and its brutality."[37] It
strikes me that, in satirizing the ambience of Charles's court,
Rochester's writings engage in the same counterhegemonic activity. In resisting his sovereign, Rochester calls into question
the very legal and cultural foundation of his society; furthermore, similar to Foucault and to Derrida and to Nietzsche,
as well as to numerous materialist and Marxist critics from
Bakhtin to Eagleton, Rochester bases his challenge upon a critique of how language and knowledge are manipulated by
those in power to maintain their ascendancy. Just as significant is the fact that Rochester voices his censure precisely at
the moment in English history when the mode in which power
was exercised could no longer be defined exclusively in terms
of the sovereign-subject relationship. The onset of the early
modern period in the West is marked by a distinct shift in the
nature and production of power. Foucault reports that "in the
seventeenth and eighteenth centuries, we have the production
of an important phenomenon, the emergence, or rather the
invention, of a new mechanism of power possessed of highly
specific procedural techniques, completely novel instruments,
quite different apparatuses, and which is also, I believe, abso-
lutely incompatible with the relations of sovereignty."[38] Foucault speaks, of course, of the formation of market capitalism

and democratic rule. Again, it seems to me that Rochester's works both exist on the brink and tellingly express the disposition of this new era of polity in England. The earl's literary rebukes of Charles as well as his Whiggish leanings are decidedly antifeudal, anticourtly, and antisovereign. Rochester assails the traditional sovereign-subject relationship. While of course no systematic capitalist or democrat, Rochester prefigures—probably without realizing it—the coming rule of parliament guided by innovative political thinkers such as Locke.

That Rochester's attacks may have been motivated more by a personal antipathy for Charles and his retinue than by his participation in global political theory does not lessen, in my view, the significance of his early modern utterance. In fact, the very particularity of his discontent with the general politics of truth in which he found himself may serve to heighten the importance of his objections. In one sense, Rochester had no choice but to attack the specific power structure in which he lived. Even when satirists write obliquely, very often their works are read by contemporaries allegorically, that is, as coded assaults on particular victims of the day. Allegorical and politicized reading was a widely practiced habit of the Restoration period. I would venture to say that many if not most of Rochester's immediate readers found civil import in the calumny of many of his satires. Contemporarily, Rochester was *bound* to be political. In another sense, too, one could argue that the more forthright the local satiric attack, the more keen and powerful is its ultimate political consequence. (A quality, I would contend, not lost on Andrew Marvell contemporaneously or, later, on Swift.) If Rochester really wanted to get under the skin of Charles and his crew, what better way than to scour their very hides? The painter Henri Matisse remarked once that all art bears the mark of its historical surroundings, but that great art is that in which this mark is most deeply imprinted. Likewise, it seems to me that the greatest satire is that which has embedded in it most deeply synchronous manifestations of folly and knavery. If as subsequent readers of this satire we have difficulty appreciating its coeval targets and issues, that is our fault and problem, not those of the satire. Again, I see the particular and the general in Rochester's writings being vitally linked and cosupportive, not mutually exclusive.

To address finally a related matter of satiric theory, I see, if not an absolute divide, at least a clear distinction between what I assert as Rochester's Foucauldian project against Charles and the normal debunking function occurring in satire. If not entirely extrageneric, Rochester's satire is extreme in its exfoliation of social convention (see chapter 3 for a discussion of my take on Rochester's place in contemporary and current satiric theory). Rochester's radical view of language best accounts for this difference. While satirists such as Dryden, Marvell, and John Oldham alongside Rochester, John Cleveland and Abraham Cowley before him, and Alexander Pope and Jonathan Swift after him work essentially within the superstructure of the dominant belief system (which includes contending political factions) when penning their satires, Rochester not only calls into question that current system, but, as I hope to show, calls into doubt all system whatever. During the period only the now little-read miscellany satires of Samuel Butler share somewhat, in my view, in Rochester's politicized deconstruction of the English state. Moreover, recent critical thinking about satire raises the possibility that, contrary to New Critical or structural or psychological interpretations of the genre, the normal debunking function of satire is often closer to Rochester's radical project than critics hitherto have taken the time to notice.[39] Rochester's Foucauldian satire then may not be extrageneric at all; instead, it might well belong to—if not significantly innovate upon—an important strain of satire that always has been with us and that has become increasingly prominent—both in artistic production and in critical recognition—during the modern and postmodern (and post-postmodern?) eras.

The matter of current theory having been addressed, then, I begin in the following chapter my consideration of the historical site in which Rochester encountered the machinations of Restoration truth and power.

2

Contemporary Idiom

Nay so confirm'd was he in Sin, that he lived, and oftentimes almost died, a Martyr for it.
                                    —Robert Parsons, *A Sermon preached at the*
                                                   Earl of Rochester's Funeral

ROCHESTER's contemporary reader is quite a specific creature. Dustin Griffin defines the court poetry of Charles II's reign as that

> circulated at the court (if not actually produced there), *about* life at court, *by* highly placed courtiers, not senior ministers to be sure, but intimates and social equals of the king who read and enjoyed their work and distributed to them royal favors in the form of gifts, titles, and places. Court poems are designed initially for an intimate audience of friends and social equals.[1]

Primarily, Rochester writes for virtually a captive audience of sophisticated, privileged, socially powerful men who to one degree or another consider themselves libertines.[2] Perhaps most familiar to us of the verse produced and consumed by this circle of wits is curiously erudite obscenity that displays, among other things, the educated mind at lascivious play (e.g., "In the Fields of Lincoln's Inn"). Such cosmopolitan dirty word games are a signature mark for this association, and Rochester plays the game dexterously. In fact, I believe Rochester never writes with this genre completely out of his mind. However, as asserted in chapter 1, Rochester's writings also comprise a notable strain of that which dismantles the very core of Charles's hedonistic elite—to include both all those who participated in it as well as all those would-be rakes who aspired to its ideals. Rochester's lyrics often perform a surreptitious function of superficially celebrating the libertine cult while in

26

fact advancing devastating criticism of it. Far from pandering to an audience biased toward witty, sexually explicit verse, these works covertly reveal that same appreciative, ostensibly urbane male readership, to include the king, to be in truth self-deluding and ignorant. Via irony, ambiguity, narrative self-deprecation (a peculiar trait for sexual verse), and cognitive mayhem, the poems set a linguistic trap for the unwary reader. That trap is, simply enough, if the reader is titillated by this, the reader is a fool. Rochester's game is subtle and, if appreciated, personally humiliating and intellectually devastating. Moreover, it is played out not only in the obscene lyrics, but within the philosophical and skeptical setting of the major satires, within the banter of Rochester's prose and dramatic farce as well as in the one serious tragic piece he wrote for the stage, and within the seemingly innocuous political squibs and impromptus penned at court. Exploiting the various mediums of courtly literature, Rochester attacks the hegemonic fraternity of the day. In his role as acknowledged high priest of Charles's profligate courtiers, the earl is icon and iconoclast at once.

Let us call the specific object of these attacks the target fop. He is the reader being placed under explicative pressure by Rochester's works. Like Rochester himself, the target fop may be characterized as a highborn, well-educated, egocentric man, much of whose behavior is prompted by a combination of social position and carnal pleasure. Carnally, he both oppresses women and simultaneously is a slave to the object of his oppression.[3] Socially, his entitled status enables him to indulge in actions and in a self-image beyond those of the normal citizen. However, I will expand somewhat on Griffin's characterization of the audience for court poetry by extending that readership downward along the aristocratic pecking order. Included among target fops, I believe, should be all of those members of the gentry with aspirations of gaining positions within courtly circles. Recently, Timothy Raylor has demonstrated a well-established tradition prior to the Restoration of clubs and fraternities among precisely these types of men. Essentially conservative groups, such gatherings of young men were eager to elevate themselves as part of a gentlemanly social and literary culture distinct from, and in opposition to, the rising "bourgeois Puritanism and enthusiasm" of the city.[4] After 1660, this kind of clubbing gained in significance in England. I see these men keen on participating in

Charles's regime of truth as potential victims of Rochester's writings as well. In short, then, the target fop is the smart libertine gentleman of the court and, by extension, of the town. Whether a courtier; an idle aristocrat; a civil servant; a career officer, or cleric, of the judiciary; or a student at the Inns of Court, this manner of rake and would-be rake, wit and near-wit (and often nitwit) was ubiquitous in the salon, on the Mall, in the coffeehouse, at the playhouse, and about the stews. Educated, powerful, and to varying degrees beyond the reach of social sanction, the target fop represents an unequivocal political force in Restoration London.[5] He is Rochester's fellow gang member, of a rival foppish faction to the Ballers, or someone hopeful of initiation into that privileged league in general. Whichever, he is celebrated constantly in the comedic drama of the period—sometimes extremely ambivalently, as in the case, I believe, of Etherege's *Man of Mode* or of Wycherley's *Country Wife*.

The predicament Rochester's works pose to the target fop is this. If the fop does not realize what the piece is on about with regard to exposing the mechanics of power and the manufacture of truth, he condemns himself a fool—similar to those ridiculed in, say, *Tunbridge Wells* and *Timon*.[6] If the fop does understand the nature of the linguistic showdown before him, he is rendered foolish again, but in a different way. Once he comprehends that chaos prevails over all attempts at human order, when, as Nietzsche says, "truths are illusions of which one has forgotten that they *are* illusions,"[7] then intellectually he is left hopelessly afloat in "Doubt's boundless sea." As indicated by *A Satire Against Mankind* (see 8–24), reason and "bladders of Philosophy" will then do him no good. Thus Rochester's poems anticipate in two vital ways Nietzsche's assertion that humans, like cognitively dysfunctional moths, continually flutter to and fro around the flame of Vanity. Either they exercise their reader, depending on his critical acumen, in excessive pride and conceit, or they reveal to him that all human endeavor lacks real value, that civilization is in fact something worthless, trivial, or pointless. When Marianne Thormählen astutely describes Rochester's political satire as "topical innuendo, easily lost on a reader unfamiliar with Restoration history, fused with personal malice, often on a sexual basis,"[8] I would include in that category all works that assail the target fop; these are political statements as well. Equally, I would add to that poetic formula a clandestine agenda of iconoclastic

Pyrrhonism. Altogether, these qualities prevail over the whole of Rochester's canon.

Furthermore, I believe contemporaries, if not recognizing these qualities in Rochester's writing, had vigorous inklings of their presence. Critics often cite Andrew Marvell's alleged characterization of Rochester as "the best English Satyrist" who "had the right veine" of satire.[9] I wonder if Marvell, most adept at linguistic play himself, in fact praises the exfoliative nature of the earl's verse. Friends and enemies alike (save for Mulgrave) credit Rochester with sparkling and matchless wit. More than a bromide, the comment grants insight into the *nature* of Rochester's thinking. Francis Fane, who apparently knew Rochester personally, ascribes to the nobleman an unusual combination of unorthodoxy and orthodoxy at once. Calling Rochester the Lord Bacon of his times, Fane remarks:

> that if ever there were a beam of Knowledge, immediately deriv'd from God, upon any Man, since the Creation, there is one upon your self . . . you are an Enthusiast in Wit; a Poet and Philosopher by Revelation; and have already in your tender Age, set out such new and glorious Lights in Poetry, yet these so orthodox and Unquestionable, that all the Heroes of Antiquity, must submit, or Homer and Virgil be judg'd Nonconformists.[10]

According to Fane, Rochester's views are classical *and* radical, of God yet new to humanity. Moreover, the politico-religious terms used to describe Rochester and his verse—*Enthusiast, Revelation, Lights,* and *Nonconformists*—normally denote disparagement of canting puritanism. However, here they praise the individual lights of Rochester's unique mind—a mind so fine that even Homer and Virgil must fall into the orbit of its thoughts. Undoubtedly Fane's descriptive Enthusiasm gets the better of him in this dedication to Rochester; still, his comments illustrate a potentially telling feature of Rochester's works. As in the case of Bacon's innovations toward experimental science, in challenging the status quo Rochester's writings also examine the fundaments of a traditionally empowered view of the world and reveal cracks in its foundation.

Contemporaries and near-contemporaries also give much play to the notion of the originality of Rochester's expression. Comparing satires by Rochester and Nicolas Boileau-Despréaux, Thomas Rymer asserts that "My Lord *Rochester* gives us another Cast of Thought, another Turn of Expression, a strength, a Spirit, and Manly Vigour, which the *French* are utter strangers to" (*Heritage* 168). Similarly, an anonymous essayist of 1707 declares that whereas Boileau "has spar'd no Pains to dress the Satires of *Horace* in good *French*, yet it smells too much of the Lamp." In contrast with Rochester, "when any Thought of *Horace, Juvenal, Persius,* or *Boileau*, falls in my Lord's Verses, it is plainly his Lordship's, without any Marks of Borrowing it from any other, the Spirit and Easiness of the whole being of a Piece" (*Heritage* 184–85). By "Spirit," both commentators seem to have in mind a distinguishing disposition or special bent of mind animating Rochester's verse. Besides independent thinking, perspicacity is normally attributed to Rochester's particular "Spirit" as well. Even Pope, no great fan of Rochester although he learned much from his verse, acknowledges the earl to possess "more delicacy and more knowledge of mankind" than other poets of the era of Charles II—this despite the fact that he also considers Rochester to be "of a very bad turn of mind, as well as debauched."[11] In relationship to the other satirists of Rochester's day—an era he characterizes as being "very rich in satire"—Joseph Spence also finds Rochester "more perceptive of the characters of men; he had a more penetrating force and was more polished" (*Heritage* 194). Likewise, the earl is credited with having the courage of his convictions. Thomas Brown maintains that Rochester's "Wit was often Profane, and he neither spar'd Prince nor God, from whom he receiv'd both the greatest Abilities, a splendid Title, and a magnificent Fortune" (*Heritage* 176). In his *Dictionnaire Historique et Philosophique*, Pierre Bayle notes that Rochester was "one of those atheists who live according to their principles" (*Heritage* 183). Thus far, then, we have seen Rochester's turn of mind as expressed in his writings described as singular, momentous, insightful, petulant, adroit, and unflinching.

Bayle also defines Rochester as a "man distinguished by his wit and by compositions full of pungency and gaiety." In his observation we encounter perhaps Rochester's outstanding trait: his ability to mask attack with wit. In *The Princess of Cleves* (1681), Nathanael Lee has Nemours lament the dead "Count *Rosidore*"—meaning the recently deceased Rochester— as "the Spirit of Wit" whose "Imperfections were catching" (*Heritage* 29). Paradoxes such as attractive imperfections or gay pungency occur frequently in assessments of Rochester and his poetry. Anthony Hamilton, recounting the life of his brother-in-law the count de Grammont, a frequent visitor to the court of Charles II, portrays Rochester as "the most dangerous enemy in the universe: never did any man write with more ease, humour, spirit, and delicacy; but he was at the same time the most severe satirist" (*Heritage* 187). It seems that contemporaries recognized in Rochester an imperiling capacity to lure readers rhetorically to unsavory conclusions. Just as John Dryden prescribes the proper formula for satire to be the ability to make a malefactor die sweetly rather than the slovenly butchering of a man, Rochester, upon inspection, reveals himself through his work to be the kind of delicate enemy Hamilton describes. The earl is an easy and humorous, not to mention insidiously clever, satiric nemesis. A satanic likeness is apparent in such characterizations. Writing in 1720, Giles Jacob says of Rochester's verse:

> He had a strange Vivacity of Thought, and Vigour of Expression; his Style was clear and strong, and his Figures very lively, and few Men ever had a bolder Flight of Fancy, more steddily govern'd by Judgment than his Lordship. He laid out his Wit very freely in Libels and Satires, in which he had a peculiar Talent of mixing his Wit with his Malice, and fitting both with such apt words, that Men were tempted to be pleased with them. (*Heritage* 189)

Rochester displays technical mastery over the satiric device of rendering calumny charmingly: the sophistication of his wit acts to obscure—but not to lessen—the ferocity of his attack. This paradox of dealing in pleasing enormities, combined with the cognitive properties of his writing frequently identified by contemporaries, situates Rochester's work ideally, I believe, to perform the type of Foucauldian and Nietzschean cultural critique I have suggested.

Perhaps the religious men with whom Rochester had contact near the end of his life have special insight into Rochester's take on truth and power. Robert Parsons, preaching the earl's funeral sermon, may afford us the most valuable intuition yet on Rochester as an agent of chaos set against the forces of order. Parsons reports of his late spiritual charge:

> He seem'd to affect something singular and paradoxical in his Impieties, as well as in his Writings, above the reach and thought of other men; taking as much pains to draw others in, and to pervert the right ways of virtue, as the Apostles and Primitive Saints, *to save their own souls, and them that heard them.* For this was the

heightning and amazing circumstance of his sins, that he was so
diligent and industrious to recommend and propagate them; not
like those of old that *hated the light,* but those the Prophet men-
tions, *Isiah 3.9. who declare their sin as Sodom, and hide it not,* that
take it upon their shoulders, and bind it to them as a Crown; framing
Arguments for Sin, making Proselytes to it, and writing Panegy-
ricks upon Vice; singing Praises to the great enemy of God, and
casting down Coronets and Crowns before his Throne.

Nay so confirm'd was he in Sin, that he lived, and oftentimes
almost died, a Martyr for it. (*Heritage* 46)

Rochester as a Martyr for Sin, framing "Arguments for Sin,"
living, as noted by Dr. Johnson, in "ostentatious contempt of
regularity," figures more than the rake's life. More urgently, it
entails an intellectual invalidation of Restoration culture as
well. At some level, Parsons obviously senses in Rochester a
personal *and* textual agenda that runs contrary to Christian
social order and morality. What he may not recognize in Rochester is that in attacking rakehood as well as what was regarded as more standard and acceptable cultural behavior, the
earl does not merely offer a sinful alternative to Christianity.
Rather, in binding sin to him "as a Crown," Rochester works
to plunge his reader into near-total anarchy. Similar to the
Marquis de Sade, Rochester in his writings approaches libertinism as "a combination of lawless obscenity and the denunciation of religion, consciously and systematically pushed to
its farthest limit."[12] Rochester emphasizes civil over ecclesias-
tical government, however, in his denunciations. Unlike James
G. Turner, I do not see Rochester merely as an aristocratic
child testing the boundaries of his proxy royal father's tolerance.[13] Instead, via a critical procedure at once less reductive
and psychoanalytically based and more political and rhetorically based, Rochester's wit can be seen as applied toward the
demolition of Charles's libertine sway. In a departure from the
earlier drolling and clubbing tradition of gentlemen,[14] Rochester's verse (and even his personal behavior) turns away from
the fundamentally conservative pre-Restoration comic idiom
of his predecessors and toward a decidedly skeptical and radical post-Restoration satiric expression. If during the second
half of the seventeenth century court wits came to occupy the
same carnivalistic position formerly fulfilled by the court
jester, as Sir William Temple suggests,[15] Rochester is a jester
gone awry—something akin to Lear's fool. Far from farcically
upholding the values of the dominant society, Rochester's

raillery-cum-railing subverts the contemporary status quo. His writings stalk rather than entertain the courtly and para-courtly target fop. Parsons's characterization of the earl as a martyr for sin aptly summarizes the key traits and the critical agenda of Rochester's militant project.

The other notable encounter between the declining profli-gate and a clergyman, of course, is the interviews of Rochester and Gilbert Burnet. In these, Rochester's aggressively unor-thodox views emerge with great force. Burnet's long-winded arguments for Christian morality and precepts sounded to Rochester "like *Enthusiasme*, or *Canting*" (*Heritage* 59). Amaz-ingly, even through Burnet's contrivance of speaking for the dying earl in his *Life and Death of Rochester*, Rochester's rejec-tion of conventional Christianity remains cogent. Rochester terms religion "the effect of Fancy" and acknowledges that "they were very happy whose Fancies were under the power of such Impressions; since they had somewhat on which their thoughts rested and centered" (60). Virtually all parts of wor-ship Rochester deems "the Inventions of Priests, to make the World believe they had a Secret of Incensing the Appeasing God as they pleased"; the earl also specifically rejects such doctrines as Providence, intercession through prayer (61), original sin, and prophecy or miracles (65). Of those last two notions, Rochester comments: "for the boldness and cunning of Contrivers meeting with the Simplicity and Credulity of the People, things were easily received; and, being once received, passed down without contradiction." Rochester goes on to question the "Incoherences of Stile in the Scriptures, the odd Transitions, the seeming Contradictions" (65). In brief, Roches-ter recognizes organized religion as a mechanistic discourse of constraint, as a mere illusion of truth, and condemns as miscreants those who are charged with saying what counts as true. In linguistic terms, Rochester speaks of the impossible presence of a center or origin to language. His works embrace what Jacques Derrida calls

> the Nietzschean *affirmation*, that is the joyous affirmation of the play of the world and of the innocence of becoming, the affirmation of a world of signs without fault, without truth, and without origin which is offered to an active interpretation. *This affirmation then determines the noncenter otherwise than as loss of the center.*[16]

Similar to the early Sophists, Rochester does not lament our linguistic maze; rather, he savors the intellectual demands it exacts upon us. Reading the world or the word is a dynamic, not a compliant process.

Predictably, Burnet responds to Rochester's remarks with both Christian and positivist party line—interestingly bringing politics into the debate for the first time as well. For Burnet, accepting matters on the testimony of others is not only reasonable, "but it was the hinge on which all the Government and Justice in the World depended: Since all the Courts of Justice proceed upon the Evidence given by Witnesses." Therefore, when events seem credible, witnesses disinterested and numerous, and depositions sufficiently public, "it is a vain thing to say, because it is possible for so many men to agree in a Lye, that therefore these have done it. In all other things a man gives his assent when the credibility is strong on the one side, and there appears nothing on the other side to ballance it" (*Heritage* 66). Following this same centrist formula, Titus Oates had just caused hundreds of Catholics to be imprisoned and twenty-four to be executed while bringing panic to the government and to the nation. In our own century, Hitler used such rationale to execute millions. Burnet describes perfectly here not just Foucault's insidious regime of truth, but more fundamentally what Derrida describes as an absurdity: "The concept of centered structure is in fact the concept of a play based on a fundamental ground, a play constituted on the basis of a fundamental immobility and a reassuring certitude, which itself is beyond the reach of play."[17] And in fact certain of Rochester's writings offer, to echo Burnet's assertion, nothing and chaos on the other side to balance and counter such false mechanics of power and such a naive belief in the centered structure of language.

As final arguments against Rochester's views, the clergyman proposes rather unconvincingly the Wager: it is prudent to believe in God in case God exists. Building to his final ad hominem attack, Burnet muses with regard to *"Libertines"*:

> I wish they would consider that by their own Principles, they cannot be sure that Religion is only a Contrivance, all they pretend to is only to weaken some Arguments that are brought for it: but they have not Brow enough to say, They can prove that their own Principles are true. So that at most they bring their Cause no higher, than that it is possible *Religion* may not be true. But still it is possible it may be true, and they have no shame left that will

deny that it is also probable it may be true; and if so, then what mad Men are they who run so great a hazard for nothing? (*Heritage* 90)

As one of these "mad Men," as indeed a martyr for what Burnet and Parsons would term sin, Rochester suggests no countertruth to religion; he asserts no alternative vision of order to replace that of Christianity; in fact, he proposes no *center* whatever to take the place of Burnet's basis for linguistic certainty. Instead, Rochester recommends rhetorical and interpretive chaos over binary opposition. Thus Rochester *does* run so great a libertine hazard for the sake of what later philosophers would term *Nothingness*—that is, for the sake of a conviction that the human constructs of religion, government, and society are arbitrary and driven by political gain. I doubt Burnet grasped, to recall Barthes, Rochester's countertheological refusal to countenance God's hypostases. That might be why in the account he permits Rochester to air his views so freely—though I suspect Burnet edited heavily their conversations. Even if Burnet were aware of the sophistication of Rochester's stance, he must have been confident that few of his readers would take—or even understand—the mad earl's opinions seriously. (To be sure, these are not pedestrian concepts Rochester entertains.) As a result, like the target fop of Rochester's verse, Burnet and his readership unknowingly and ironically are exposed to the cerebral puzzles insinuated by this rhetorically engaging freethinker.

According to Burnet, ultimately it was Rochester's experience of the position-seeking clergy at Charles's court that convinced him that religion was a "mere Contrivance" (see *Heritage* 77–78). Rochester also tells Burnet that "He never improved his Interest at Court, to do a premeditate Mischief to other persons" (51). In other words, Rochester did not participate in the customary political practice of back-stabbing in order to advance himself at Whitehall. More of Rochester's observations about court life are vividly available to us in his correspondence. Often quoted as proof of his apoliticality are various remarks made by Rochester, usually to Henry Savile, about the hollowness and mendacity of statesmanship.[18] Other remarks by Rochester suggest, however, that his eschewal of political maneuvering at court was *not* a dissociation from politics per se; rather, Rochester took part in polity in another way. It seems that Rochester found the climate at court a singularly inhospitable one, particularly with regard to trust and friendship. In 1671, when reflecting to Savile upon the phenomenon of *in vino veritas*, Rochester writes:

> oh that second bottle Harry is the sincerest, wisest, & most impartiall downwright friend we have, tells us truth of our selves, & forces us to speake truths of others, banishes flattery from our tongues and distrust from our Hearts, setts us above the meane Pollicy of Court prudence, wch makes us lye to one another all day, for feare of being betray'd by each other att night; And before god I beleive the errantest villain breathing is honest as long as that bottle lives and few of that tribe dare venture upon him att least among the Courtiers & statesmen.

Likewise, sometime between 1673 and 1675 during a more serious meditation on the rarity and good fortune of friendship, Rochester tells Savile that "this thought has soe intirely possest mee since I came into the Country (where only one can think, for you att Court thinke not att all or att least as if you were shutt up in a Drumme, you can thinke of nothing but the noise is made about you)." Whitehall epitomized, then, insincerity and cacophony for Rochester. Yet far from withdrawing from that environment, Rochester satirizes it; writing seemingly for the amusement of a court audience, he in fact inculpates the target fops of that locale, using in effect insincerity and cacophony toward that purpose. Writing to Savile in 1677 that only sickness has been able "to depress the natural alacrity of my careless soul," Rochester asserts:

> You who have known me these ten years the grievance of all prudent persons, the byword of statesmen, the scorn of ugly ladies (which are very near all) and the irreconcilable aversion of fine gentlemen (who are the ornamental part of a nation), and yet found me seldom sad, even under these weighty oppressions.

In other words, for a full decade Rochester has been heedless— "careless"—of the adverse consequences of writing against the affectations of such highborn marks. Writing from London to Savile in Paris in 1679, Rochester similarly sums up his own capacity as social and political censor: "that if it were not for sickness I could pass my time very well between my own ill-nature, which inclines me very little to pity the misfortunes of malicious mistaken fools, and the policies of the times, which expose new rarities of that kind every day."[19] Rochester seems fully to have appreciated the social and political dimensions and nature of his satiric undertaking. So did the literati around him.

Writing posthumously of Rochester, Robert Wolseley in his "Preface to *Valentinian*" (1685) both notes that Rochester's verse was intended "for the private Diversion of those happy Few, whom he us'd to charm with his Company and honour with his Friendship" and that the earl drew his pen "to stop the progress of arbitrary Oppression" (*Heritage* 140, 155). Significantly, Wolseley collocates these two pursuits in what I have termed the *target fop*. According to him, Rochester wrote "good Sense" in order

> to do his King and Countrey justice upon such publick State-Thieves, as would beggar a Kingdom to enrich themselves, who abusing the Confidence, and undeserving the Favour of a gracious Prince, will not be asham'd to maintain the cheating of their Master, by the robbing and starving of their fellow-Servants, and under the best Form of government in the World blush not to live upon the spoyl of others, till by their impudent Violations of Right, they grow like Beasts of Prey, *Hostes humani Generis*. These were the Vermin whom (to his eternal Honour) his Pen was continually pricking and goading. (140–41)

At first glance, such praise seems more suited to Marvell than to Rochester. The upshot of *The Last Instructions to a Painter* is condemnation of the Court party for steering Charles in the wrong political direction. I believe Rochester undertakes similar censure of, if not the ministers around the king, then specifically the inner circle of courtiers around him—namely the Ballers, of which Rochester himself was more or less ringleader, and their like.[20] Other literary people who knew Rochester personally demonstrate awareness of this social agenda as well. Friends such as Francis Fane, Anne Wharton, John Oldham, and Aphra Behn see amelioration and guidance at the heart of Rochester's satire. In his elegy to Rochester, *Bion*, Oldham comments that the earl's verse "woo'd our Souls into our ravisht Ears"(39).[21] Calling Rochester "The last Reproacher of your Vice," meaning the fools and knaves attacked in his satire, Behn laments upon the death of Rochester:

> Satyr has lost its Art, its Sting is gone,
> The Fop and Cully now may be undone;
> That dear instructing Rage is now allay'd,

And no sharp Pen dares tell 'em how they've stray'd;
Bold as a God was ev'ry lash he took,
But kind and gentle the chastising stroke.[22]

Recognizing the negativity and paradox of Rochester's project, they nonetheless feel its utilitarian value as well. Enemies such as Dryden and Mulgrave, on the other hand, perceive dangerous and unjustified defamation in Rochester's writings. In an extraordinarily cautious letter Dryden wrote to Rochester in 1673, the laureate expresses the view that he wished the earl had remained at court where he had *less* time to contemplate the world—an intriguing counterposition to Rochester's own sentiments about court life expressed to Savile.

> In the meane time you have withdrawn your selfe from attendance, the curse of Courts. You may thinke of what you please, and that as little as you please, (for in my opinion), thinking it selfe, is a kinde of paine to a witty man; he finds so much more in it to disquiet, than to please him.[23]

I have argued elsewhere that Dryden worries in this letter over potentially unpleasant results if negotiations with Rochester to become his client-poet fail. By suggesting that Rochester thinks too much for his own good, Dryden perhaps indicates to Rochester an awareness of the nobleman's habit of retiring to the country to write lampoons and hopes he does not soon find himself among the victims.[24]

Dryden's eventual patron, Mulgrave, meanwhile attacks Rochester openly in *An Essay upon Satire* (1679) for his poetical and personal habits of belligerence and dissimulation.

> For while he mischief means to all mankind,
> Himself alone the ill effect does find,
>
> *   *   *
>
> False are his words, affected as his wit,
> So often he does aim, so seldom hit;
> To ev'ry face he cringes whilst he speaks,
> But when the back is turn'd the head he breaks.
> Mean in each motion, lewd in ev'ry limb,
> Manners themselves are mischievous in him.[25]

The description is more than an apt characterization of Rochester's rhetorical snare when stalking the target fop—of whom Mulgrave in most respects might serve as archetype. Simulat-

ing the accoutrements of court poetry, Rochester's verse sub-
versively attacks the unwary courtier reading it. In his
subsequent castigation of Rochester coming with *An Essay
upon Poetry* (1682), Mulgrave pronounces of the dead earl's
love lyrics:

> Such nauseous Songs as the late Convert made,
> Which justly call this censure on his Shade;
> Not that warm thoughts of the transporting joy
> Can shock the Chastest or the Nicest cloy,
> But obscene words, too gross to move desire,
> Like heaps of Fuel do but choak the Fire.
> That Author's Name has undeserved praise,
> Who pall'd the appetite he meant to raise.[26]

With these lines Mulgrave appears to fall neatly into the trap
of Rochester's obscene lyrics. By judging Rochester's songs to
be only "Bawdry barefac'd" and therefore unwitty, Mulgrave
reveals himself to be, in the words of Wolseley's eventual retort
to these lines, "among unthinking, half-witted People, who
judge without examining and talk without meaning" (*Heritage*
148). Where some might pant over the "obscene words" of the
lyrics, mindlessly consuming the pornography of the material,
Mulgrave equally unthinkingly rejects the works as smut without considering the possible intricacy of the matter within.
Either reaction misses the point of Rochester's linguistic
games that exploit perceivable gaps in Restoration elite culture and society. The poems are not "too gross to move desire."
Instead, they make the reader question appetite in the first
place: Rochester's lyrics expose the mindlessness of Charles's
sensual and self-aggrandizing circus—a circus in which Mulgrave, by the way, performs as a prominent clown.

At once reporting but equally advancing a theoretical matrix
for their views on Rochester's writings, I have tried thus far
to let Rochester's original readers speak. I will end this chapter
on the contemporary idiom of Rochester's works by considering briefly the broader literate culture in which these people
lived, read, wrote, and interpreted.

Recently, R. W. F. Kroll has offered a significant reassess-
ment of our views on early modern neoclassical culture. Contending that we have grown too comfortable with our
distanced interpretation of this age, Kroll insists that a "read-
justment of assumptions must occur in the way that literary
critics and theorists read neoclassical literature by learning

to scrutinize more patiently the local intellectual conditions under which discursive attitudes are forged."[27] For Kroll, the Restoration period is a particularly dynamic one in English social, intellectual, and literary history. During this time, Kroll argues, "English society strenuously reconstructed a new cultural rhetoric, forging a system of symbols by which to define itself and creating a comprehensive mechanism by which individuals could navigate within that society" (8). I believe that Rochester is thoroughly a creature of this new cultural rhetoric Kroll proposes. Persistent inquiry into the synchronic circumstances of Rochester's expression reveal his writings to partake of the innovative early modern discursive landscape then emerging.

To begin with, Kroll believes that contrary to many assumptions made about it, neoclassical discourse is aware of its own artificiality. Far from treating "language as transparent or referential," the "empiricism that informs this culture is neither naïve nor absolutist, but is consistently sceptical about the powers of the mind" (3–4). A scientific "plain style" use of language, then, is not to be assumed as the standard for the age. Instead, literati recognized the limitations of language and the essentially disconnected relationship between words and objects in the world. Recognition of these sophisticated attitudes toward language, moreover, can significantly alter the way we read a neoclassical text (see 3–7). Kroll also emphasizes the vital importance of the neo-Epicurean movement at the Restoration.[28] In questioning and strategically revising the inherited grounds of their cultural practices, neoclassical writers worked from various classical models, to include Stoicism, Skepticism, and Epicureanism. Many thinkers found in ancient Epicureanism not only "a highly sophisticated view of how the physical world was constructed from atoms and the void" but "a self-conscious cultural ethic that dissented from the surrounding Hellenistic culture" (9). Kroll maintains that out of Epicurean attitudes toward cognition and language materializes at this time an "Epicurean poetic" that approaches knowledge as superficial and language as provisional. Perfectly matching other anti-Aristotelian views of the seventeenth century, Restoration neo-Epicureanism calls into question certainty and knowability while following the current philosophical precepts of Gassendi rather than Descartes (see 10–15). This "contingent epistemology," in fact, Kroll characterizes as "the dominant discourse of the age" (16–17). It should be obvious that my reading of Rochester situates his works explicitly within the literate culture Kroll describes. An understanding of the cognitive and linguistic mayhem at work in the colloquy of Rochester's writings alters, often radically, the surface meaning of his verse. Displaying many traits of neo-Epicurean thought (to include two fragmentary translations of Lucretius' *De Rerum Natura*), many of Rochester's texts overwork a reader's response and in the end summon disturbing unknowability.

What is more, Kroll sees the neo-Epicurean ethos of Restoration literate culture as having both origins and consequences in the momentous political events that mark the age. Kroll characterizes neoclassical culture not as the product of a single Foucauldian rupture, but as

> a series of dramatic epistemological and linguistic revisions in response to the Civil War and Interregnum. Those revisions, which together produce a powerful orthodoxy, occurred as a sequence of tectonic shifts in the culture between 1640 and 1680, often in strategic debates between promoters of the preferred discourse of contingency and those espousing alternative models of knowledge and language. (17)

Counter to typical poststructuralist suppositions about the "Enlightenment," Kroll finds that hegemonic factions and institutions *did not* usually subscribe to positivist, Cartesian doctrine concerning knowledge and language. Just the reverse. Those institutions returned to power after 1660—the monarchy, the Anglican Church, and eventually the Royal Society—habitually deployed a contingent epistemology as a means of acquiring and maintaining power. Skepticism and relativism became a convenient tool for royalist coalitions to use when impeding attempts to innovate upon their status quo. Those in power found that what we now generally term deconstruction could be used as an instrument of oppression as easily as structuralism and dogmatism (53). Normally, opposition groups—according to their own lights, Catholics and radical Protestants sects alike—adhered to beliefs that entailed nonrelativistic truth and transparent language (see 16–18). Thus Kroll concludes that the dominant contemporary view of language at the Restoration was one of words being phenomenal, material, in the public (as opposed to the purely private) realm, and therefore supremely *negotiable* entities. Otherwise, language became "the secret and insidious instrument of radical or tyrannical control" (20). At the same time, however, in the struggle to impose on any given sign the generalized concept for its signified, established agencies usually prevailed. Material language may have been negotiable and relative, but equally it was "the possession of visible, public institutions" (see 19–27).

Within the neo-Epicurean intellectual, linguistic, and political climate Kroll describes, Rochester spent his entire life. He perhaps knew no other form of discourse. The reading I propose for his works, therefore, is *not* contemporaneously unfounded. Rather, Rochester's procedure can be seen as thoroughly conventional—though not uncomplex—for his time. Iconic and iconoclastic at once, Rochester participates in the prevailing contingent epistemology of the Restoration era. It was the literate habitus in which he matured; both he and his readers were acclimated to the war for control over the signified—what Kroll depicts as the cultural upset of debate, confrontation, and realignment that marked the years from 1640 to 1680. Where Rochester's particular use of this dominant discourse becomes both remarkably labyrinthine and deliberately political, however, is in the possibility—a strong one, I believe, and one in the following chapters I will attempt to demonstrate—that Rochester employs the dissimulative, relativistic, deconstructive discourse of Charles's status quo *against* Charles's status quo. Rochester's writings not only demand extraordinary readerly scrutiny and subvert positivist notions about "truth"; they ironically deploy the linguistic tactics used by the hegemonic powers of the day in an effort to expose the fraudulent nature of that group's hold on power. More simply and inelegantly put, Rochester bullshits the bullshitters. If the written, material word were valued as a medium for negotiation—that is, for *reading*—during the second half of the seventeenth century, then ultimate importance was placed on the *sophisticated* act of interpretation. Sign and signified could not be collapsed; neoclassical theorists, Kroll believes, "sought to expose this figural claim as a cognitive chimera, connoting some politically motivated attempt to coerce the reader by aesthetic means, and so to deny him or her true liberty of readerly judgment." As a result, Restoration discourse "treated as tantamount to an ethical or political failure the failure to read with sufficient empirical rigor"; it was the reader's business and, moreover, "responsibility to educe general principles from partial but suggestive signs" (22). In setting a trap for the target fop, Rochester's writings at once depend on and disrupt this general practice of reading. If one did not read Rochester's verse, drama, and prose with sufficient empirical rigor—the type of rigor the reader *him*self was likely to employ elsewhere as a hegemonic libertine or as part of the Stuart ascendancy—then that reader fell victim to Rochester's subterfuge. Those anxious to condemn others as enthusiasts for empirically baseless "truths" were themselves rendered guilty of the same interpretive crime—an uninspected belief that their worldview was *the* worldview. As evidenced by the accounts of contemporaries just reviewed, several of Rochester's textual constructions seemed elaborate enough indeed to make monkeys of many if not most readers in this fashion.

However tempting it might be, I am unsure that we know enough about Rochester's candid political views to place him with entire confidence in what Kroll calls "an influential group of English thinkers and writers" for whom, as a generation reacting to national crisis, "Epicureanism articulated a cultural model that they felt to symbolize a resistance to cultural fragmentation (associated with the Civil War) on the one hand, and tyranny (associated with the radical sects or Louis XIV's France) on the other" (9). The earl's behavior and articulations display perhaps a proclivity for this relativistic and centrist political outlook; however, Rochester both as a person and as an author lacks the outright civic activism that might qualify him for complete membership in Kroll's association. With far more assurance I think we can characterize Rochester as someone who targeted for intellectual and political censure that prominent part of early modern English society James G. Turner identifies as the "half libertine" or "social libertine." Citing Sir William Temple as an example, Turner characterizes the half libertine as "amphibious men who moved freely between the demimonde and the politest circles, and for whom libertinism was a sort of dressing-up box of rakish attitudes and gestures." Mixing business with pleasure, such men attended with equal ardor, as it were, the cabinet room and the pit. The social libertine, then, "respects the pales and partitions that society has constructed to allow the coexistence of lust and respectability; he knocks against them, playing a milder version of the Restoration testing game."[29] It strikes me that what Turner calls the social libertine and what I have described as the target fop are fundamentally one and the same creature. Sexually, each will have his cake and eat it, too. Socially, each flaunts convention while living deeply staked in convention. Intellectually and politically, each balks at the idea of pursuing libertine and neo-Epicurean metaphysics to their ultimate effect. Namely, each is afraid to stare into the completely empty box of language; each is afraid to acknowledge the wholly arbitrary nature of human constructions. In writings at once playful and vicious, Rochester confronts his king and his fellows—if they were to exercise sufficient empirical rigor—with just these incapacitating possibilities.

The following chapters will illustrate, then, the rhetorical possibility of a Foucauldian assault on Restoration elite culture available to the courtly and townly readers of Rochester's works. In chapters 3 and 4, the qualities of narrative alienation and textual/linguistic chaos in the major satires are explored. In chapter 5, I demonstrate the previously underappreciated political project in Rochester's sexual lyrics as well as in his less studied works of prose and drama. A sixth and final chapter will offer some concluding thoughts about Rochester's project and, perhaps, how it relates to us today.

3

Narrative Angst

Bless me, thought I, what thing is man that thus
In all his shapes he is ridiculous?
—Rochester, *Tunbridge Wells*

THE majority of critical attention paid to Rochester's works focuses upon four or five of his compositions written between 1674 and 1676 that could be called his major satires.[1] Critical approaches to these poems largely involve assessing them within the traditions of formal verse satire as they had come down to English poets via the classical sources of Greece and especially Rome as well as from the new satiric innovations of France. While this strategy is of course a vital and worthy way to inspect these works, it can tend to universalize them. We search for Horace, Juvenal, and Boileau in Rochester's satires more than we search for a contemporary English setting. Certainly, Rochester writes self-consciously within a literary tradition of verse satire in these compositions. Equally, however, I believe his satires execute the kind of extremely localized debunking of Restoration elite culture outlined in chapters 1 and 2. If there is a universal satiric matrix at work in the satires, there is also particular satiric matter filling that framework. If I had to place weight of importance on one over the other, I would chose that of the specific content of these works above that of their general form—in other words, the reverse of most critical appraisals. Such a project goes beyond merely glossing the many local references in Rochester's major satires: it entails reconstructing what impressions those local references might have added up to for his contemporary readers—the majority of whom, while not completely ignorant of satiric tradition, would have been more interested in the present import of the piece than in its satiric ancestry.[2] In doing

45

this, however, I do not want to dismiss or negate the consequence of inherited satiric tradition in Rochester's writings. Therefore, before discussing the possible native impact of *Timon* and *Tunbridge Wells* on readers of the 1670s, I will suggest a way to reconcile the universal with the particular in Rochester's satire.

By the end of the seventeenth century, the essential characteristics of the two giants of Roman satire, Horace and Juvenal, were well set in critical opinion.[3] However, judgments of who is a Horatian and who a Juvenalian satirist based on stylistic considerations alone—which is how most critics tend to proceed—can be misleading. For example, Raman Selden calls Rochester and Butler "low-style" satirists in association with the Horatian plain-style norm—which means simply that, according to Selden, they are Horatian satirists. At the same time, however, Selden also states that, during the Restoration, Rochester and Butler begin a satiric practice based upon "a *low view of man*"; this is something decidedly not part of the Horatian tradition. Because of this, Rochester is characterized, somewhat bafflingly, as having literary values rarely in harmony with his moral and philosophical ones. Selden tags him as "England's most subversive Horatian satirist."[4] Instead of this obvious waffling, would it not be more useful and accurate to form an opinion on Rochester and Butler based both on *what* they say in their satires and on the style *in which* they write? The relationship between content and form is a complex and vexed critical issue. I have to favor materialist theories, however, holding that content in the end is the more significant element of a literary production. Ideas give a satire its most distinctive qualities.[5] In the critical rush to assert a prosodic shift in English satire after 1660 away from the harshness of Juvenal and toward the refinement of Horace—that is, to affirm the transcendence of new French civility over native English savagery—many critics have overlooked the fact that the *tenor* of a significant portion of English satire after 1660 not only remains solidly Juvenalian, but also elaborates upon Juvenal's Cimmerian view of the world.[6] I believe Rochester's verse to be a leading if not wholly innovative exponent of such a strain of English satire.

According to conventional wisdom of the seventeenth century, Horace's satiric perspective—as opposed to style—could be described as normative and cultivated. Fundamentally, his satires were regarded as medicinal: curative in the sense that they afforded a remedy to specific defects; restorative in that they were intended to bring us back in line with rational conduct. The normative aim of Horatian satire was effected best by its narrative persona—primarily, the cultivated tone of a good, honest man. Amused, somewhat detached, urbane, and educated, the *vir bonus* of Horatian satire optimistically offered a remedy to an individual's impaired but not irreclaimable condition.[7] In contrast to Horace's satiric demeanor, two words that might define the seventeenth-century estimation of Juvenal's outlook are frenzied and incensed. Juvenal's satires commonly employed the narrative persona of the *vir iratus*, the indignant man. This narrator was regarded as a latter-day Archilochus whose rage and acerbity frequently loosed on Rome the primitive terror of the curse. Juvenal's principal rhetorical device was the perpetual torrent of caustic observations, arguments, and examples delivered by his narrator (e.g., Satire 6). Juvenal was always "on the Gallop," as Dryden remarks; his frenetic wit gave the laureate "as much Pleasure as I can bear."[8] Such unending vituperation, delivered with indefatigable passion, often was described with the standard epithet *saeva indignatio*—savage indignation—an attitude that, in its energy, simply overwhelmed considerations of style.[9]

I see a similar kind of savage indignation operating in Rochester's major satires. More unbridled intellectually than metrically, the outrage expressed in Rochester's verse embraces the idea that no phase of human activity is sacrosanct. Society is an arbitrary, even absurd construction resulting from human ignorance, and, what is worse, even if we discover this circumstance, we must submit to its awful reality. Possibilities for deliverance are slim or none. Furthermore, I believe that such a view of humanity is available when reading Juvenal's satires. More than the moralist that traditionally he had been taken to be, Juvenal functioned perhaps with greater force during the later seventeenth century as a poet who revealed in full the unpalatable bleakness of our human condition. John Oldham felt inklings of this gloom; Samuel Butler positively reveled in it in his miscellany satires. Rochester seems to have recognized this quality as well in the most infamous ancient satirist and applied it to his own assault on elite London culture.

Just as Juvenal departed from the Roman tradition of writing satire in a low, plain style by writing in a high, exaggerated

style instead, it could be argued as well that he subverted the
traditional rectitude of Roman satire. Lofty morality and
tragic dignity—through the ages, the conventional qualities
ascribed to Juvenal—often are not the real hallmarks of his
satire; rather, I see an unmitigated attitude of irreverence col-
oring much of what he writes. This trait distinguishes his verse
from that of Persius, Horace, and even Lucilius. Often, nothing
is sacred in Juvenal's satires—not the gods, not the old days,
not even what he might lead us to believe is his own social
plight in Rome. Anything that might stand as a cultural or
personal ideal in his satire is likely at some point to be dimin-
ished by ridicule.

For example, the gods and religious ceremony are Juvenal's
frequent targets: numerous impious swipes at both punctuate
the satires (e.g., 1.128–31; 6.14–16, 55–59; 10.7–8); sustained
diatribe appears (6.511–41); and at one point, when a clear
opportunity exists to juxtapose the new bad with the traditional religious good, Juvenal's narrator undercuts the occasion by the inclusion of one too-realistic detail.

> quandoquidem inter nos sanctissima divitiarum
> maiestas, etsi funesta pecunia templo
> nondum habitas, nullas nummorum ereximus aras,
> ut colitur Pax atque Fides Victoria Virtus
> quaeque salutato crepitat Concordia nido.
>
> 1.112–16

> [Though as yet, pernicious Cash, you lack
> A temple of your own, though we have raised no altars
> To Sovereign Gold (as already we worship Honour,
> Peace, Victory, Virtue, or Concord—whose roosting storks
> Rattle and flap on the roof when you salute their nest),
> Still it is Wealth, not God, that compels our deepest
> reverence.][10]

It seems that temples to the gods, which the speaker cannot
help noting also provide roosts for birds, compel as little rever-
ence in him as the new worship of pelf. Equally, the good old
days, the mother of all satiric commonplace, fare no better in
Juvenal's satire. His compositions do not partake steadfastly
in the golden age fantasy of an idealized past when men were
braver and more just while women were chaste and more sub-
missive. The innocent age described at the beginning of Satire
6, for instance, is something less than idyllic or heroic.

> Credo Pudicitiam Saturno rege moratam
> in terris visamque diu, cum frigida parvas
> praeberet spelunca domos ignemque Laremque
> et pecus et dominos communi clauderet umbra,
> silvestrem montana torum cum sterneret uxor
> frondibus et culmo vicinarumque ferarum
> pellibus, . . .
> sed potanda ferens infantibus ubera magnis
> et saepe horridior glandem ructante marito.

6.1–7, 9–10

[During Saturn's reign I believe that Chastity still
Lingered on earth, and was seen for a while, when draughty
Caves were the only homes men had, hearthfire and household
Gods, family and cattle all shut in darkness together.
Wives were different then. . . .
Bred to the woods and mountains, they made their beds from
Dry leaves and straw, from the pelts of savage beasts
Caught prowling the neighbourhood. *Their* breasts gave suck
To big strong babies; often, indeed, they were shaggier
Than their acorn-belching husbands.]

As with the rattling storks' nests atop the temples, Juvenal's narrator cannot resist poking fun at Rome's rube forbearers. Finally, even the complaints of what could otherwise serve as Juvenal's social alter ego, Umbricius in Satire 3, do not escape belittling irony. Umbricius bemoans when ousted by a Greek:

> perierunt tempora longi
> servitii; nusquam minor est iactura clientis.

3.124–25

[my years of obsequious
Service all gone for nothing. Where can a hanger-on
Be ditched with less fuss than in Rome?]

Everywhere Juvenal displays a brutal frankness hardened by the realism of experience that produces in his works perhaps their most distinctive quality: an air of abstract gloom piqued with an edge of bitter wittiness. The construction of shining ideals, or, it would seem, any positive assertion at all, is nearly impossible for Juvenal. Moral norms exist but are strangely irrelevant; seemingly, they can never be attained. Unlike Horace, Juvenal gives no truly serious indication that he believes a commonsensical ethical mean would have a positive effect on the behavior of people. However, Juvenal's callous and sometimes delirious irreverence is not pointless gibe or extravagant buffoonery. On the contrary, it is a reflective, iconoclastic, and, at bottom, nihilistic intellectual stance.

Philosophy per se held little meaning for Juvenal; generally in his satires he adheres to the popular Roman view (still alive today—sometimes with justification—with regard to academics) of philosophers as muddleheaded pedants. However, one notable exception to this attitude occurs in Satire 10. In a lengthy passage (10.28–53) comparing the casuistic views of Democritus, the "Laughing Philosopher," and Heraclitus, the "Weeping Philosopher," only the latter is ridiculed.

> sed facilis cuivis rigidi censura cachinni:
> mirandum est unde ille oculis suffecerit umor.
>
> 10.31–32

> [The cutting, dismissive sneer comes easily to us all—
> *But wherever did Heraclitus tap such an eye-brimming*
> *Reservoir of tears?*]

At the end of the passage, in contrast, Democritus is praised as a man of exceptional insight insusceptible to the vagaries of Fortune.

> tunc quoque materiam risus invenit ad omnis
> occursus hominum, cuius prudentia monstrat
> summos posse viros et magna exempla daturos
> vervecum in patria crassoque sub aere nasci.
> ridebat curas nec non et gaudia vulgi,
> interdum et lacrimas, cum Fortunae ipse minaci
> mandaret laqueum mediumque ostenderet unguem.
>
> 10.47–53

> [Democritus long ago
> Found occasion for laughter in all human intercourse,
> And his wisdom reveals that the greatest men, those destined
> To set the highest examples, may still be born
> In a land with a sluggish climate, a country of muttonheads.
> The cares of the crowd he derided no less than their pleasures,
> Their griefs, too, on occasion: if Fortune was threatening,
> "*Up you,*" he'd say, and give her the vulgar finger.]

Two points stand out in this passage. One, Democritus is distinguished as an example of the most estimable type of person:

through him Juvenal's narrator prescribes the supreme pattern for sound conduct—even if that conduct is only flipping the bird at fate. Two, Democritus' criteria for rational behavior is to scorn in the normal course of human events the concerns and perturbations, the amusements and desires, and even certain mishaps and sorrows of people at large. Human existence *itself* is belittled. In effect, then, human life is not so much rejected as human society is in a sense dismantled. All we do is, at bottom, ludicrous. And, like Democritus, Juvenal in his satires frequently works to disconfirm various accepted social actions and viewpoints which, upon inspection, are nonsense. As Democritus derided the cares, pleasures, and griefs of the crowd, so too Juvenal mocks "all human endeavours" (*quidquid agunt homines,* 1.85). What is prior and privileged in the current social hierarchy is thus devalued and shown in fact to hold its false prominence whimsically, even fatuously and shamefully. Juvenal's satire undermines the supposedly unassailable thought-systems of his society: law, religion, government, custom, and ethics themselves.[11] Moreover, Juvenal does not effectually replace these shattered idols; rather, for the most part, his satires simply and forcibly *deconstruct.* Human action is not corrected, only revealed for what it actually is: nothing much at all. Implicit in these works is a sense of resignation and, perhaps, a touch of despair. People are incorrigible creatures existing in irremediable circumstances. They will always value falsely; they will always construct capriciously. According to Juvenal, the only sane response to such a circumstance is Democritean laughter—although, in Juvenal's satire (and as Dryden may have sensed), this laughter at times becomes manic and nearly unbearable.

Juvenal's satiric perspective is obviously grimmer and, in the end, perhaps more perplexing than Horace's medicinal satiric approach: Juvenal *affects* the posture and the passion of a moral reformer; however, his purpose is repeatedly *not* one of reform but instead one of revelation. Juvenal's startling innovation with respect to the traditional function of Roman satire is that he treats satire not so much as an occasion for ethical correction, but as a source of existential disclosure. Horace (and Persius) often functions as the moralizer: he deals in practical matters and presents us with an ethical imperative. Juvenal, differently, is an observer: he deals in abstract insights and informs us with dismal realizations about our life on earth. Such satire is sensitive to the profound fragmenta-

tion of human existence and experience. The concept of socie-
tal or moral structure itself is attacked. Viewed in this way,
Juvenalian satire becomes an often extreme expression of irri-
tation and frustration over the human vanity and blindness
that works to lock us in our own foolish perceptual prisons.

Given the irreverent nature of Juvenal's satire, given his un-
precedented praise of a single philosopher, and given that this
praise of Democritus occurs in Satire 10, his most serious and
reflective poem, it is appropriate, I think, to speak of the Democritean quality of Juvenal's satire. The term usefully defines
what I feel is his predominant deliberative perspective. More
to the point, I believe this outlook also to be the characteristic
of Juvenal most exploited by English satirists after the Restoration. Far from offering moral self-help, Juvenal speaks, in the
estimation of Boileau, "d'affreuses véritéz" and "de sublimes
beautéz," which, translated freely by William Soames and
Dryden, read "horrid Truths" in which "there's something of
Divine."[12] Prettified by French poetic sensibilities, the traditional Anglo-Juvenalian satiric strain became after 1660—
however locally and politically applied by specific satirists—
largely acrimonious and dispiriting attacks on the impotence
of human discernment and erudition. (Such elements figure
prominently, for example, in Dryden's *Mac Flecknoe* and *Absalom and Achitophel*.) During the Restoration era, as discussed
at the end of the previous chapter, the cultural penchant for the
epistemology of Epicurus—himself a student of Democritus—
would likely have predisposed satirists to this pyrrhonistic element in Juvenal.[13] In the hands of Rochester, Juvenal's Democritean stance becomes, first, a pitiless divestiture of the trivial
and dogmatic madness inherent to human conduct and thinking; finally, his satiric vision encompasses a kind of semiotic
escapade where the hollow sign system of language itself collapses. Moreover, the unmistakable target of this destructive
satiric perspective is the regime of truth of Charles II. Whether
or not Rochester acted upon this particular interpretation of
Juvenal's satire just sketched is of course matter for conjecture.
Regardless, both the term and the concept of Democritean
satire serve usefully as a way to describe the satiric agenda of
Rochester's written critique of his cultural milieu. It is to his
appraisal as expressed in *Timon* and *Tunbridge Wells* that I
now turn.

In both satires, immense cognitive tension is generated in
the contemporary narratee via the device of the narrator. For

each piece, the narrator figures Rochester's localized target fop. However, the narrator is a target fop who undergoes and, as a result, suddenly recognizes the kinds of "horrid Truths" about human (and more particularly Restoration) society communicated by Democritean satire. The fear and loathing that are the products of the narrator's new and discomforting insights, in turn, potentially threaten the naive worldview of the Restoration narratee. More than ecumenical alienation amid humanity at large, these satires feasibly trigger in their reader angst over living within his own privileged class stratum. The effect is more emphatic in *Tunbridge Wells* than in *Timon;* if Rochester carries out the learning process of imitating a satire by Boileau then attempting an original piece on his own in these two works (as well as with *Satire Against Mankind* and *Artemisa*),[14] then the earl improves as he goes.

For Rochester's target fop, the experience of reading *Timon*[15] could function as an exercise of imaginatively suffering what might have been for Rochester the actual intellectual frustration and social distress of living in close proximity to Charles II. Thormählen comments: "Generally speaking, *Timon* has more to offer the historian than the poetry lover—or the true misanthropist."[16] I am tempted to heighten further her emphasis on locality in the work to call *Timon* a full-blown political and social satire directed against Charles and his confidants. Much of caliber has been written about the poem's relationship to Boileau's third satire as well as to the literary criticism of current dramatists carried out over the second half of the text. I find no need here to rehearse those literary subjects. Instead, it seems to me that in the portrait of the narrator's host, hostess, and dining companions exists a vague but telling portrait of Charles and his court. Politically, under express satiric scrutiny is the empty noise of battle and the hypocrisy of international relations at the time of Charles's second Dutch war (1672–74). Socially, certain vagaries and pitfalls of the libertine life-style tellingly are brought to light.

Thormählen makes two excellent points when she observes both the lack of critical comment about the host in *Timon* and his importance of place in the satire.[17] Nearly a third of the poem is taken up with his portrayal, yet no one seems to want to say much about him. The most evocative lines about this "dull, dining sot" (5) are these:

> mine host
> Had been a colonel; we must hear him boast,
> Not of towns won, but an estate lost

For the King's service, which indeed he spent
Whoring and drinking, but with good intent.
He talked much of a plot, and money lent
In Cromwell's time.

                                                    95–101

At first glance, this boorish master of ceremonies seems to be merely a stock character of Restoration literary culture: the old Cavalier, something of a dinosaur from an era gone by. Under closer scrutiny, however, a case could be made for the host's politically signifying Charles. In this one short passage, the number of similarities between them are striking. Both are of a generation older than that of Timon (whom the hostess indicates is a young man; see 64–66) and Rochester (at the time of the poem in his midtwenties to Charles's midforties). Both fought in the civil war. Neither enjoyed much success as a royalist military commander (while Charles comported himself well during the battle of Worcester, nevertheless the operation was a martial disaster). Both lost wealth and power as a result of the war (Charles spectacularly so). Both found the Restoration settlement to be a less than satisfactory financial arrangement (so much so for Charles that he sought to escape his fiscal dependence on Parliament by striking secret deals with Louis XIV; Charles often complained of his poverty as monarch). Both whore and drink (in "Verses for which he was Banished" Charles is characterized as being equally "scandalous and poor"). Both plotted and lent—as well as borrowed— money during the Interregnum to restore the monarchy. Both showed "good intent" in their pursuit of the royalist cause but without significant consequence. Cromwell's government did not fold until after the lord protector was dead; a political vacuum brought Charles back to the throne.

Other textual hints for the host's being a likeness of Charles exist in the satire. Next to Timon, the host is the most prominent and fully drawn character—perhaps even better delineated than the narrator. (I will comment more on this point later.) During the literary discussion, the host exercises his evidently superior judgment and authority by terminating the debate over who is the best playwright with a resounding vote for Dryden. He is the only diner not to misquote his playwright—even though he selects an unfortunate simile by the laureate; neither do the other diners challenge the host's critical acumen. In bestowing the laureateship on Dryden, had not

Charles in a sense similarly—and perhaps unsatisfactorily—
ended that same debate?[18] The host also turns the conversation
back to international affairs, a move that will bring the dinner
party to fiasco and the satire to its climax. If I am justified in
suggesting that the host and his four bullies caricature Charles
and his ministers, then this action imitates the king's presiding
over a meeting, perhaps, of his Privy Council or his Foreign
Affairs Committee. Finally, when the scuffle breaks out among
the dinner guests, the host (along with Timon) stays out of
the fray. Charles had a similar habit of remaining above the
infighting of his advisors. The one obvious difference between
the host and the king is the fact that the former is rendered as
thoroughly countrified and English in his manner and tastes,
positively eschewing new French fashion. When it is time to
dine, the host declares:

> As for French kickshaws, Sillery and Champoon,
> Ragouts and fricassées, in troth we 'ave none.
>
> 73–74

Charles, on the other hand, was thoroughly courtified and
French in his manner and tastes; indeed, at the Restoration,
the mania for all things French accompanied the returning
monarch across the Channel. Could this glaring difference,
though, not be a political jab in itself? Does the satire suggest
that Charles is not only out of touch with his subjects—in fact,
aloof from a segment of the population vital to his power base
in the kingdom—but also that in his current international
dealings Charles works toward something less than the English
national interests? Of course, absolute proof of the host's fig-
uring the king in *Timon* is impossible. However, evidence internal and external to the poem renders the suggestion, I think,
intriguing.

The character of the hostess, too, though perhaps more problematic as a figure of direct political parallel, contributes to
the satire's criticisms of the current royal court. While most
commentators are quick to castigate her as a depraved old
lecheress,[19] I wonder if her function might not approximate
the opposite of such a charge. Judged fairly (i.e., *not* through
the eyes of the narrator), the lady does or says nothing objec-
tionable; in fact, the contrary occurs. It is Timon's mean and
sexist characterization of her as a dried-up coquet who was
once "Fit to give love, and prevent despair" (48), as well as

Huff's crude response to her questioning (61–62), which bring an unsavory air to her portrait. The hostess is not a participant in, but a victim to, the libertine mode of Charles II's circle of wits. Opposing this new court fashion, she stands as a forlorn and not unsympathetic survivor of the more cordial retinue of Charles I.

> My lady she
> Complained our love was coarse, our poetry
> Unfit for modest ears: small whores and players
> Were of our hair-brained youth the only cares;
> Who were too wild for any virtuous league,
> Too rotten to consummate the intrigue.
> Falkland she praised, and Suckling's easy pen,
> And seemed to taste their former parts again.
>
> 101–8

Where in her depiction of the sexual and literary practices of the Ballers does the hostess speak falsely? Her lament for the lost arts of love and poetry is not unlike that of Artemisa. In fact, the hostess may occupy a rare place in Rochester's satire as a plain dealer whose position is *not* adulterated by irony or ambiguity. If so, the direction of the satire runs not in sexist reflection upon her, but in cultural censure of Charles's minion. The hostess also might serve to remind readers that compared to his father's tender regard for his queen, Charles II's relationships with women were nothing short of scandalous. By the early 1670s, the king had developed his curious sentimental/ brutal treatment of his barren queen; had retired in style one royal mistress in Barbara Villiers (of whom he was willing to admit five of her children as his own); had fathered children on at least two actresses, Nell Gwyn proving to be more of a survivor than the less-fortunate Moll Davis; and, aside from any number of less well-recorded infidelities, had recently brought to bear the combined pressure of some of his top ministers as well as the French ambassador to coax Louise de Kéroualle, a young newcomer to the entourage of the queen, into his bed.[20]

It is, however, with the hectors and their politically motivated brawl that *Timon* scores its best hits against the government of Charles II. While the king is credited with the political acumen of an outmoded clown, his ministers are cast as dimwitted and puffed-up supporters of faction. Their debate centers on the valor of the French—a particular sore point in the

administration of Charles at the time. In his alliance with the
English against the Dutch, Louis was not anxious to see the
domains and European influence of his royal cousin enlarge.
On more than one occasion during the war, the French king
maneuvered to ensure that English interests were not served.
This fact dawned only slowly on Charles and his advisors, and
even then there was little they could do about the situation.
They had developed a taste for the secret money supplied by
the French for the war effort—an effort that could not misfire
without their losing crucial stature with the nation and with
Parliament. Thus when Huff and Dingboy exchange words over
the ability of the French army in battle, their topic is no satiric
abstraction about the folly of war, but rather the most vexed
international issue of the day. While it would be glorious to
be able somehow to identify these four characters with real
ministers in Charles's service—the pro-French Huff, for example, with the royal brother James, who had fought as a member
of the French army before the Restoration; or the anti-French,
and therefore by implication pro-Dutch, Dingboy with Shaftesbury, the future leader of the Whig opposition—such a possibility seems remote to me (although James and Shaftesbury
had developed quite an antipathy for one another by this time),
and also not the real point of Rochester's satire.[21] Rather, I
believe the poem solicits the generic, idiotic quality given to
the four ruffians. Regardless of factional bias, the courtiers are
of a kind—in conventional but localized satiric terms, Restoration political fools and knaves.

Huff rebuts Dingboy's aspersion of the French as being cowards throughout military history. The confrontation leads to
upheaval.

> "What they were then, I know not, now they're brave,
> He that denies it—lies and is a slave,"
> Says Huff, and frowned. Says Dingboy, "That do I."
> And at that word, at t'other's head let fly
> A greasy plate, when suddenly, they all
> Together by the ears in parties fall.
> Halfwit with Dingboy joins, Kickum with Huff;
> Their swords were safe, and so we let 'em cuff
> Till they, mine host, and I had all enough.
>
> 165–73

Although the four combatants fall into parties, both as individuals and as political factions they remain indistinguishable in

their fundamental inanity. Their altercation, at heart, is an exercise in big talk and small action. As character types, they recall Bulkeley's description in his letter to Rochester of fops who "woud make ye World believe they are not afraid of dying, & yet are out of heart if the Wind disorders their Hair or ruffles their Cravatts" (see chapter 2, note 3). Huff, Halfwit, Kickum, and Dingboy argue about military courage, then resort to throwing dishes and attempting to box one another's ears. Their swordless melee is a mock reenactment of the real carnage taking place on the continent. As surrogates for Charles's ministers, their paltry efforts at engagement perhaps reflect England's inability to project military might. The English fleet never was able to engage the Dutch fleet decisively during the war, and the planned invasion of Zealand was little more than a fantasy in the minds of Charles's military strategists. Just as the host presides over the meaningless feud of these roaring hectors, so Charles conducts an unproductive war with his incompetent officials.

The diners add knavery to folly in the way they bring their combat to a close. Reports Timon:

> Their rage once over, they begin to treat,
> And six fresh bottles must the peace complete.
>
> 174–75

After expending directionless fury, they negotiate. One has the feeling that their drunken peace will be neither a sincere nor a lasting one. Such a suggestion aptly incriminates king and ministers during this period. Treating as well as double-dealing in place of outright military victory had become a particular specialty of Charles's government. During its second war with the Dutch the Stuart regime made clandestine pacts with the French, broke a previous Anglo-Dutch alliance, entered into war without the consent of Parliament (the first war with the Dutch had ended in English humiliation), when the war dragged on carried out peace negotiations with the Dutch more or less behind the backs of the French (who were doing the same behind English backs), and finally, with the Treaty of Westminster (February 1674), had a not very satisfactory separate peace imposed upon it by a combination of being outmaneuvered militarily and diplomatically by the States-General and by not being able any longer to manage Parliament effectively.[22] Not only is Charles's war meaningless noise, but his treaties are empty machinations. Moreover, the depiction of a dinner party in extreme disarray is a germane image of the administration in 1674. Contrary to the view that after the autumn of 1673 Charles shrewdly engineered an English withdrawal from the conflict, the king's most recent biographer has found evidence to indicate that he appears at this time "not so much as a consummate politician carefully moving his nation out of war as a desperate man obsessed with finding any possible means of continuing a conflict upon which his honour had become staked."[23] In January 1673–74, French agents at Whitehall had the impression that Charles was losing control of not only the situation but of himself. "This sense of royal weakness was borne out by the well-informed correspondents at court of Essex and Williamson, who found it impossible to determine which ministers were in favour as the King swung wildly from one to the other."[24] Though the war ended in a nominal victory for England, the popular impression was that the good of the nation had not been served; rather, many believed that the only concern of Charles and his retainers was for the enrichment of themselves. Many also believed that Charles and his inner circle were plotting to turn the government into an absolute monarchy and the nation back to Catholicism. Ronald Hutton comments of popular opinion at this time: "There was no escaping the sense that during the war years the restored monarchy had entered a new and profoundly uncomfortable era."[25] Both Shaftesbury and Buckingham had been dismissed from Charles's government. James had openly declared his Catholicism. The king had lost his control over Parliament. As a result, one insider at Whitehall observed in February 1674: "There will be a new game played at court, and the designs and interests of all men will be different from what they were."[26] That contest would lead in time to the Exclusion Crisis. Like *Timon*, other of Rochester's commentaries on the king and his counselors charge underlings with vanity and stupidity, while Charles himself is praised mockingly as "a grand politician."[27] At the moment when the nation felt the reign of Charles Stuart take an ominous turn for the worse, it is not unreasonable to postulate that, amid the range of rhetorical play *Timon* provided Rochester's reader in 1674, political comment was a distinct possibility.

What does *Timon* as a political satire, however, have to do with its narrator/narratee being subjected to the social shocks of Democritean satire? Everything, really. Timon begins the

satire elementally as Rochester's reader; he is evidently a
pintle-poet, a writer of libels, a rake, a member of the inner-
circle gang of wits. However, because of what he undergoes
during the course of the satire, he begins to understand the
hollowness and hypocrisy of his own patrician society. More
than a social satire that sneers at upwardly aspiring bourgeois,
which is a reasonable way to read Boileau's third satire, *Timon*
focuses on the education of its narrator, and by extension of its
narratee. Timon, and more expressly the narrator of *Tunbridge
Wells*, becomes the target fop who *sees*. Unwittingly, his tutor
is his host.

As Thormählen comments, this gentleman "is the root cause
of Timon's woes."[28] The host is the controlling entity in the
satire; he presides over the dinner party, indeed, over the society into which Timon finds himself unwillingly transported.
He seizes Timon on the Mall and presses him into his company
and, in effect, into his service. The narrator seems strangely
powerless to resist.

> He runs upon me, cries, "Dear rogue, I'm thine,
> With me some wits of thy acquaintance dine."
> I tell him I'm engaged, but as a whore
> Whose modesty enslaves her spark, the more,
> The longer I denied, the more he pressed;
> At last I e'en consent to be his guest.
>
> 7–12

During the coach ride to his residence, the host attributes a
libel to Timon's hand. Timon denies his authorship, but
frankly as readers we cannot settle the case; for all we know,
Timon might be lying to protect himself. In any event, his
denial is irrelevant. The host has decided the matter already,
not only for himself, but for the entire town.

> He knew my style, he swore, and 'twas in vain
> Thus to deny the issue of my brain.
> Choked with his flattery I no answer make,
> But silent leave him to his dear mistake,
> Which he by this has spread o'er the whole town,
> And me with an officious lie undone.
> Of a well-meaning fool I'm most afraid,
> Who sillily reports what was well-said.
>
> 25–32

Two items from this passage want particular inspection. One is the characterization of the host's lie as "officious." Beside the current meaning of the word, the *O.E.D.* informs us that another was available at the time: "Pertaining to an office or business, official; hence, formal." A magisterial inference perhaps can be read into the host's actions here. Secondly, *what* exactly was "well-said" and *how* exactly is it being "sillily" reported? Is it the libel in question that was well-said, meaning somehow accurate or skillfully trenchant? Might this not suggest that it was Timon's issue after all? And at whom was the libel directed? From the text, we cannot know these things. Equally cryptic, is it the host's alleged misattribution that Timon designates as a silly report of—for the sake of argument— the libel? It would seem to be. But again, facts about the case are oddly irrelevant here.

The host has fabricated a truth that, no matter how inaccurate, nonetheless has genuine consequences for Timon; the host's is a "dear mistake" in the sense that it will have ill consequences not for himself but for the young wit. Moreover, there is the hint that the host has carried out this imaginary act within some sort of official or formal context. Just as the host might personate Charles II in a political reading of Rochester's satire, so he might do the same in a social reading of *Timon*. Over the first thirty lines of the poem, the relationship established between Timon and his host is unusually parallel to that between a court wit (Rochester himself?) and Charles. The host has the leverage to command, to silence, to make, or to break Timon. He pulls the reluctant youth into company that will prove to be to his detriment.[29] Identifying the authorship of libels is a prominent and hazardous pastime of the host's community. The host also has a fatal attraction to wits; he plays the spark to their whore. The host can assemble his circle of wits—regardless of what Timon might think of their quality— at will. He has the authority to mandate fact. When Timon remarks of the host that it is "Of a well-meaning fool I'm most afraid," could not most of Charles's courtiers (as well as ministers and minor officials) say the same? The host/king sets the rules in his society; everyone must play his game or play no game at all. Timon represents, then, the target fop in his predicament of being enthralled—in both senses of that word— in the regime of truth of Charles II. At bottom, Timon/target fop is a victim.[30]

Two major deviations from Boileau's satire heighten Timon's victimization within the purview of Stuart society. One involves reader response to the narrator; the other entails rearrangement of plot.

One feasible reading of Boileau's enactment of *le repas ridicule* is to expose extremes in social behavior and thus imply an Horatian golden mean of correct conduct. On the one hand, a group of vulgar fools, led by the ostentatious dinner host, is held up to ridicule for its vain efforts to ape haute couture, in particular haute cuisine. On the other, the peevish tone of the narrator, who must suffer these fools, serves to chide overzealous epicures such as Boileau had experienced firsthand in the close circle of gourmets centered about the *Croix-Blanche* in Paris. Both pretentious social climbing and elitism are satirized, and the middle way is recommended. Boileau can be seen, then, to employ irony against his narrator, who is made responsible for his own predicament. It was the promise of Boucingo wine and the opportunity to hobnob in the company of Villandry (the famous epicure), Molière, and Lambert (the renowned musician) that inveigled him to accept a dinner invitation from a fop whose solicitations he had been dodging for nearly a year (3.14–28).[31] In contrast, Rochester's satire fosters no irony at Timon's expense. As we have seen, Timon is virtually ambuscaded on the street and, despite protestations, dragged to his epicurean and hospitable undoing. The situation is comic—not ironic—when the entrapped Timon arrives at his host's to find that "Sedley, Buckhurst, Savile" have not come but "Halfwit and Huff, / Kickum and Dingboy" are there instead (34–36). Groans Timon:

> I saw my error, but 'twas now too late:
> No means, nor hopes appear of a retreat.
>
> *   *   *
>
> A wife, good gods! A fop and bullies too!
> For one poor meal, what must I undergo?
>
> 41–42, 45–46

In fact, Timon has committed no error in the satire other than stepping out for a stroll that morning. Neither is there any sense of Timon's own snobbish attempts at self-aggrandizement being foiled. He may look down his nose at the fools surrounding him, but in his entanglement he is at the mercy of the host. The entire scene where the host takes Timon to the doomed meal in his coach, on the way producing the libel, is a departure from Boileau. Significantly, Boileau's narrator is neither a poet nor has the particular reputation for being a man of wit and known to the intimate friends of the king, as does Timon. Neither do culinary improprieties send Timon into seizure, as they can Boileau's narrator (3.81–84). While both speakers find themselves in ludicrous situations, we might tend to feel that Boileau's faultfinder gets what he deserves. For Timon, however, our inclination might be one of commiseration. After all, the former suffers nothing more serious than the indignity of an unremitting use of nutmeg and pepper; the latter is taken prisoner amid company whose master holds sway over palpable nonsense. Readers brought into Timon's narrative confidence empathetically suffer as well at the hands of this collusion of upper-crust blockheads.

Timon also inverts the order of Boileau's original after-dinner conversation. Politics briefly then literature at length constitute the deliberations of the guests in Boileau's satire. A conflict of literary opinion sparks fisticuffs between two guests at the end of that poem. As just discussed, playwrights then party politics occupy Timon's codiners, the second topic precipitating the brawl among all the guests. I do not want to slight the importance of the literary discussion in *Timon*. Not only is it engaging dramatic criticism from the era, but it serves to illustrate the predilection of the host's society to found fashion and popular opinion. (Grave error, as we will see, when *Satire Against Mankind* and *Artemisa* are examined.) However, I want to concentrate instead on the effect Rochester's structural transposition has on Timon and, potentially, on readers.

Once the row ends, the narrator of each satire makes his escape. Boileau's speaker slips away unnoticed and vows epicular mortification should he ever be lured into such company again.

> En pareille cohue on me peut retenir,
> Je consens de bon coeur, pour punir ma folie,
> Que tous les vins pour moi deviennent vins de Brie,
> Qu'à Paris le gibier manque tous les hivers,
> Et qu'à peine au mois d'août l'on mange des pois verts.
> 3.232–36

> [In such a rabble rout you'd catch me nevermore.
> And if you do, I stand content henceforth to see

> All wines alike converted into sour Brie,
> That Paris in the winter void of ven'son be
> And that next August I shall eat not one green pea.]

He is unlikely to undergo his ordeal a second time: having blundered into the disastrous dinner engagement of his own accord, Boileau's narrator is wiser now for the experience and will not repeat his mistake. He is safe in the sanctuary of his snobbery. Timon, on the other hand, bursts from the host's town house with a similar oath.

> I ran downstairs, with a vow nevermore
> To drink beer-glass, and hear the hectors roar.
>
> 176–77

How likely is it, though, that he can maintain his pledge? Timon is vulnerable to being accosted on the Mall in the same way tomorrow. The host and his crew represent not so much a social class that can be snubbed indefinitely, but rather the lion's share of Restoration elite culture. They are Charles and his courtiers; they are Charles and his ministers; they are the beau monde and aspirant beau monde about town—and everything that comes with such privileged society. For Timon, there is no real escape from the din of the symbolic dinner party—just as, perhaps, Rochester complained to Savile of being "shutt up in a Drumme" when at court (see chapter 2) but equally seemed incapable of permanent retirement to the country. Thus with these disturbing social and political reenactments of genteel vanity and diplomatic bedlam in Restoration London emerges the sting of Rochester's Democritean satire in *Timon*. Whatever English high society does may be derisible, but, as Timon discovers, it also can be personally menacing as well as tormentingly unavoidable. This localized insight into the world is the discomforting lesson that suddenly breaks upon the unsuspecting narrator/narratee. The host/Charles stays out of the fray because, as the truth-maker, he controls the fray; he is above the fray. Timon/the edified target fop flees the fray because, now, he knows to fear the fray; he loathes the arbitrary and pointless nature of the fray. But his flight is to no purpose. Conceivably, then, Rochester's satire simultaneously brought anxiety and futility to its immediate readership.

If *Timon* seems probationary in its denunciation of Charles's

mechanics of power, *Tunbridge Wells* is unequivocal in its exposé of the social elite. As the interpretant, Rochester's reader
is subjected to stress which, once more, exceeds gibes at social
inferiors and invites instead a complete reevaluation of the
narratee's cultural habitat. The satire also introduces the basis
for narrative angst present in many of Rochester's most disturbing poems, namely, the misapplication of human reason.
This predicament induces the epistemological resignation expressed in *Satire Against Mankind* and in *Artemisa*. Again, the
figure of the narrator is the primary rhetorical tool of the
satire for bringing all of these issues to light.

Just as Timon is not, as he has been characterized, "a malevolent atom," neither is the narrator of *Tunbridge Wells* the
"querulous, foul-mouthed, and dyspeptic" narrative persona of
native lampoon.[32] Such assessment of their narrative roles is
insufficient; neither is limited to the part of a malcontented
sot venting spleen. (Rochester demonstrates his familiarity
with that device in "A Ramble in St James's Park.") Instead,
both satires concentrate on provoking anxiety and alienation
within their narrative personae.[33] Timon and the narrator of
Tunbridge Wells are estranged observers in the world. They
move uneasily in an environment they find both disconcerting
and vaguely sinister. Trepidation becomes more acute for the
speaker of *Tunbridge Wells;* he satirically emulates the empirical seeker of knowledge who eventually arrives at a repellent
conclusion. That both portraits include an image of the narrator as drinker, gambler, poet, lover, rake, and wit—in short,
the entire courtly libertine *jeu de théâtre*—should not confine
our view of him to biographical sketches of his author or the
superficial instrument of lampoon. Rather, I read this device
as a summons to the target fop to empathize with these speakers. If Rochester wanted to critique and even inform his special
audience, his poetry had to do so in a manner that it would
attend. Either the snare is used contemptuously or as a teaching agent. Probably it is intended as both.

Like *Timon*, *Tunbridge Wells* is dense with Restoration locality.[34] Here I am interested not so much in who are the particular fools bringing distress to the narrator's visit at the wells,
but what exactly he learns from his observations of Restoration gallant society. For *Tunbridge Wells* is not a satiric investigation of humanity at large or even late seventeenth-century
English civilization in general; instead, it is a pointed study
of Rochester's own fashionable community recreating itself.

Thormählen may discern a "certain animus against the gentry" and social climbers in the satire,[35] but except for the group of Irish maligned at lines 77–82, all other casualties of the narrator's comments come from the privileged segment of the English populace, even the second sons suffering humiliation as a result of the practice of primogeniture.[36] I believe the satire is less concerned with splitting hairs about who among these affluent people is slightly more advantaged than the rest than it is with leveling the fraud of entitled society altogether. Therefore, I will focus on the mental journey of the narrator/narratee.

The narrator starts his day as a member in good standing of this select society.

> At five this morning, when Phoebus raised his head
> From Thetis' lap, I raised myself from bed;
> And mounting steed, I trotted to the waters,
> The rendezvous of fools, buffoons, and praters,
> Cuckolds, whores, citizens, their wives and daughters.
>
> 1–5

At this point, his wry aspersions against fellow spa-goers establish the narrator as a wit, not a nihilist. Like Timon, he seems a member of the merry crew of Rochester's own cronies.

> My squeamish stomach I with wine had bribed
> To undertake the dose it was prescribed.
>
> 6–7

However, today something would be exceptional about his traffic with the other members of his caste. Friction quite beyond the scope of routine cutting remarks is abruptly announced by the following triplet.

> But turning head, a cursed sudden crew
> That innocent provision overthrew,
> And without drinking made me purge and spew.
>
> 8–10

It is as though Sartre's sense of nausea suddenly, literally, and without explanation has overtaken the narrator. His initial reaction to his disquiet, naturally enough, is to flee its source. Over the first half of the satire, the narrator actively balks, slinks, and runs from one "new scene of foppery" (47) to the next, but to no purpose. Like Timon, he is unable to disentangle himself from the company of fools. Then, at the center of the poem, both the verbs and the narrator become passive with regard to the society around him. The "silly Macs *were offered to my view*" (78; my italics). Assuming a new mode of deliberate investigation rather than wild evasion, the narrator takes *himself* into the assembly.

> Amidst the crowd next I myself conveyed,
> For now there comes (whitewash and paint being laid)
> Mother and daughter, mistress and the maid;
> And squire with wig and pantaloons displayed.
> But ne'er could conventicle, play, or fair
> For a true medley with this herd compare.
> Here lords, knights, squires, ladies, and countesses,
> Chandlers, mum-bacon-women, sempstresses,
> Were mixed together; nor did they agree
> More in their humours than their quality.
>
> 83–92

Ostensibly, *Tunbridge Wells* locates us in this passage amid the benighted rabble so common to Roman satire. The narrator's description seems to epitomize *lanx satura*—verse filled with many fools. However, Rochester's speaker remarks no chandlers, mum-bacon-women, or seamstresses at close quarters. Rather, he contemplates, at lowest on the social scale, the squirearchy in the form of belles and beaus, ladyships and daughters, and subsequent sons condemned to the military life. The first of these he studies scrupulously. The passage (93–120) of the gallant wooing the young damsel is the longest portrait of the piece and occurs at the middle of the satire. Often celebrated by critics for its affinity with Restoration comedy, the section signals as well, in my view, a crucial moment of transfiguration for the narrator. If he has tried to avoid the unpleasant realities of his social group hitherto, now he takes a good, hard look. As would Pope in *The Rape of the Lock*, he sees only callow, trivial, self-indulgent, unthinking, and undiscerning youth applying their social entitlement and immunity toward sexual romp. (Similar to observing a modern-day fraternity party.)

> With mouth screwed up, and awkward winking eyes,
> And breasts thrust forward—"Lord, sir," she replies,

> "It is your goodness, and not my deserts
> Which makes you show your learning, wit, and parts."
>
> 105–8

Far from condoning this scene of libertine nirvana, as his initial characterization might lead us to expect, the narrator finds their libidinous negotiations intolerable as the "same dull stuff, a thousand different ways" (118). If we must take the narrator for the rake critics make him out to be, in condemning this flirtation, does he not in a sense condemn himself as well? After all, the young gallant scores his carnal hit; in Charles's libertine culture, I doubt womanizers were overweening about style points. The narrator's objection to the tryst is not a taunt at neophyte hedonists; rather, it strikes at the heart of target foppery.

After witnessing how privileged society perpetuates itself, the narrator takes to his heels one more time. He contemplates the next step in the beau's progress: wives who will supply an heir by means of adultery (121–55). At this point, however, the spectacle of his fellow patrons at the wells seems to have wearied him. Growing acquiescent, the narrator surrenders himself to his final group of tormentors: "Some warlike men were now got to the throng" (156). By the end of the satire, after scrutinizing eight or nine different manifestations of upper class frippery, the narrator-educatee arrives at his finding. It comes in the form of an epiphany:

> Bless me, thought I, what thing is man that thus
> In all his shapes he is ridiculous?
> Ourselves with noise of reason we do please
> In vain: humanity's our worst disease.
>
> 173–76

The realization that has rushed into his head is that reason, as used by humans to order their lives—specifically, their Restoration patrician lives—is mere clamor. Not only do we chase egocentric and asinine ends with it, but fruitlessly. We cannot even gratify our own folly. Moreover, since reason is the special attribute of humanity, it is therefore our downfall as well. Thus the comparison of human with bestial happiness.

> Thrice happy beasts are, who because they be
> Of reason void, are so of foppery.
>
> 177–78

The formula of reason = foppery in this couplet is imperative. More than reason and humanity being our bane (as though these horrid insights are not enough), foppery—coxcombry and dandyism; pretensions to wit, wisdom, and accomplishments—plague our existence particularly. In *Tunbridge Wells*, this foppery can only be that of the social milieu of Charles II— the etiquette and affectations of his power elite. Rochester's Democritean satire draws a bead explicitly at Restoration practitioners of truth and power.

Following this new and dispiriting existential cognizance, the narrator, as he began the piece, rides away on his horse. Now, however, he understands that incongruously he travels on the back of his intellectual better.

> Troth, I was so ashamed that, with remorse
> I used the insolence to mount my horse;
> For he, doing only things fit for his nature,
> Did seem to me by much the wiser creature.
>
> 179–82[37]

While this ending adds nothing more to the narrator's new understanding of his society, it does supply the reader with essential information about how the narrator *feels* after his unexpected educational episode at the springs. He admits to guilt and sorrow for his own foppish human behavior; he recognizes the audacity of his misguided human reason. The narrator of *Tunbridge Wells* has seen his world turn trivial before his eyes. Like Timon, he has heard the hectors roar; more than Timon, he knows now that the hectors include himself. The full and harrowing implications of this new knowledge will be explored in Rochester's other major Democritean satires. The main function of *Timon* and, in particular, *Tunbridge Wells* would seem to be to administer a rude wake-up call to their narratee.

4

Linguistic Iconoclasm

And all the subject matter of debate
Is only, who's a knave of the first rate?
                    —Rochester, *A Satire Against Mankind*

IF the satires *Timon* and *Tunbridge Wells* serve to notify the
target fop of his precarious social and intellectual position in
the Restoration world, then *A Satire Against Mankind* and *A
Letter fancied from Artemisa in the Town to Chloe in the Country*
create an even more threatening and thoroughgoing local
habitation and a name for his predicament. In chapter 2, I
commented how Rochester's verse often mimics the insincerity and cacophony of court life in order to satirize that same
noise and hypocrisy. In these two Democritean satires, this
circumstance occurs in the extreme. *Satire Against Mankind*
presents the reader with a rational impasse; *Artemisa* renders,
in the end, textual and linguistic anarchy. Both compositions
are apt to drive the interpretant to distraction in his quandary
to locate system and meaning, for at the heart of each satire
is the collision of falsely reasoned order with naturally sensed
chaos—something only implicit in *Timon* and *Tunbridge Wells*.
This confrontation is played out not only at the abstract, philosophical level of ideas, but principally at the social and political level of Restoration England—that is, on the target fop's
home turf. The particularities of Charles II's oppressive gov-
ernmental rule and libertine court culture provide the ultimate source of both rational failure and textual disorientation
in these works. Charles's regime of truth appears as a vast
masquerade, an elaborate cognitive and factional sham that
benefits some to the great cost of most. Moreover, the fabrication of such jurisdictions of truth and power seems to be an
inescapable fact of human existence. With these Democritean

70

themes, Rochester's verse engages not just the sensual libertine of the age (see chapter 5), but the freethinking *libertin
érudit* as well.[1]

Locality is so dense in *Satire Against Mankind* that the modern reader's initial response might be to ignore it altogether
in favor of a more universalized reading of the poem.[2] While
a similar generalized comprehension of the satire might be
reached in this way, certainly the contemporary reader of
Rochester's verse did not arrive at an understanding in such
a manner; neither with this imprecise method of reading can
one appreciate as much the attack mounted in the poem
against the power elite of the day. Rochester's satire confronts
the reader with an intolerable choice as late seventeenth-
century Englishmen: either impose spurious, ludicrous, and
destructive order on the world via the misapplication of reason, or cope with earthly chaos. The false order assailed in
the satire is personified primarily by a narrative *adversarius*
representing the currently ascendant orthodoxy of the Anglican clergy. Natural chaos, on the other hand, may be dealt with
via a vaguely delineated "right reason" upheld by Rochester's
narrator and resembling prevailing libertine freethinking and
extreme skepticism. In the end, even though over the first part
of *Satire Against Mankind* Rochester's narrator seems to offer
a positivist alternative to corrupt conjectural thinking, such a
pleasing notion nowhere is validated over the second part of
the satire. When the narrator declares "Thus I think reason
righted, but for man, / I'll ne'er recant, defend him if you can"
(112–13), he effectively annuls right reason as a workable
countersolution to contemporary paranoia and will-to-power.[3]
According to Rochester's satire, English society is inextricably
ensnared in a Hobbesian and Machiavellian web of fear and
hypocrisy; the only way to rise above it is not to be part of
it—in other words, not to be English, even arguably human.
Such an elective is hardly feasible. In *Satire Against Man*, patrician society's lot is to reason foppishly and to systematize fal-
laciously. This conviction reiterates and elaborates upon the
afflictive conclusion of *Tunbridge Wells:* existence itself is the
narratee's defect.

Rochester's narrator opens with a general assault on human
reason. We are described as "strange, prodigious creatures"
and summarized as "that vain animal, / Who is so proud of
being rational" (2, 6–7). "Prodigious" implies amazing in a
monstrous, nearly criminal sense (*O.E.D.*); our ratiocination is

vain both in its egoism and in its ultimate incompetence. Our inherent foppery is to ignore our proper five senses to be guided instead by our reason, which we fashion into a bogus sixth sense.[4]

> His senses are too gross; and he'll contrive
> A sixth, to contradict the other five;
> And before certain instinct will prefer
> Reason, which fifty times for one does err.
>
> 8–11

This sixth sense will prove to be in the satire a capacity that allows humans to imagine and contrive reality rather than actually experience the world—a human quality that Marxists often define as ideology. The narrator does not claim our instinct to be infallible; however, our five natural senses are not nearly and wildly erratic as our contrived sixth. The former he calls our "light of nature" (13); the latter, in a justifiably celebrated passage (12–24), he characterizes as the "*ignis fatuus* of the mind" (12). The result of our delusion is a life spent reeling amid the confusion and mistakes of mere conjecture.

> Then old age and experience, hand in hand,
> Lead him to death, make him to understand,
> After a search so painful, and so long,
> That all his life he has been in the wrong:
> Huddled in dirt the reasoning engine lies,
> Who was so proud, so witty, and so wise.
>
> 25–30

As will become plain during the second part of the satire where the narrator delineates the brutal nature of human social order, we are perhaps less to be pitied for our dear fallacy than condemned. Our facility for groundless reasoning enables certain people to invent and impose false systems in the world that manifest themselves as oppressive social constructions.

For the first time in the satire Rochester's narrator brings these contentious notions closer to home for the narratee target fop when he pauses to examine the role of wit in this calamity.

> And Wit was his vain, frivolous pretence
> Of pleasing others, at his own expense.
> For wits are treated just like common whores,

First they're enjoyed, and then kicked out of doors;
The pleasure past, a threatening doubt remains,
That frights th' enjoyer with succeeding pains:
Women and men of wit are dangerous tools,
And ever fatal to admiring fools.
Pleasure allures, and when the fops escape,
'Tis not that they're beloved, but fortunate,
And therefore what they fear, at heart they hate.

35–45

Suddenly with these lines we are returned to the specifically fashionable world of *Timon*. As a man of wit, Timon compares himself to a whore who attracts the spark or admiring fool—in his case, his host (9–11). Like Charles, Timon's host has a strong attraction to wits, and his fondness has the effect of subjecting Timon (and the narratee) to an unstable and irksome social environment. The practice of wit in *Satire Against Mankind* portends, however, a far more sinister outcome than that of suffering through a ridiculous meal. In this passage, more than a well-meaning fool such as was Timon's host, the enjoyer of the man of wit somehow is vitally threatened by his pleasure and threatens the man of wit in return. Wit, like the venereal disease carried by whores, somehow works on the mind of the fop. Where sexually his health is menaced by the one, intellectually his well-being seems to be jeopardized by the other. The "threatening doubt" and "succeeding pains" that frighten and might prove fatal to the fool probably suggest the cynicism and skepticism associated with the atheistic wit of Charles's court.

As a result, the man of wit (like the whore) is feared and hated, exploited by the patron then as quickly repudiated. Where Timon was an innocent victim of his tribulation, the practitioner of wit in *Satire Against Mankind* makes himself a dangerous plaything in the hands of those more powerful than he. Falling prey to the enticement of his sixth sense, the man of wit, in a "frivolous pretence / Of pleasing others" and thereby gaining security (the motivation for all human action according to the second part of the satire), ironically only works his own demise. Again, the most conspicuous example of an aficionado of wits (and whores) during the age was Charles. Not so much for Rochester personally as for his companions and intended readers generally, this odd passage dwelling on the danger of wit serves to situate that special segment of Restoration society—the courtier and patrician rake—within the bleak, contemplative arguments of the satire as well as within the real social peril it outlines. Rochester's own well-being depended on how well or ill Charles received his vassal's volleys of wit. Rochester's verse asserts that, like the fools at Tunbridge Wells, the court and town wits vainly please themselves with the noise of their own reason. Perhaps not quite as recognizably as *Timon* and *Tunbridge Wells, Satire Against Mankind* nonetheless speaks directly and ultimately more exigently to the target fop.

With the interlocutory challenge of the "formal band and beard" (46), Rochester's satire both personifies and specifies its attack on reason. Thormählen has identified the adversarius ultimately to represent "post-Restoration Anglicanism with its consistent emphasis on reason."[5] Though the satiric portrait is distorted, the Latitudinarian or Cambridge Platonist faction of the church is unmistakable in him.[6] The tenets he champions, however, are broad enough to signal "middle-of-the-road views which any clergyman at the time could have uttered, whether he was an ex-Covenater or a bred-in-the-bone Anglican. Some of them would have been voiced by a Roman Catholic priest, too."[7] Rochester's narrator goes up against, in essence, the Christian orthodoxy of later seventeenth-century England—God and his hypostases in its current habit. The adversarius's speech amounts to an encomium to speculative reasoning.

> *Blessed glorious man! To whom alone kind heaven*
> *An everlasting soul hath freely given;*
> *Whom his great maker took such care to make,*
> *That from himself he did the image take;*
> *And this fair frame in shining reason dressed,*
> *To dignify his nature above beast.*
> *Reason, by whose aspiring influence*
> *We take a flight beyond material sense,*
> *Dive into mysteries, then soaring pierce*
> *The flaming limits of the universe,*
> *Search heaven and hell, find out what's acted there,*
> *And give the world true grounds of hope and fear.*
>
> 60–71

Humans have been made in God's rational image; we occupy therefore a station above the beasts; provided with the ability to reason, we necessarily "take a flight beyond material sense" and pierce the "flaming limits of the universe"—namely, we

profess to comprehend God's master plan. The narrator immediately rebuts each assertion.

To the notion that "Blessed glorious man" is made in the
godhead's rational likeness, he replies that reason in fact
causes such a delusion:

> And 'tis this very Reason I despise,
> This supernatural gift that makes a mite
> Think he's an image of the infinite;
> Comparing his short life, void of all rest,
> To the eternal, and the ever-blessed.
>
> 75–79

To annul the idea that humans, dressed in "shining reason,"
are superior to beasts, Rochester's narrator provides quite a
different portrait of rational humanity.

> This busy, pushing stirrer-up of doubt,
> That frames deep mysteries, then finds them out;
> Filling with frantic crowds of thinking fools
> The reverend bedlams, colleges and schools.
>
> 80–83

To his adversary's highest praise of reason, that with it humans
can understand the great mysteries of existence, he retorts
sardonically:

> Borne on whose wings each heavy sot can pierce
> The limits of the boundless universe:
> So charming ointments make an old witch fly,
> And bear a crippled carcass through the sky.
> 'Tis the exalted power whose business lies
> In nonsense, and impossibilities.
>
> 84–89

The mocking oxymoron of piercing the *limits* of a *boundless*
universe at once derides and reverses the clergyman's conception of the universe as finite and comprehendible and echoes
the phrase "Doubt's boundless sea" (19) used earlier to describe
the predicament of humanity misled by reason. Speculative
reasoning arrives at nonsense and impossibilities; it yields
conceptions of reality which, since they are formulated beyond
material sense, have nothing much to do with materiality.
Rochester's narrator prefers to keep the narratee's feet on the
ground instead.

> But thoughts are given for action's government;
> Where action ceases, thought's impertinent:
> Our sphere of action is life's happiness,
> And he that thinks beyond thinks like an ass.
>
> 94–97

The vital point of difference between these two views of human reason, then, boils down to this: what is the proper source of information on which to base correct conduct in the world? Action, government, and the pursuit of happiness both individual and communal are the real issues under debate in the satire. *Satire Against Mankind* radiates questions of polity. The disputants posit acutely conflicting ideas on how we should determine the course of these matters.

Specifically, when the adversarius avows that human reason can "Search heaven and hell, find out what's acted there, / And give the world true grounds of hope and fear," he argues in practical terms that the groundwork of proper government exists in the minds of the educated, moneyed, and thereby entitled minority of the nation. *They* determine right from wrong; *they* furnish us with the "true grounds" for correct conduct; *they* frame our social order. And they do so not only magnificently divorced from material reality but with decided prejudice toward their *own* well-being. Given the fact that religion and politics were virtually interchangeable concerns during the seventeenth century, we should not persuade ourselves that Rochester's satire engages only in the abstractions of theological and philosophical polemic. Practical and crucial issues of who should hold sway over whom and why are at stake in *Satire Against Mankind.* I believe the poem represents Rochester's most detailed portrait of political England, and it is a bleak picture indeed. His narrator offers an alternative view as to the source of credible ordinance in the world. Rather than springing from the deluded and self-serving fantasies of the elect and the immune, our behavioral impetus fittingly arises from material nature. "Right reason" is defined as

> That reason which distinguishes by sense,
> And gives us rules of good and ill from thence;
> That bounds desires, with a reforming will
> To keep 'em more in vigour, not to kill.
> Your reason hinders, mine helps to enjoy,
> Renewing appetites yours would destroy.
> My reason is my friend, yours is a cheat,

Hunger calls out, my reason bids me eat;
Perversely, yours your appetite does mock:
This asks for food, that answers, "what's o'clock?"

100–109

Just as in the case of Rochester's conversations with Burnet—
another debate involving a practitioner of wit and a clergyman—the dispute between narrator and interlocutor revolves
around the former's unwillingness to accept as valid anything
beyond human perception. For him, right reason is an a poste-
riori proposition, not the a priori formula of the adversarius.
Nothing exists in the mind prior to, or independent of, experience; our actions in the world should not be based on phan-
toms of the human brain.

Critics who find nothing more than a doctrine of hedonism
in the narrator's position take the passage both too lightly and
with too much of Rochester's reputation as a rake in mind;[8]
one wonders how these lines would be received had they been
written by Pope. Rochester's satire argues not against all reason, nor does it advocate unthinking sensual abandon; on the
contrary, a "reforming will" that "bounds desires" is advocated. Ultimately what his narrator calls for is a marriage of
mind and body—precisely those things Descartes had considered hopelessly divorced—or, more exactly, for the mind to
act as *part* of the body. Rochester's narrator is unprepared to
countenance doctrines formulated outside of, to use an unusual phrase, the physical reach of the mind. His position perhaps is unorthodox, possibly extreme even for freethinkers on
both sides of the Channel.[9] But, like neo-Epicureanism, it is
not merely about food, wine, and mirth and thus devoid of
political insinuation. Tangible "rules of good and ill" originate
from a study of nature via our five senses. Elements of the
social theory of Hobbes and Montaigne help actuate the narrator's stance.[10] In leading a sensible life of temperance accomplished through the balance of reason and appetite, it seems
that the evils of repression and hunger are avoided. Reason
becomes our private friend rather than "a cheat" artificially
regulating our public lives. Such a scenario of sentient personal security in conflict with methodical social oppression
strikes me as fundamentally the same argument elaborated at
great length by John Locke in his *Two Treatises of Government*
where he advocates constitutional versus absolute monarchy.
In different ways, both pieces of writing revolve around the

issue of private property. Rochester's narrator is anxious to gain the right to possess and to act upon his *own* rules of good and ill, not those handed him by the church and state. While in our century we might be inclined to see anarchy and nihilism only in such an assertion of intellectual private property, to readers at the court of Charles II and in the sophisticated and politicized coffee and ale houses of Restoration London, equally available readings might include the clash of clergyman and Epicurean, of established church and dissenting creeds, as well as hints of the mounting tensions between crown and Parliament. Rochester's satire is not concerned with just anyone's operation of speculative reasoning, but expressly with those men, namely clergymen, schoolmen, and politicians, who control the state *via* the exercise of speculative reasoning.[11] Like Locke's *Second Treatise*, Rochester's *Satire Against Mankind* courts a sense of generality and even, if read wrongly, ahistoricity. Beneath its surface, however, a severe case is made against Stuart society. Also like Locke's essay, Rochester's satire willingly and forcibly embraces the chaotic implications (for Locke, the possibility of civil war) of its organic and individualistic right reason as a preferable alternative to subjugation at the hands of the current regime.[12] Rochester's narrator concludes with regard to his opponent's hypothetical thinking, "'Tis not true reason I despise, but yours" (111).

What particularly drives home the satire's critique of the Restoration social order is the fact that as soon as the narrator's concept of right reason is sketched out, it virtually drops from sight for the remainder of the poem.[13] Instead of praise or elaboration of his heretical doctrine, the narrator returns to consideration of the theriophilic opening of the satire and quickly shapes his *quaestio* ("disputed question")[14] into an exposé of the misery caused to humanity by speculative reasoning. Once again, this portrait of human nature can be read at the universal level of conventional satiric misanthropy; however, we must keep in mind that the depiction leads us squarely to the precincts of Charles's court. Not only is right reason never satisfactorily demonstrated, but it becomes by the end of the satire an asset unattainable to the general community. At best, it might serve as a way for the rare individual to live somewhat more sanely within the dementia of highborn society.[15] Could this idea be a bit of counsel intended for Rochester's brother wits? Given the passage just discussed concerning wit as a self-destructive pursuit in patrician society, such a surmise is not unrealistic. Any indication that right reason could be practiced by humanity at large—or, more precisely, by the Restoration ruling class in particular—is crushed, however, under the iconoclastic millstone of Democritean satire.

According to Rochester's satire, what distinguishes beast from human is necessity from wantonness.

> Birds feed on birds, beasts on each other prey,
> But savage man alone does man betray:
> Pressed by necessity, they kill for food,
> Man undoes man, to do himself no good.
>
> 129–32

Animals engage in an instinctive war for survival; perversely—both in the sense of mulishly and degenerately—humans pursue empty supremacy over their fellows.

> With teeth and claws, by nature armed, they hunt
> Nature's allowance, to supply their want.
> But man, with smiles, embraces, friendships, praise,
> Inhumanely his fellow's life betrays;
> With voluntary pains works his distress,
> Not through necessity, but wantonness.
>
> 133–38

Through unfounded and childish behavior, we cruelly and capriciously seek to undo others before they can undo us. Ironically, our inhumane hunt for power results in no personalized good: because everyone is engaged in the same blood sport, rather than securing our own well-being we involve ourselves in perpetual collective strife. Unlike Hobbes in *Leviathan*, Rochester's satire holds out to us no prospect of a superstate into which to entrust, perforce, our care.[16] Just the opposite, Rochester's satire insists that those who devise the superstate by means of the nonsensical fabrication of truth—namely, the statesman and the clergyman—are chiefly *responsible* for our predicament and misery. This sobering revelation is why "in their own degree" (115) beasts are wiser and of a superior moral nature than people. Animals are not innately better than humans, but because "man" in "all his pride, and his philosophy" (114) engages in disastrous speculative reasoning, he makes himself less instinctually intelligent than beasts. In eschewing right reason, that hybrid of instinct and intellect, humans demote themselves from the obvious apex of animals, having the greatest mental capacities coupled with their natural sensorial capabilities, to the basest creature on earth. Moreover, we accomplish this horror systematically and as a species under the auspices of those contrivances we call society and politics.

The sole motivator of our reckless behavior is fear for our private security.

> For hunger or for love they bite, or tear,
> Whilst wretched man is still in arms for fear.
> For fear he arms, and is of arms afraid:
> From fear, to fear, successively betrayed.
>
> 139–42

Both anticipating the arguments of the National Rifle Association and contradicting a future slogan of FDR, the narrator's claim that fear herds us into the delusional sphere of speculative reasoning at a stroke reduces human society to a tiresome and wretched fraud. Even what we typically consider the more worthy qualities of humanity in fact are products of dread. "Base fear" is the source of honor, fame, power, bravery, generosity, affability, kindness, and wisdom (143–49). Because of fear a man "screws his actions, in a forced disguise" (150). Our social and political life is therefore a masquerade wherein a fragile veil of sentimentality conceals a predatory community of stupid brutality. Under this guise of culture, a person "Leads a most tedious life in misery, / Under laborious, mean hypocrisy" (151–52). Fraudulent social order, which we ourselves generate from gross assumption, in turn creates, more, *forces* us into our miserable condition of endless and precarious counterfeit. The self-inflicted catastrophe is a peculiarly human trait; no other animal contrives its own ruin.[17] Our bathetic/pathetic drama plays on a civic stage.

> Look to the bottom of his vast design,
> Wherein man's wisdom, power, and glory join:
> The good he acts, the ill he does endure,
> 'Tis all from fear, to make himself secure.
>
> 153–56

The logical conclusion of this tale of dullness and panic is that human community is nothing more than a conglomerate of ignorant cowards.

The narrator concludes his portrait of social order with profoundly disturbing vituperation. The picture he makes us see runs contrary to all fond images of ourselves. Consummate cowards, we are not even brave enough to be cowardly: "Merely for safety after fame they thirst, / For all men would be cowards if they durst" (157–58). Human consternation runs so deep that even our natural fear of harm is overwhelmed by the mandate to participate in tangibly deleterious social pretense—another example, like the epiphany that grieved the narrator of *Tunbridge Wells*, of how far beneath the natural wisdom of beasts we have slipped. Within this climate, anything like instinctual goodness becomes suicidal.

> And honesty's against all common sense,
> Men must be knaves, 'tis in their own defence.
> Mankind's dishonest: if you think it fair
> Among known cheats to play upon the square,
> You'll be undone.
>
> 159–63

Humans, and especially Rochester's Restoration narratee, live tangled in a web of terror and hypocrisy without practical means to break free. Proposing alternative versions to conventional wisdom leads virtually to crucifixion.

> Nor can weak truth your reputation save,
> The knaves will all agree to call you knave.
> Wronged shall he live, insulted o'er, oppressed,
> Who dares be less a villain than the rest.
>
> 164–67

Such a pragmatist will find himself suppressed, out of favor, remote from power, excommunicated, banished—all acutely recognizable perils of courtly vocation. These lines speak of partisan repression as much as moral or philosophical isolation. The socially distressed narrators of *Timon* and *Tunbridge Wells* have been lowered to the condition of political prisoners in *Satire Against Mankind*. Further, at this point, hopes of the narrator's previously stated right reason providing us with rational relief must disappear. Such "weak truth" could not survive our ruthless, insensible travesty. Still addressing his adversarius, the narrator mordantly replaces the interlocutor's earlier vaunted opinion of humanity with his own grim summary.

> Thus sir, you see what human nature craves,
> Most men are cowards, all men should be knaves;
> The difference lies, as far as I can see,
> Not in the thing itself, but the degree;
> And all the subject matter of debate
> Is only, who's a knave of the first rate?
>
>   168–73

Coward or knave is merely semantics; all are of a kind, and who manufactures truth the readiest and manipulates power the best will lead our parade of imbeciles. The word "craves" is particularly damning in this account: it designates volition. Humans—courtiers even more—do not passively suffer their fate, but actively facilitate their distress. Reasoning beyond the ken of physical knowledge seems to be a human fetish.[18]

If the narrator's pronouncements sound like overstatement to twentieth-century readers—come on, we aren't *that* bad—I suggest this is because we are not the satire's intended audience. Calibrated in the narrator's satiric cross hairs instead is Rochester's target fop. His description of a pack of paranoid scoundrels and poltroons sounds nothing so much like Rochester's description of life at Charles's court (see chapters 2 and 6). While we may be tempted to apply the narrator's remarks to power brokers on and about our own Capitol Hill, *Satire Against Mankind* closes by deliberately locating the phenomenon of speculative reasoning and of the fabrication of man-made order at the seat of Restoration power. The narrator begins his coda defiantly.[19]

> All this with indignation have I hurled
> At the pretending part of the proud world,
> Who, swollen with selfish vanity, devise,
> False freedoms, holy cheats, and formal lies,
> Over their fellow-slaves to tyrannise.
>
>   1–5

The "indignation" of the narrator culminates a movement throughout the satire from an ethos of wry observer at the beginning of the poem—in essence, Horace's *vir bonus*—to one of perturbation at the narrator's account of corrupt human nature. A tone of Juvenal's *vir iratus* accompanies the mounting horrid truths of Democritean satire. The "pretending part of the proud world" that causes his satiric fury refers explicitly to authority-wielding speculative reasoners in their hypocriti-

cal efforts to subjugate their fellow beings. Marianne Thormählen's reading of "False freedoms, holy cheats, and formal
lies" as signaling, respectively, the manipulative lies of statesmen, clergymen, and university professors is admirable.[20]
Rochester's satire affronts the mechanics of truth and power
square in the face. In particular, the opening remarks of the
Addition hark back to the speech of the clerical *adversarius*
where he asserts that his a priori reasoning can "give the world
true grounds of hope and fear" (71)—in other words, stipulate
the laws of religion and society. The narrator has since savagely debunked this fallacy. Not only is the assumption motivated by human conceit, but, at the level of political
consequence, it is swollen as well by "selfish vanity." Officers
of various human institutions may protest to serve king and
country, God, or the pursuit of knowledge; in fact, they serve
themselves by ruthlessly acquiring and maintaining a hold on
privilege. Precariously, as the narrator has contended, these
men undo others to do themselves, in the end, no durable good.
The laws, rituals, and protocol of society represent nothing
more than the pathetic exhibition of one slave of humanity's
fearful natural condition fabricating rules with which to tyrannize his "fellow-slaves." All suffer as a result of this charade
of civilization. Rochester's narrator seems to regard clergymen
as one of the most pernicious breeds of knave-of-the-first-rate.
In the *Addition*, one other kind is appended by implication.

Mocking the "whimsical philosopher" Diogenes once more
(cf. 90–91), the remainder of the *Addition* conducts an ironic
search through the court for one good man whose example
would force Rochester's narrator to recant the opening paradox of the satire—that is, that he would rather be a beast than
a human. The narrator first conjures a picture of the ideal
politician.

> But if in Court so just a man there be,
> (In Court, a just man—yet unknown to me)
> Who does his needful flattery direct
> Not to oppress and ruin, but protect;
> Since flattery, which way soever laid,
> Is still a tax on that unhappy trade.
> If so upright a statesman you can find,
> Whose passions bend to his unbiased mind,
> Who does his arts and policies apply

To raise his country, not his family;
Nor while his pride owned avarice withstands,
Receives close bribes, from friends corrupted hands.

6–17

This characterization of an imaginary just minister amounts
to condemnation of Charles's actual ones (similar to the censure implicit in the hectors of *Timon*). Such a paragon is a
mirage at court, unknown to the narrator. What this politician
would do if he existed in fact delineates what current administrators *should* perform, but don't. While "needful flattery" is a
regrettable fact of Restoration political life, it should be applied not to "oppress and ruin," but to "protect." We have seen
that within the argumentative framework of *Satire Against
Mankind*, political evil results from the wanton misapplication
of human reason in contriving a regime of truth: speculative
reason is the authoritarian's specific method of bringing about
oppression and ruin. I believe as countermeasure Rochester's
narrator suggests here that political benefit will come only as
a result of the preservation of an individual's right to understand and to maintain his own view of the world: this asset is
the basic human liberty that must be safeguarded. Only then
will slaves cease to tyrannize fellow-slaves. The ideal politician
achieves his *right reason*—in the narrator's earlier definition
of that term—by regulating his passions with "his unbiased
mind."

At this point in the poem(s) we find exemplified, however
vaguely but in expressly *political* circumstances, the mind-
body union advocated earlier by Rochester's satire. An unbiased mind implies that the good statesman does not participate in the prejudice and partiality of the adversarius's
baseless reasoning; instead, he harnesses his desire for advancement or certainty with a reforming will that submits his
speculations to the reality check of actual cases—that is, to
political experience. What really *does* bring about civic, famil-
ial, and individual good: false elevation of me and mine that
arouses discord—recent examples being Charles's two Dutch
wars—or applying "his arts and policies" in order "To raise his
country, not his family"? Clearly, the narrator believes that
corporate strength breeds individual security; the inverse of
that formula, the Machiavellian pursuit of private fortune,
breeds tyranny. Therefore, the just politician exercises natural
sense to promote the advancement of the commonwealth. The

unjust politician leaves the perfidious status quo unaltered in order to profit from the subterfuge. In *Last Instructions to a Painter,* Andrew Marvell contrasts the Country with the Court party in exactly the same terms. With "gen'rous Conscience" and "Courage high" the former serves the king "with clear Counsells" (983–84; see also 287–92).[21] The latter are portrayed as "scratching Courtiers" and the "smallest Vermine" who, in "Burr'wing themselves to hoord their guilty store," undermine "the Palace's Foundations" and so bring destruction to the government and the nation (976–80). Not only would receiving bribes from friends be unworthy conduct on the part of the narrator's ideal politician, conduct motivated by "his pride owned avarice" and illusions of entitlement, but such action would reveal impaired reasoning on his part as well. Like the adversarius, he would be thinking foolishly beyond material sense and, ultimately, cultivating his own adversity. Since the narrator's fictional statesman practices right reason, Rochester's satire charges that the factual statesmen at court, to include the king, practice instead this literally senseless form of speculative self-deceit.

The narrator's other facetious quarry is the good churchman. Here perhaps Stillingfleet comes in for scathing censure for his "vain prelatic pride" and "obstreperous, saucy eloquence"; from the pulpit he dares "To chide at kings, and rail at men of sense" (see 20–24).[22] Whether attacking this contemporary or further stigmatizing Latitudinarian clergy as a group, the passage, roughly twice as long as that on the statesman, asks and answers negatively two questions: "Is there a churchman who on God relies? / Whose life, his faith and doctrine justifies?" (18–19). Obviously, both inquiries are pointed. The first wonders if clergy actually receive their true grounds for hope and fear from God, as they claim, or if they rely on their own whimsies to concoct them. The second then demands to see a churchman whose own conduct lives up to that he would impose on the rest of us. The ideal clergyman is as much a reverie as the ideal politician. He would be:

> But a meek, humble man, of honest sense,
> Who preaching peace does practise continence;
> Whose pious life's a proof he does believe
> Mysterious truths which no man can conceive.
>
> 43–46

Notably, such a clergyman would have "honest sense" as opposed to the patently dishonest sense of the adversarius; moreover, Rochester's narrator does not demand or even imply that
he seeks proof that the "Mysterious truths" professed by the
good churchman be revealed as fact. Such revelation is impossible and unknowable; "no man can conceive" the infinite. All
the narrator would enjoy witnessing is one clergyman whose
faith—as opposed to reason—is such that he conducts his life
in absolute practice of what he believes and preaches. What
the narrator surveys instead is clerical hypocrisy and, worst
of all, political ambition. (I think it pertinent to keep in mind
here as well Rochester's telling Burnet that what most turned
him toward irreligion was the observation of clerical behavior
at court; see chapter 2.) By the end of the passage, churchman
and statesman become one essential creature in lines that
might well attack Charles's archbishop of Canterbury, Gilbert Sheldon.[23]

> Nor doting bishop, who would be adored
> For domineering at the Council board;
> A greater fop, in business at fourscore,
> Fonder of serious toys, affected more,
> Than the gay, glittering fool at twenty proves,
> With all his noise, his tawdry clothes and loves.
>
> 37–42

Political, religious, and social vanity combine in the old
bishop. The "Council board" he seeks to dominate is the king's
Privy Council; the "business" and "serious toys" he adores are
schemes of political and religious intrigue; in his love of the
trappings of power, his foppery is more intolerable than that
of the young blade. In this single portrait, perhaps, exists a
mosaic of all target foppery.

At the close of the *Addition*, Rochester's narrator anticipates
no likelihood ever of recanting his original position. If the im-
peccable statesman and churchman were ever to come to light,
they would be worthy of the narrator's political and ethical
alliance *only* because such figures would be, in effect,
extrahuman.

> If upon Earth there dwell such god-like men,
> I'll here recant my paradox to them,

Adore those shrines of virtue, homage pay,
And with the rabble world their laws obey.

47–50

The narrator will retract his theriophilic paradox *to them* alone, never to the deluded mass of humanity; he will obey *their laws*, not those of the current status quo. Only under the guidance of these suprahumans would he be willing to take a place in "the rabble world"; until that time, he will have no business with the credulous hoi polloi or its calculating overlords. The implicit *rejection* of mundane shrines, homage, laws, and obedience in these lines countenances rebellion, not capitulation, on the part of Rochester's narrator. He insists of the flawless pair:

If such there are, yet grant me this at least,
Man differs more from man than man from beast.

51–52

In other words, if such governors did exist, they would be so exceptional that the ordinary human would have far more in common with the beast than he or she would with these chimerical people of godlike understanding. Truth may exist on a supranatural level, but Rochester's narrator is convinced that we are not equipped with the intellectual means to grasp it. Like the beast, the material world is our lot. To the material world we must confine our thoughts and actions.

But the political fact of the matter is that humans do not constrain themselves to their five senses. Fabricating truth as a device to gain security is our distinctive and immutable trait.[24] Unfortunately, in that gambit to assuage our fear, we create confederations of miserable hypocrisy. Given the depth of human depravity that comes as a result of our impertinent pursuit of truth and power, the narrator's alternative of coping with natural chaos as experienced by the senses seems the height of sanity. However, as *Satire Against Mankind* makes abundantly clear, such rational behavior at best might be the province of a special few. Even then, those few would not be immune to the insanity of the larger community; there is no escape from the Democritean insight that the noise of reason is our worst disease. In the satire, that lethal commotion is incarnated by the entourage of Charles II—by the churchmen, statesmen, and wits of the royal fraternity. When noting that

the events of the Popish Plot have been described as "an extraordinary tale of human credulity, knavery and folly," Ronald Hutton comments: "It might be added that it would have
been extraordinary if those three qualities had not characterized most of the politics of Charles's reign."[25] Rochester's
model of human unreason was the very life he led at the hub of
English statecraft. Indeed, in its endorsement of right reason,
Rochester's satire may advise courtiers to dare to imbibe that
second bottle of wine, but the purpose behind that sensorial
policy extends beyond mere drunkenness. In a courtly setting
where good fellowship is mere ruse and oppressive convention,
where wit is a self-destructive prerequisite for inclusion, right
reason is offered as an alternative admonition to that of the
formal band and beard. Both the narrator and the adversarius
denounce wit; the latter cries: "anything that's writ / Against
this jibing, jingling knack called Wit / Likes me abundantly"
(48–50). However, the clergyman attacks wit as part of a killjoy
creed that demands, more seriously, knuckling under to an
anesthetizing status quo. The narrator's warning, on the other
hand, calls for a more rational and humane mode of living
based on the doctrine—as Locke, too, contends—that ultimately all knowledge is derived from sensation. Howsoever
without expectation of its attainment, Rochester's satire calls
for good fellowship well surpassing that of drinking companions; it calls for a degree of liberty apparently unavailable to
Englishmen of the time as social animals.

If *Satire Against Mankind* abandons us in predicament, *A
Letter from Artemisa to Chloe* engulfs us in conundrum. In
Rochester's most meditative and challenging poem, a reader
might recognize the clash of sensorial versus speculative reasoning and the political consequences of the latter overpowering the former. In Rochester's longest, most dramatic, and
thereby most convoluted poem, a reader detects similar con-
tests between dissenting perspectives of the world. However,
arriving at consequence or outcome or even at a point to it
all proves a more difficult project. Thormählen observes that
"there is a lack of incisive critical analysis" of *Artemisa* and
indicates that the main obstacle is "due to critics finding Artemiza's own stance and credibility difficult to define." Where
scholars such as D. M. Vieth, H. D. Weinbrot, and Dustin Griffin dismiss Rochester's narrator as herself an object of satire,
Thormählen argues for our accepting her not as vulnerable or
sentimental or unreliable but as heartily and quite reasonably

disillusioned about love. Suddenly, according to Thormählen, the critical fog lifts from the poem. *Artemisa* can be investigated as a more or less straightforward thesis-exempla satire where Rochester's speaker "makes her point clearly and goes on to prove it with energy and panache." While Weinbrot, Vieth, J. H. Wilson, and others sexistly dismiss Rochester's creation because her "peculiarly feminine, whimsical humour has failed to communicate itself to these men," Thormählen presents Artemisa as the cynosure of the satire.[26]

While in no way wanting to denigrate Thormählen's views of Artemisa—essentially I believe she is correct in most of them—I am reluctant nonetheless to abandon the puzzling quality of *Artemisa* in favor of a less complex reading of the poem's structure. I am also hesitant to make genre out of gender in this case. Without scorning Rochester's narrator as a dizzy blond, I find that the textual chaos generated by the satire nevertheless swallows up Artemisa along with the less estimable female characters of the piece, the fine lady and Corinna, as well as with all the male characters of the poem—to include the monkey. Thormählen rejects the "Chinese-boxes" schemata many critics have devised to explain Rochester's composition, saying that if one accepts Artemisa's "position as the argumentative basis of *Artemiza to Chloe,* no elaborate structural devices seem necessary."[27] However, Thormählen herself is unable to avoid the confusing textual folds of the poem. For example, when examining the effect of the fine lady's exemplum of Corinna on Artemisa's thesis about love, Thormählen's argument seems to me strained; aspects of the passage "could . . . be regarded as evidence of Artemiza's fair-mindedness, in which case it supports rather than undermines her trustworthiness." In her final analysis she admits: "An attempt to imagine the Corinna tale told by Artemiza herself on the basis of her own observations indicates the degree to which the poem's success is indebted to this 'voice within voice' structure."[28] Thormählen both slights and affirms the multi-layered construction of the satire.

A potentially more troubling gap in her case comes with Thormählen's reading Rochester's speaker as an authentically feminine voice. It is not. Artemisa is a feminine mask imagined and deployed by a male poet. Like Cleland's *Fanny Hill,* Rochester's *Artemisa* pretends to speak woman-to-woman, but in fact emphatically speaks man-to-man. Both authors base their works on the device of a woman narrator writing a letter to (and at the request of) another woman in the country wherein the lewd ways of love in town are surveyed. In fact, both texts represent an act of masculine arrogation of the utmost literate act then tolerated of women, namely letter writing. There *are* no women's voices speaking in these pieces, only feminized puppets. Where Cleland's novel gives its male consumer pornography, Rochester's verse satire, like *Timon, Tunbridge Wells*, and *Satire Against Mankind* beside it, addresses the target fop. Had Aphra Behn written *Artemisa* instead of possibly serving as a model for its narrator,[29] I might be more inclined to accept Thormählen's frank reading of the poem's argumentative line. (Though, in a sense, mine could be construed as a sexist statement, suggesting that the woman, Behn, was incapable of writing with the intellectual sophistication of the man, Rochester.) Because Rochester wrote it—and *not* because he is male but because of the tenor of everything else he wrote—I am inclined instead to propose the absentee man of wit, oddly enough, as the cynosure of this most intricate and confusing satire. I see no compelling reason why Rochester, whose works I find uniformly sexist, suddenly should wax feminist in *Artemisa*.[30] I agree that, as a narrator, Artemisa must be accorded the same fair hearing as Timon or as the narrators of *Tunbridge Wells* and *Satire Against Mankind*. But this fair treatment does not mean necessarily that the palpable textual abstruseness of the poem be dismissed by Thormählen as sexistly motivated misunderstanding on the part of male critics. Rochester's satire, among other topical ventures, sustains the Foucauldian critique of hegemonic cultural and intellectual shenanigans that we have seen in his other major satires.[31]

Despite the fact that a host of recognizable Restoration social and literary conventions operate in *Artemisa*, a troubling impenetrability prevails upon the composition. What I see at work in the poem is a thoroughgoing deconstruction of the language of the elitist power structure of the day—a truly politicized application of the techniques of deconstruction. This procedure is not carried out in any anachronistic postmodern sense;[32] our angst is no more rarified than that of people of the late seventeenth century. Instead, Rochester's demolition razes the local setting of entitled Restoration London. The text of *Artemisa* folds in upon itself and finally collapses. As a textual construct, Rochester's satire renders three concentric circles of perception and behavior, each ring personified by one of the three central female figures of the poem, and at the center of this design places the neither seen nor heard man of wit. Once this structure becomes evident, however, it immediately commences to implode. The poem seeks to create, rather than to camouflage, cognitive and interpretive mayhem. As the hinge pin of the composition, the phantom man of wit eventually functions as a transcendental signifier without a palpable transcendental signified to sustain it. Far from advocating ultimate presence that acts as a foundation for human society, Rochester's satire demonstrates the ultimate truancy of such agency. "Truth," though we can speak the *signifier*, has no *material* presence in the world, just as the man of wit is deliberated in the satire but never actually perceived—either visually *or* cognitively. In current critical parlance, Rochester denies in *Artemisa* the notion of logocentrism—even phallogocentrism; the concept is condemned as the idle construct of speculative reasoners and as an example of slaves tyrannizing fellow slaves. Highborn Restoration life is represented instead as a maladroit embroilment of open-ended—and sometimes terrifying—linguistic play. Like all the narrators of Rochester's satires, Artemisa is an affiliate victim of Democritean ground zero. Where *Satire Against Mankind* attacks speculative reasoning, *Artemisa* goes further: it questions our means to reason—rightly or otherwise.

As just indicated, *Artemisa* carries an elaborate textual design. Unlike *Satire Against Mankind*, it tends to dramatize its themes rather than put them into the bifurcated voices of narrator and adversarius (although to an extent Artemisa and the fine lady participate in those traditional satiric roles). In its concentric structure, the poem could be characterized not as a play within a play, but as an exemplum within an exemplum. The first exemplum occurs in Artemisa's letter to her friend. Offered as proof for her assertion to Chloe that love in the town has grown to be "an arrant trade" (51), it constitutes the overriding argumentative concern of her epistle. The subject of Artemisa's exemplum is the fine lady—and here's where the satire grows complex. The second exemplum of the satire, the anecdote within the anecdote, is told by the fine lady herself. Offered as proof for *her* assertion to Artemisa and to other women at a social gathering that it is better for a woman to love a fool than a man of wit, her subject is the story of Corinna undone by the man of wit and in turn undoing a fool. When reading *Artemisa*, then, it is important to keep in mind that the second exemplum, that of the fine lady, is subservient to the purposes of the first, that of Artemisa. Within the construct of the epistle, the fine lady's statements are to be taken ironically, not straightforwardly; in other words, according to Artemisa's exemplum, what the fine lady blames should be taken as praise and what she praises should be seen as blame. What the satire *itself* indicates, as distinct from Artemisa's letter (perhaps Thormählen confuses the two language acts, one fictitious and one real), is more difficult to apprehend. Where Rochester's creature, Artemisa, argues matter-of-factly to her narratee, Chloe, Rochester's satire operates obliquely on its narratee, the target fop. Again as just indicated, I propose that Rochester's verse intentionally locates that male reader in an informational void. He gropes his way through three successive layers of increasingly confounding evidence to find (or rather not to find) at the core of the satire the profound absence of the man of wit. As he goes, Charles's cult of wit is dismantled as itself an empty language act.[33] The only way to demonstrate my supposition is to journey to the center of the poem. The footing is treacherous and gets worse as it goes.

Artemisa occupies the outer circle of the satire. With it comes the broadest vantage point and so the most sensible point of view. Though a woman, Artemisa resembles the narrators of *Timon* and *Tunbridge Wells*. Just as critical objections have been raised against her character and reliability as a narrator, so Timon has been called a snob and the narrator of *Tunbridge Wells* a sot. Like these men, Artemisa is the one who is subjected to the experience of the ruling culture; more than these men, she as a poet orders her experience as she relates it to her correspondee. She has greater autonomy than those two masculine narrative counterparts. This autonomy, however, should not be mistaken for control. Even though her account of town fashion is recollected in tranquillity in her letter to Chloe, Artemisa is no more in command of her situation than Timon, nor can she effectively act to correct the existential enormities she discerns any better than the narrator of *Tunbridge Wells*. She, too, is a victim. She, too, although her gender is wrong, serves as a satiric proxy for the narratee target fop. She places readers in a familiar perspective and locale. More than serving just as a proxy for the narratee, however, as a woman of wit Artemisa also serves to *ridicule* men of wit in a way more explicit than Timon or the narrator of *Tunbridge Wells*. Although contemporary male readers of the poem were likely to disparage her character as a "philosophical lady," I find much more biting derision running in the opposite direction—that is, if one thinks about it, Artemisa's aping the target fop to *his* disadvantage.

Reflecting on the "lofty flights of dangerous poetry" (4), Artemisa observes:

> Amongst the men—I mean, the men of wit—
> At least they passed for such, before they writ—
> How many bold adventurers for the bays,
> Proudly designing large returns of praise,
> Who durst that stormy, pathless world explore,
> Were soon tossed back, and wrecked on the dull shore,
> Broke of that little stock they had before?
>
> 5–11

Her ensuing comment about how "a woman's tottering bark" would be tossed even more savagely on the wild sea of poetic endeavor than these "stoutest ships—the men of wit" is but drollery compared to the derision aimed at men of wit in the preceding passage. Nor does Artemisa stop here in her remarks about the male domain of wit and verse. Offering herself farcical warning, she says:

> Dear Artemisa, poetry is a snare:
> Bedlam has many mansions: have a care.
> Your Muse diverts you, makes your reader sad;
> You fancy you're inspired; he thinks you mad.
> Consider too, 'twill be discreetly done,
> To make yourself the fiddle of the town;
> To find th' ill-humoured pleasure at their need,
> Scorned if you fail, and cursed though you succeed.
>
> 16–23

Read carefully, these lines do not serve as caution to Artemisa or to would-be women-poets at all. Rather, they notify men of the dangers of taking up the pen, particularly with regard to the potential demands and reproofs of submitting to the dull-witted male readership of the town. Timon, for example, would have fared better to heed Artemisa's advice. Neither do her final comments serve necessarily as self-indictment.

> Thus, like an arrant woman, as I am,
> No sooner well-convinced writing's a shame,
> That 'whore' is scarce a more reproachful name
> Than 'poetess':

> As men that marry, or as maids that woo.
> 'Cause 'tis the very worst thing they can do,
> Pleased with the contradiction, and the sin,
> Methinks I stand on thorns till I begin.
>
> 24–31

Readers would have to be convinced indeed of Artemisa's womanish stupidity to find in these lines only a self-damning confession of titillating impetuosity. For one thing, they are written with too much wit.[34] For another, in them she draws the same parallel between poet and whore made also by the narrators of *Timon* and *Satire Against Mankind.* Like whores, poets both place themselves at the mercy of a rapacious male clientele and promote their own disaster by soliciting the favor of patrons who by nature must hate whores and wits for who they are and for what they do. Once more, Artemisa's observations speak less in disparagement of women-poets than they offer a sharp combination of ridicule and warning to the target fop. The satire begins, then, straightforwardly enough (for satire) with subtle but cogent narrative reproof of Restoration elite society.

Only when Artemisa begins her lament for "that lost thing (Love)" (38)—the thesis of her letter—does her power as a narrator become really problematic. Doubts arise not because of her gender, but, as in the case of the narrator of *Satire Against Mankind,* because of the tenability of her precepts. She avers:

> Love, the most generous passion of the mind,
> The softest refuge innocence can find,
> The safe director of unguided youth,
> Fraught with kind wishes, and secured by truth,
> That cordial drop heaven in our cup has thrown,
> To make the nauseous draught of life go down,
>
> * * *
>
> This only joy, for which poor we were made,
> Is grown like play, to be an arrant trade:
> The rooks creep in, and it has got of late
> As many little cheats and tricks as that.
>
> 40–45, 50–53

In speaking of love as a "passion of the mind"—a concept that traditionally might be taken as oxymoron—Artemisa allies herself with the consolidation of body and mind found in the narrator's "right reason" of *Satire Against Mankind*. However, like that doctrine, Artemisa's credo of love is both somewhat vague and ultimately impossible to implement in the false-reasoning world. The sentiments expressed in the passage are estimable. Some details, perhaps, give us pause. Artemisa associates love with "innocence"—a good thing—but also with "unguided youth"—something not so good. Similarly, she maintains that it is laden with "kind wishes" but also guaranteed "by truth." The first element indicates circumstances that as yet are not so, while the second supposes a fixed condition. Like the narrator of *Satire Against Mankind*, Artemisa theorizes remarkably but imprecisely; more notably, with her letter to Chloe she likewise attempts direct linguistic action to enact her views—a language act comparable to if not better than that narrator's debate with the clerical adversarius. Her venture fails no more because she is a woman than the narrator of *Satire Against Mankind*'s project fails because he is a man. Both her endorsement of love and his for right reason fall short as policy due to the tide of human senselessness that in the end must overwhelm their stands.

A reader would have to be sexist herself to discover only satire against women in Artemisa's complaint that it is "Our silly sex" (56) that is chiefly guilty for recent offenses against townly love. Though born "like monarchs, free," London women have turned "gypsies for a meaner liberty, / And hate restraint, though but from infamy" (56–58). They chafe at the threat of disgrace according to conventionally accepted behavior—their new "meaner liberty"—rather than act according to their own intellectual and perceptual lights. Such conduct makes them speculative reasoners.

> They call whatever is not common 'nice',
> And deaf to nature's rules, or love's advice,
> Forsake the pleasures to pursue the vice.
> To an exact perfection they have wrought
> The action love, the passion is forgot.
> 'Tis below wit, they tell you, to admire,
> And e'en without approving, they desire.
> Their private wish obeys the public voice,
> 'Twixt good and bad, whimsy decides, not choice.
> Fashions grow up for taste, at forms they strike:
> They know what they would have, not what they like.

> Bovey's a beauty, if some few agree
> To call him so; the rest to that degree
> Affected are, that with their ears they see.
>
> 59–72

In this passage we find exemplified by feminine behavior in the salon precisely the same state of perpetual, miserable, and deleterious hypocrisy instigated by fear and experienced by men at court living under the domain of false order and speculative reason outlined by the narrator of *Satire Against Mankind*. Similar to the disastrous statecraft pursued by those men, these women have lost all natural sense of love and pursue only the current custom, not the object itself. Public voice, whimsy, and fashion determine their tenderness and desire. They are deaf to their own five senses, that is, "to nature's rules, or love's advice." As a result, pleasure is displaced by vice; real passion of love is replaced by mere action of sex; what they like is supplanted by what they are supposed to like. As in *Satire Against Mankind*, then, action not guided by the senses leads to rational abominations. These wrong-judging women of the town ignore their senses so grossly "that with their ears they see." Where in that other satire an adversarial debate is established between falsely reasoned order and naturally sensed chaos, in *Artemisa* a similar clash between fashion (speculative) and love (instinctive) is arranged within the fiction of the narrative epistle.[35] Rochester's satire is too sophisticated to adjourn at the simplism of satire against women— though it permits its reader that simplistic interpretation. At this point in our amble toward its center, the poem's chief concern is with exposing false modes of reason—again, a common pursuit of satire. However, as we enter into the next circle, that of the fine lady, the satire begins to push the envelop of its Democritean insights to inspect the fraudulence of language itself.

Inhabiting the second level or ring of the satire's structure, the fine lady suitably personifies Artemisa's thesis of the senseless behavior of town ladies brought on by the adherence to fashion. She is an intelligent false reasoner extremely similar to the adversarial clergyman of *Satire Against Mankind*. The subject matter of her monologue is quite different from that of the clergyman; however, it derives from the same source— a fundamental misapplication of rationality compounded by a lack of self-awareness. Artemisa calls the fine lady "this mixed thing" (148) of wisdom and folly. In her worldview, she is "So very wise, yet so impertinent" (149)—that is, experienced yet also audacious and irrelevant in her outlook. Artemisa reflects that this woman is

> One who knew everything, who 'twas thought fit
> Should be a fool through choice, not want of wit:
> Whose foppery without the help of sense
> Could ne'er have rise to such an excellence.
> Nature's as lame in making a true fop
> As a philosopher; the very top
> And dignity of folly we attain
> By curious search, and labour of the brain,
> By observation, counsel, and deep thought.
> God never made a coxcomb worth a groat;
> We owe that name to industry and art.
> An eminent fool must be a fool of parts.
>
> 150–61

In the fine lady's "foppery without the help of sense" we return to the observations of high society made by the narrator of *Tunbridge Wells*. Likewise, the distinction made between a true fop and a true philosopher implies the studied foolishness of thinking beyond material sense—the crime of clergymen, statesmen, and schoolmen in *Satire Against Mankind*—versus the application of right reason. Throughout the passage, the idea of industriously procuring our own harmful triviality of thought is reiterated. The fine lady does not lack worldliness or intelligence, only the ability to train her discrimination upon herself.

> And such a one was she, who had turned o'er
> As many books as men, loved much, read more,
> Had a discerning wit; to her was known
> Everyone's fault and merit, but her own.
>
> 162–65

As with the interlocutor of *Satire Against Mankind*, she is sufficiently clever to twist her native intelligence into opinions that contradict what is plainly evident. Speculative reasoning led that clergyman to believe that humans could transcend sense to discover unknowable truths on which to base their lives. The fine lady's less cosmic postulate is that it is better for a woman to love a fool than for her to love a man of wit.

One might take the fine lady's thesis, similar to the narrator's opening stance in *Satire Against Mankind*, for a *quaestio*—
a paradoxical defense of an outrageous position that in the end
will produce startling insights. This reading, however, neglects
the fact that the fine lady speaks as part of Artemisa's controlling exemplum proving love to be debased in the town; what
she asserts as true should be read as false. Her commendation
of the fool as a lover amounts not to a *quaestio*, but to a
mock encomium.

> But the kind easy fool, apt to admire
> Himself, trusts us: his follies all conspire
> To flatter his, and favor our desire.
> Vain of his proper merit, he with ease
> Believes we love him best, who best can please.
> On him our common gross dull flatteries pass,
> Ever most joyful when most made an ass.
> Heavy to apprehend, though all mankind
> Perceive us false, the fop concerned is blind,
> Who doting on himself
> Thinks everyone that sees him of his mind.
> These are true women's men—
>
> 124–35

The fine lady is not Rochester's spokeswoman for Hobbesian
and libertine values, as some critics have read her.[36] Rather,
she is Artemisa's creature of social orthodoxy thinking and
speaking within the inane fashions of the town. She even has
married a fool herself because, at the time, it was considered
"*à la mode*" (103). In her shrewd false reasoning, the fine lady
is a formulator and proponent of false order. Opposing her is
Artemisa as a champion of knowledge and action founded on
the senses. If Artemisa (really Rochester) had allowed the fine
lady to speak as little as the narrator of *Satire Against Mankind*
allowed his adversarius to voice his opinion, the signification
of Rochester's satire would not exceed the monologic "dialogue" of that earlier poem. That is to say, *Artemisa* and Artemisa's letter would remain much more one in the same language
act, and Artemisa's narrative thesis concerning the debased
practice of love in the town would be the primary import of
the composition. However, Rochester permits the fine lady to
speak over half of the poem's 264 lines. Her prolonged voice,
even though ostensibly under the control of Artemisa's pen,
has the effect, I think, of sending the satire into its linguistic

and cognitive tailspin. Artemisa's thesis-exempla satiric epistle maintains its integrity only *until* the fine lady launches into her own extended thesis and accompanying exemplum. With these two sections, Rochester's satire propels its reader toward the enigmatic core of the satire—the man of wit; along the way we must pass through the troubling ambit of Corinna. At this point in the satire the analytical seams of Artemisa's epistle rend. And here I think it best to pause, not only for breath but to contemplate for a moment the view.

If Artemisa proposes that we base our conduct on what is plainly evident, Rochester's verse makes certain that what we most need to judge with our own five senses—the man of wit—is nowhere to be found. How can we apply right reason to a mirage? The impasse, I believe, duplicates that of our own dilemma in apprehending the world outside us. If thinking, like reading and writing, is a language act, then our knowledge of the world depends on words as signs for reality. Literally, language creates our world and our worldview. However, as Locke—and many others—worries (see note 15 of chapter 1), words and ideas are general and universal concepts; as signs, they do not belong to the real existence of things. Rather, they are applicable "indifferently to many particular things." Our *concept* of a real object, what Ferdinand De Saussure calls the signified, has only an arbitrary connection with the object itself. Our sound-image for that concept, the signifier, has even less actual connection to the external object. If our intake of sensory information is subsequently ordered into understanding by this unstable process of determining meaning through the abstractions of signs, one can appreciate the notion of language, and the human mind, as a closed system operating distinct from an external reality we can only imagine and debate imperfectly among ourselves. We exist in a linguistic cave—what Hume in the next century would designate "the universe of the imagination."[37] Exterior sensations come to us, but we can only make sense of them within the confines of our own walls of signification. Our minds blend together a series of distinct sensations; from these, we imagine we perceive a continued reality. Language itself is metaphor, an act of speculation and then fabrication of bogus harmony. Right reason is thus illusion and allusion at once—a vain and passing reference to what we *cannot* do as language-dependent creatures. Pressing skepticism to its limit, Rochester's *Artemisa* effectually fractures human language and reason, replicating this crisis of human knowledge. Once the fine lady begins to support her contention that fools are preferable to men of wit, percipient mayhem ensues for the interpretant. Each of us is left stranded in a dim, private cave.

For example, in the fine lady's praise of fools (*her* thesis) as "true women's men" quoted earlier, do we detect satire against men? According to the fine lady, certain men of fashion confute their own five senses by fancying themselves to be specimens of desirable manhood. "Heavy to apprehend," these fops then mistake as women in love with them women who are resolved on beguiling and manipulating them; this duplicity occurs in spite of the fact that "all mankind / Perceive us false." Clearly, these gentlemen are as asinine, if not more so, than the ladies of fashion. Yet are we to take seriously something put in the mouth, according to the design of Artemisa's epistle, of an ironic speaker? Possibly the fine lady's remarks serve as further proof of Artemisa's thesis to Chloe that love has grown an arrant trade in town. Perhaps men no less than the arrant society women are shallow-thinking creatures of vanity. Between Artemisa's attestations of feminine folly and the fine lady's asseverations of masculine arrogance, a picture of fashionable London emerges as a scene of gross analytic and communicative delusion.[38] If the reader accepts this interpretation, however, the exclusively sexist reading of *Artemisa* as satire against women, narrated by a bimbo, vaporizes. Furthermore, a reader now must grant credence to the assertions of both the satire's narrator *and* adversarius—something that certainly does not happen in *Satire Against Mankind* or in satire as a general rule. Perhaps Artemisa uses the fine lady as a satiric mask through which to speak out against men. But then again, the narrator is only an amateur and arrant poetess—or maybe this is a sophisticated poetic device she has pulled on us? Suddenly things are getting complicated—more complicated than normal even for satire.

Midway through the poem the fine lady (really to be taken as Artemisa now?), Circe-like, turns men into monkeys.

> She to the window runs, where she had spied
> Her much esteemed dear friend the monkey, tied.
> With forty smiles, as many antic bows
> As if't had been the lady of the house,
> The dirty chattering monster she embraced,
> And made it this fine tender speech at last:

'Kiss me, thou curious miniature of man.
How odd thou art! How pretty! How japan!
Oh I could live and die with thee—'

                                                            137–45

The fine lady practically climbs into bed with the "dirty chattering monster"—or has she already, in effect, by marrying
her foolish husband, her "necessary thing" (92) that she manipulates as a means to her desires?[39] Is the fine lady an agent
or an object of satire? Is she both? Is she someone whose opinion we can take seriously at all—either at face value *or* as a
narrative stand-in for Artemisa? And if men are made monkeys
by the satire, which men specifically are targeted for abuse?
Only country boobies, such as the fine lady's husband or the
young dupe Corinna masters? (Another example in the satire
of a woman making a monkey out of a man.) Or are all men
indicted by the fine lady's words? Do fools and men of wit
become one and the same? Is *Artemisa* in fact a satire against
men? Thormählen believes that the fine lady "is primarily concerned with the establishing of female hegemony in the sex
struggle."[40] If true, are not *all* men at risk of knowing, in the
fine lady's words, the "perfect joy of being well-deceived" (115)
at the hands of a calculating woman? And are we sympathetic
to the fine lady's deceptive, totalitarian tactics in gaining female hegemony in the sex struggle? As the new oppressor, is
she palpably different or better than the former male oppressor? One gleans from the fine lady's speeches the mounting
tension of sexual politics and male paranoia—elements abun-
dant in Rochester's lyrics (see chapter 5). Yet is this anxiety
created within the fine lady's oration, or within the compass
of Artemisa's argument against ladies of fashion in the town,
or have we exceeded the dimensions of her missive altogether?
Questions overwhelm us. I could go on and on, and indeed
critics have. At this point, however, I believe it should be plain
that we have been led into an elaborate verbal maze wherein
we could chase our critical tails indefinitely. The longer the
fine lady speaks, the more amazing the poem becomes. But we
should resist the temptation, I think, to regard the project of
the satire as *only* to deposit its reader in inescapable conundrum. Although the poem certainly enacts the chaos of textuality, equally compelling in it is the presence of the depravity—
both rational and social—of Restoration high society. As Foucault insists, history must be taken as more than language; it

demands to be studied as a chronology of war.[41] The chaos of language has real, worldly consequences of power in our political lives. These issues of fairness or oppression, I believe, are played out most dramatically in the third and deepest concentric ring of the satire—that of the fine lady's exemplum of Corinna. To become only tangled in the words of *Artemisa* misses the more fundamental political signification of the satire played out, albeit in an attenuated way, at its base. To resume our rigorous journey, we now must step down into that lowest circle of the satire's vortex.

The fine lady's story of Corinna takes up approximately a third of the composition. Here Rochester's satire renders a combined rake and whore's progress in which *both* young people fall victim to the powerful cult of wit and words that epitomize fashionable Restoration London. To speak of Corinna especially as dissipated or brutal is a sexist exercise in blaming the victim. Shaped by accident of birth and by social forces beyond her control, she finds herself trapped in that miserable human condition of fear and hypocrisy, of struggle for survival, outlined by *Satire Against Mankind*. Pursuing one of a handful of career opportunities open to her as a sparkling mistress of the town, Corinna prospers within the limitations of that role until she encounters the man of wit.

> Gay were the hours, and winged with joy they flew,
> When first the town her early beauty knew;
> Courted, admired, and loved, with presents fed,
> Youth in her looks, and pleasure in her bed
> Till fate, or her ill-angel, thought fit
> To make her dote upon a man of wit,
> Who found 'twas dull to love above a day,
> Made his ill-natured jest, and went away.
> Now scorned by all, forsaken and oppressed,
> She's a *memento mori* to the rest.

193–202

Within the complicated framework of the poem—at this point we face a secondhand account of a secondhand account—knowing precisely what transpired between Corinna and the man of wit is difficult. The man of wit never speaks; neither does Corinna give her direct account of the affair nor Artemisa her indirect impressions of it. Either woman's version would be preferable to the equivocal report from the fine lady. She simply asserts that the wit ruined Corinna, making some manner of "ill-natured jest" before forsaking her. Did he deflower Corinna, making her a social pariah? It seems not; before doting on the man of wit she was "Courted, admired, and loved" and described as having both youth in her looks "and pleasure in her bed." These factors suggest real rather than potential pleasure. (But as we've seen, can we *trust* the fine lady's account?) Did the wit give her the pox, thus rendering her a "*memento mori*"? Did he impregnate her? No evidence exists for either reading. (But then again the fine lady may not want to name such deeds amid her modish assembly.) Rather, the problem seems to have been that the libertine "found 'twas dull to love above a day." In other words, the witty pleasure-seeker acquires and dispenses with women as casually as he draws and expels breath. But even if Corinna suffered heartache at their separation, that would not prevent her from resuming her career. The man of wit actively had to impede Corinna's future livelihood. Presumably, he did so by revealing her dusky feminine wonders under the glaring light of his masculine reason. (The fine lady's specific objections to men of wit will be discussed presently.) That is, he exposed her in some way to his comrades in pleasure, perhaps by writing a libel against her, thereby causing her sexual appeal to decline on the open market.[42] Rochester's target fop doubtlessly would favor this reading and, indeed, approve such action: it serves the trollop right. The word "oppressed" in line 201, however, blunts the fraternal jocularity of the passage. By definition, the term designates political consequences: according to the *O.E.D.*, the wrongful exercise of authority or superior power or strength; the condition of being downtrodden, especially harassed or crushed by tyranny or unjust treatment. Certainly that is the result of the wit's jest:

> Diseased, decayed, to take up half-a-crown
> Must mortgage her long scarf and mantua gown.
> Poor creature! Who, unheard of as a fly,
> In some dark hole must all the winter lie,
> And want and dirt endure a whole half-year,
> That for one month she tawdry may appear.
>
> 203–8

Like Defoe's Moll Flanders and Cleland's Fanny Hill—other male-imagined prostitutes—Corinna is born into sexual subservience, exploited and persecuted by the masculine power structure, and when forced to fend successfully, and in her case viciously, for herself, repudiated by the very society that engendered—literally—her original maltreatment. A case might even be made for "young Master Worship," the unsuspecting country squire whom Corinna cozens and murders, being less fool than victim of the same dominant London culture. In coming to town where he "Turns spark, learns to be lewd, and is undone" (223), he merely engages in the social norm and the sexual politics of the day by attempting to play the role of the man of wit—the icon of Charles's reign. I do not want to dismiss the idea of individual responsibility for one's actions when it comes to these youngsters; merely claiming they are "victims of society" is not enough. However, clearly both the country husband and Corinna are out of their depth in relationship to the man of wit and to the hierarchical structure of the contemporary society he represents—a power structure that in any society is such a forcible determinant of individual agency. Clearly, power is tilted in the man of wit's direction. The imbalance causes them to be casualties of fashion as defined by Artemisa, of speculative reason as defined by *Satire Against Mankind*, of the "general politics" of truth as defined by Michel Foucault. When Corinna, according to the fine lady, pretends to praise her booby squire for his simple goodness and untownish ways, could Rochester's satire not present its reader in fact with an expression of the needed antithesis to Charles's libertine dominion? Read through the dark lens of double irony, the passage takes on a peculiar pathos.

> This o'ergrown schoolboy lost Corinna wins,
> And at first dash, to make an ass begins;
> Pretends to like a man who has not known
> The vanities nor vices of the town,
> Fresh in his youth, and faithful in his love,
> Eager of joys which he does seldom prove;
> Healthful and strong, he does no pains endure
> But what the fair one he adores can cure;
> Grateful for favours, does the sex esteem,
> And libels none for being kind to him.
> Then of the lewdness of the times complains,
> Rails at the wits and atheists, and maintains
> 'Tis better than good sense, than power or wealth,
> To have a love untainted, youth, and health.
>   226–39

Spoken apparently unwittingly by Corinna and reported ironically by the fine lady, these lines seem to express the ideal of "that lost thing (Love)" upon which Artemisa builds her complaint to Chloe. Here we have a lover described as undebauched, faithful, vital, appreciative, respectful, and not inclined to kiss-and-tell. Would not Corinna have fared better in the first place to encounter such a person? Is not such a one—another "god-like" man as at the end of the *Addition* to *Satire Against Mankind?*—preferable either to a fool *or* to a man of wit? And given the benighted society depicted in Rochester's satire(s), should not the aphorism of the final couplet be taken seriously? Since "good sense" is overwhelmed by speculative reason in this world, and since "power or wealth" in fact assure our misery and doom, love of this nature, as Artemisa protests, might indeed be that cordial drop to make the nauseous draught of life go down.

Again, irony upon irony and exemplum upon exemplum make it difficult if not impossible to know exactly how to read these lines. The dramatic amplitude of *Artemisa* obstructs the chances of pat ratiocinative meaning emerging from the satire. However, one idea reasonably available within the example of Corinna, I think, is subtle but sharp criticism of the man of wit as sexual and social oppressor. Upon inspection, he is not a very savory character—that is, he is not if any of Rochester's readers, wits themselves, care much to inspect their own behavior. At this point then we must take the final step of our expedition, into the void at the heart of the satire. The man of wit situated at the center of the concentric circles of *Artemisa* could be described accurately either as the *primum mobile* of the piece, passively setting into motion the concerns of Artemisa, the fine lady, and Corinna, or as the black hole of the poem, sucking and crushing the entire composition into enigma. Unhelpfully, the clearest view we have of him is through the eyes of the fine lady, the notorious and possibly self-damning speculative reasoner of the satire. If we read her opinions on the man of wit straightforwardly—which within the complexities of *Artemisa* means opposite of her word according to the fine lady's being a negative exemplum working for Artemisa's thesis—then a rather flattering portrait of him emerges: a portrait that tentatively could be taken for something akin to right reason. Let's explore that commendatory reading first.

The fine lady objects to men of wit because they inquire into the true nature of things, specifically women of fashion. With

"searching wisdom, fatal to their ease" they will not unques-
tioningly admire town women; rather, these men will "still
find out why what may should not please" (108–9). In lieu of
falling prey to feminine guile, wits:

> Nay, take themselves for injured if we dare
> Make 'em think better of us than we are;
> And if we hide our frailties from their sights,
> Call us deceitful jilts, and hypocrites.
>
> 110–13

Seemingly, the man of wit demands reality over appearance
and substance over form even though outward appearance is
more pleasing. In a magnificent display of specious reasoning,
considering the fates of her husband and Corinna's lover, the
fine lady declares what a terrible mistake this intransigence
is on the part of the wit; it is infinitely more desirable to be
deluded.

> They little guess, who at our arts are grieved,
> The perfect joy of being well deceived.
> Inquisitive as jealous cuckolds grow,
> Rather than not be knowing, they will know
> What being known creates their certain woe.
>
> 114–18

In the end, the fine lady resorts to stock images of darkness and
light to denote feminine irrational versus masculine rational
behavior. She associates women with the moon, night, and
illusion, while men are amalgamated with the sun, day, and
verity.

> Women should these of all mankind avoid,
> For wonder by clear knowledge is destroyed.
> Woman, who is an arrant bird of night,
> Bold in the dusk, before a fool's dull sight
> Should fly, when reason brings the glaring light.
>
> 119–23

Reason and truth are the exclusive property of men of wit.
Fools and women—that is, the rest of society—pursue fallacy,
whether in permitting themselves to be well-deceived or in
actively playing the deceiver. Both women and the men who
allow themselves to be misled are equally "arrant"—the third

time in the satire that word has been applied to describe inadequate conduct. Thus, read ironically, the gist of the fine lady's
speech is hugely complimentary toward wits. Sensible wits
are noxious to senseless women. In the brief liaison between
Corinna and the man of wit, apparently such a confrontation
of right versus wrong reason occurred with Corinna, rightly
and naturally, coming away the loser. The attractive illusions
of Corinna's charms rightfully were dispelled by the man of
wit; all but the dullest sighted, most credulous and countrified
blockhead apprehended such. In short, rakes rule. It might
seem that Rochester's satire delivers what its libertine narratee wants to hear. But does it?

We have considered already an alternative reading of Corinna's
plight, one of oppression at the hands of the man of wit, not
banishment by his just decree. If the fashion and false wit of
the fine lady and Corinna represent a thin veneer of civilization
spread over a worse-than-Hobbesian world of cowardice and
dread, if indeed a superstructure of speculative reason has
been erected upon an infrastructure of abject brutality and
stupidity, ultimately who is responsible for this polity? Is it
Corinna and her dupe pathetically occupying a world of sexual
survivalism and predatory horrors? Is it the fine lady with her
petty and pretentious social airs? Is it Artemisa as a female
observer of the entire circus? Who indeed tyrannizes whom in
this satire? Who in fact *is* the knave of the first rate? It seems
to me that via its textual chaos Rochester's satire unveils the
man of wit to be the founding father of this vicious social setting. By presenting the reader conflicting views of, within the
exemplum of the fine lady, wits as "good" and, within the exemplum of Corinna, wits as "bad," *Artemisa* charges the man
of wit—again, *if* the narratee cares to think about it—with
creating the very being he debunks. His cult of wit and pleasure sanctions a Corinna and a fine lady; it also reviles and
despoils them when it pleases. Read in a certain way Rochester's satire unmasks this hypocrisy and debunks the debunker.
Wit becomes then speculative, not right, reason. Like the adversarius of *Satire Against Mankind*, the man of wit delves
merely into mysteries he himself invents—in this case, women
of fashion. Where the cleric concocts God, the wit contrives
Bitch. Clergyman and libertine are identical in their specious
exegesis of "reality." Rochester's satire could hardly deal a cru-
eler blow to his target fop. Linguistically, the satire reveals
the supposed transcendental signified of courtly and townly

libertine behavior as itself an arbitrary and self-contradictory concept. As the signifier for this fraudulent ideal, the man of wit functions as the center upon which the text collapses. Oppositional hierarchies such as man of wit/woman of fashion, masculine reason/feminine illusion, sophisticated rake/predatory murderess or country bumpkin dissolve once the power structure inherent to their relationships is exposed. Binary opposition, logocentrism, phallogocentrism—in short, all the linguistic obfuscation and sexual politics surrounding the man of wit—become rational fallacy once faced by political exigencies. In this satire, the man of wit is the sex-driven brute of the first rate. He literally is nonsense—but politically potent nonsense—in the poem.

In a satire that enacts a politicized deconstruction of Restoration elite society, the man of wit personates as well the target fop in his environs in and around Whitehall. Hutton summarizes the kingship of Charles II as a "monarch in a masquerade" and the personage of the king himself as enigmatic.

> The more intimate that his contemporaries became with him, the longer that they were associated with him, the more a sensation of distrust and alienation runs through their accounts. More than anything else, he was monumentally selfish. . . . At his core there lay a vacuum, and what emerges most powerfully from the accounts of those who knew him is a feeling of unreachability, a frustrating instinct that the man inside the king eluded the observer . . . he remains, for us as for contemporaries, a set of strongly marked characteristics with a cold void at the centre of them. He was a monarch who loved masks, whether of ceremony, of role-playing, or of intrigue. Behind those coverings, something was always missing.[43]

This description of Charles suits well the aura created around the absentee man of wit in *Artemisa;* it also captures the sense of frustration often experienced when trying to analyze the poem. Like Charles Stuart, Rochester's satire studiously cultivates unreachability; behind its characters, their manifestos, their exempla, something, too, is always missing. I believe the man of wit reasonably could depict Charles himself in his station as prime mover *and* black hole of the patrician and libertine coterie of the day. His toadies are inculpated as well, of course, but Charles is the definitive source of dissimulative and oppressive speculative reason in Rochester's world. Just as locality induced the rational failure contemplated in *Satire*

Against Mankind, so locality is the basis of the textual chaos in *Artemisa.* These satires both represent an extreme Democritean vision where first human reason then language itself miscarry. Within the precincts of Restoration court and town, right reason is nowhere seen and but scantly felt. Both satires are in a real sense political texts.

Artemisa is then Rochester's most perplexing and intricate poem. A reader sifts through multiple strata of voices and ironies to arrive at no certain conclusion other than a sense that something is rather sinisterly amiss.[44] The satire depicts Restoration high society as a multifarious cognitive game that resists penetration; no certain grounds for discrimination emerge. In the end, Artemisa's norm of love, perhaps expressed in those lines of reported speech where Corinna bamboozles her country gull, embodies an unobtainable state within the maelstrom of the poetic townscape.[45] As with right reason in *Satire Against Mankind,* love may represent a remedy to speculative reasoning and the oppression of the politics of truth, but we are too deeply enmeshed in our cerebral follies—specifically here the Restoration haut monde—to exercise such right feeling or thinking. Artemisa concludes her letter to Chloe by promising to compose for her entertainment more tales of town life.

> By the next post such stories I will tell
> As joined with these shall to a volume swell,
> As true as heaven, more infamous than hell.
>
> 261–63

Her poetry is not unlike Rochester's: both write intimate messages to compeers recounting folly and vice in fashionable and influential London. Rochester's poetic observations indeed swell to a volume of satires and lyrics on the subject. Unlike Artemisa's verse epistle, however, Rochester's poetry does *not* deliver what it ostensibly promises. *Artemisa* looks to be satire against wellborn women; it turns out to chide highborn men. In his carnal lyrics, Rochester's narratee finds himself similarly baited.

5

Political Sexuality

His sceptre and his prick are of an equal length.
—Rochester, "Verses for which he was Banished"

MANY critics comment on Rochester's poems not delivering what they apparently promise. Dustin Griffin notes how Rochester's love songs frequently subvert Restoration decorum with "coolly elegant wit or . . . an invasion of doubts and fears." Samuel Rogal asserts that Rochester's verse both typifies and resists its libertine milieu. Thomas Pasch finds "A Ramble in St. James's Park" to be a "series of confrontations between the reader's expectations and Rochester's intentions." Similarly, Sarah Wintle writes that Rochester's poetry "bears an oblique and complex relationship to the conventions and themes it uses, turning them upside-down and deflating them, sometimes with a certain viciousness." Felicity Nussbaum argues that Rochester often inverts reader expectations with regard to the ideal of love. Not only is love an unattainable objective in his poems, but both those who seek it and those who deny it are mocked by the poet.[1] Generally, I agree with such judgments of Rochester's writings; we have seen already this principle at work in his major satires. However, I would ascribe similarly to his "minor" works a political dimension all too often ignored. As in the major satires, three projects of immediate civic consequence play themselves out in Rochester's lyrics, prose, and drama. First, each lays a trap for the target fop; second, each creates a linguistic chaos that supersedes rational order; third, each exposes the arbitrary nature of truth as an instrument of power.

In addition, political agenda in Rochester's writings habitually is fused with sexual content. Aside from his major satires, his works rarely comment socially without also commenting

110

explicitly sexually.[2] The phenomenon is by no means unique to Rochester. As one critic recently has written:

> It was clear by the mid-1660s that a deep vulnerability in the court's armory lay in the king's morals: his appetites, his personal indulgences, and his sexual follies. The satirist is keen to lower the tone, to debunk epic gestures, to debase and embarrass, but his steady aim is to connect sexual greed and political corruption. What he angles after throughout is the matter of governance.[3]

Fairly early in Charles's reign, the notion of allegory and political application became a crucial reading habit of the age. Not merely a literary game, such poetical puzzles were a rich and messy exercise in the dense particularities of the social and political landscape. Allegory hunting was especially explosive because the interpretant was key to the process and because serious political consequences could ensue from particular readings of individual works.[4] I want to assert a place for Rochester's nonformal verse satire in this polemic fracas. License and libertinism at court remained an extremely politicized topic for the remainder of Charles's regime.[5] Who was better positioned at court than Rochester to offer commentary on the hottest political issue of the day? Along with discussing sexual politics in Rochester, therefore, it seems equally urgent to explore his own contribution to the expression of political sexuality under Charles's rule. The phenomenon occurs uniformly in his lyrics, prose, and plays.[6]

A number of Rochester's obscene songs, perhaps the distinguishing literary medium of the libertine ascendancy, unobtrusively condemn the very consumer of his smut. One poem in particular, the curious "Fair Cloris in a pigsty lay," possibly exercises its critique with utmost fluency. Spread against the backdrop of the politicality of Rochester's other works, this lyric about a pigherdess arguably could be read as conveying two primary goads of Rochester's lyrics directed at the target fop—namely, the notion of absent or missing lust and the threat of female sexual autonomy. If the rakish reader comes to Rochester's verse seeking vicarious gratification, he leaves disappointed—that is, if he applies any thought to the piece; an enormous assumption, I grant, for the typical consumer of bawdry.[7] The poem confirms standard male projections of women. Foremost is the notion of feminine lust. Even if ignorant of the fact or if they deny it, so the male logic runs, women hunger for sex as badly as men—to the point of secretly craving rape.[8] Such a projection is shown first by the maid's sweaty sex-dream had while slumbering among her grunting swine, and second by envisioning her own rape in that dream. Agreeable pastoral trappings, such as the name Cloris and the dream-rape's occurring in "Flora's cave" (15), simultaneously signal springtime and burgeoning nature—the traditional literary backdrop for matters of fertility and passion. Thus, Rochester sets the stage for conventional sexual violence against women. Yet, read another way, all this serves as well as bait for Rochester's snare. By tradition, pigs also have a literary correlation, namely, that of mindless appetite (e.g., the Circe episode in the *Odyssey*).[9] Moreover, the lovesick swain who contrives the plot to steer Cloris to the cave and there "throws himself upon her" (30) is decried as "the lustful slave" (26). The phrase operates ambiguously and, as a result, ironically. At one level, Rochester supplies a standard epithet to the sporty rascal and, in libertine parlance, a pseudopejorative adjective to go with it. After all, is not the customer of adult material assumed to be lustful as well? By the compact of pornography, it is this same fortunate swain, while he is piercing "her virgin zone" (31), who the male reader is imaginatively to personate, thereby gaining his artificial thrills. At another level, however, Rochester also accuses the young man—and, by extension, the narratee—of being a slave to lust. And here springs Rochester's net.

Not only is this saucy ravisher, as we have seen, wryly identified with classical notions of ignorant hedonism, but he is a mere figment of Cloris's—the supposed helpless female victim's—imagination. In other words, actual male puissance *and* sexual stimulation by proxy are—*if one thinks about it*—conspicuously absent in this poem. At the climactic moment of male orgasm, "Just in the happy minute" (35), Rochester's song foists a poetic coitus interruptus on the reader.

> Frighted she wakes, and waking frigs.
>   Nature thus kindly eased.
> In dreams raised by her murmuring pigs,
> And her own thumb between her legs,
>   She's innocent and pleased.
>
> 36–40

Not only is there no exhilarating piercing of virgin zones here, but Cloris attains a paradoxical state of sexually fulfilled innocence on her own through masturbation. To some readers' understandings this might imply that women are abandoned in their secret desires, confirming a fond male wish. But an attentive reader might also ken that Cloris has no need of a piglike rapist, a lustful slave, to take her by force. She is happier and better off by herself. To the aspiring womanizer, this could be construed as a rather threatening form of female sexual autonomy. Moreover, the male presence in the poem—both in its imaginary rapist the swain *and* in its narratee the target fop—are soundly condemned and rudely negated. With this defeat of male lust comes the defeat, in essence, of male power.[10]

I do not think this sexual-political reading of "Fair Cloris," though admittedly extremely—perhaps too well—veiled, is unreasonable. Very often in Rochester's productions, male lust can be viewed as a token for political dominance: the scepter and the prick are of an equal length. Moreover, similar correlations exist in the more overtly political verse of the period.[11] For example, near the end of *The Last Instructions to a Painter*, Andrew Marvell depicts Charles attempting to molest a bound, gagged, and blindfolded vision of a virgin who represents "*England* or the *Peace*" (904). While I am not suggesting that Cloris necessarily must be read as a similar symbol for the state or well-being of England under the rule of Charles, I do suggest that the connection between lust and ascendancy is much the same. As with Rochester's poem, Marvell's late-night scene in the king's private chambers involves the device of a dream-vision rape. In both, an innocent and helpless woman is threatened by a libertine of high social rank: in the case of "Fair Cloris," the subtly implied narratee target fop (not just the routine swain in the poem); in the case of *Last Instructions*, the king himself.

> Paint last the King, and a dead shade of Night,
> Only dispers'd by a weak Tapers light;
> And those bright gleams that dart along and glare
> From his clear Eyes, yet these too dark with Care.
> There, as in the calm horrour all alone,
> He wakes and Muses of th' uneasie Throne:
> Raise up a sudden Shape with Virgins Face,
> Though ill agree her Posture, Hour, or Place:
> Naked as born, and her round Arms behind,
> With her own Tresses interwove and twin'd:
> Her mouth lockt up, a blind before her Eyes,

Yet from beneath the Veil her blushes rise;
And silent tears her secret anguish speak,
Her heart throbs, and with very shame would break.
The Object strange in him no Terrour mov'd:
He wonder'd first, then pity'd, then he lov'd:
And with kind hand does the coy Vision press,
Whose Beauty greater seem'd by her distress;
But soon shrunk back, chill'd with her touch so cold,
And th' airy Picture vanisht from his hold.

883–902[12]

Note the same voyeuristic if not masturbatory sense of Marvell's presentation; note similar implications of sexual depravity. Marvell's strange tryst is not only rape and imperfect enjoyment combined but, more to the point, pornography infused into political satire. As Steven N. Zwicker comments on this scene:

> Luxury and sensuality at the center of the court are fundamentally political in character: pleasure rather than honor or abundance is the aim of this monarch; private passion rather than public trust is the principle of this court. . . . What the scene finally urges is the recognition that England herself has become matter simply for sexual consumption, the nation a body used mainly to excite and relieve the king's desires.[13]

Where Marvell emphasizes the political over the pornographic, I suggest that Rochester merely works the reverse. Where Marvell impugns the lascivious behavior of Charles, Rochester denigrates the king's roguish minion for the same behavior. Both attacks have political repercussions; both pull the rug out from underneath the feet of the panting male, denying the fulfillment of sexual and civil potency alike. The only real difference between the two poems is that Marvell's is patently linked to the political circumstances of England while Rochester's is tacitly so. Yet read in conjunction with other works by Rochester, "Fair Cloris" admits a pattern of politicized censure of Charles's licentious reign based on the unexpected reversal of male salaciousness.

The works of Rochester brim with the demolition of blind, male eroticism by twisting its own poetic terms of expression. Any number of Rochester's verses spread a savage noose for the casual, modish reader of erotic verse—nominally Rochester's libertine cohort in mayhem—to place his own head. In "A Very

Heroical Epistle," the "solid sloth" of the sultan where one "feel'st the joys of love, without the pain" (41–42) doubtlessly would appeal to the hedonist ideal of ad hoc copulation. However, the narrator imagining this nirvana is an egomaniacal blockhead whose highest elocutionary attainment seems to be tautology fobbed off as insouciance.

> How is it then that I inconstant am?
> He changes not who always is the same.
> In my dear self I centre everything,
> My servants, friends, my mistress and my king,
> Nay, heaven and earth to that one point I bring.
>
> 5–9

Moreover, the clear ideal of the speaker is both political and sexual tyranny.

> Oh happy Sultan! Whom we barbarous call!
> How much refined art thou above us all?
> Who envies not the joys of thy serail?
> Thee, like some god, the trembling crowd adore,
> Each man's thy slave, and womankind, thy whore.
>
> 32–36

Whether this portrait is intended as a confessional, as a caustic portrait of Mulgrave, or as a generic depiction of the target fop, the elements of sex, polity, social status, and ambiguity all are present.[14]

The unblushing "Régime de Vivre," while appealingly farcical, brings with it the same schizophrenic aura of attraction/repulsion to its modish narrator.

> I rise at eleven, I dine about two,
> I get drunk before seven, and the next thing I do,
> I send for my whore, when for fear of a clap,
> I spend in her hand, and I spew in her lap;
> Then we quarrel and scold, till I fall fast asleep,
> When the bitch growing bold, to my pocket does creep.
> Then slyly she leaves me, and to revenge the affront,
> At once she bereaves me of money and cunt.
> If by chance then I wake, hot-headed and drunk,
> What a coil do I make for the loss of my punk!
> I storm, and I roar, and I fall in a rage.
> And missing my whore, I bugger my page.
> Then crop-sick all morning I rail at my men,
> And in bed I lie yawning till eleven again.

The poem, if indeed by Rochester, again walks a fine line between celebrating and emasculating the particular regime of
libertine truth of the age. The narratee may simultaneously
envy and question such a luxurious expenditure of a day. "The
Disabled Debauchee" similarly places its reader under interpretive pressure.

> I'll tell of whores attacked, their lords at home,
> Bawds' quarters beaten up, and fortress won,
> Windows demolished, watches overcome,
> And handsome ills by my contrivance done.
>
> 33–36

Is this narrator commendable, bathetic, or pathetic? Are his
actions heroic or mock-heroic, erotic or mock-erotic, rakish or
mock-rakish? The reader has need to decide, for the narrator
spurs him on toward libertine behavior.

> Should hopeful youths (worth being drunk) prove nice,
> And from their fair inviters meanly shrink,
> 'Twould please the ghost of my departed vice,
> If at my counsel they repent and drink.
>
> 25–28

Is the narrator to be trusted? And if he is "statesman-like" (45),
are politicians then uselessly wise and impotently active as
well (46–48)? Does the old debauchee in ways figure Charles
himself? More questions than answers lurk within this seemingly straightforward racy lyric.

Even more problematic is the narrator of "A Ramble in St.
James's Park." Obviously he is a gentleman of station, quite
possibly a court insider. However, I believe Rochester's poem
unites narrator and narratee, not narrator and poet.[15] The narrator pursues a standard masculine complaint: "But mark
what creatures women are, / So infinitely vile and fair" (41–42).
Yet, once more, to the thoughtful reader, the poem soon becomes not raillery against women, but a frenetic piece of irony
directed at the fragile male pride of the overthrown libertine
swiver. Way-of-the-world wisdom and devil-take-it jocularity,
upon inspection, become instead altogether conventional
marks of a wounded male ego. The narrator's upset comes
chiefly from the fact that his mistress has hooked up with three
other wits or, in his estimation, pretenders to wit. One is described as "of your Whitehall blades" (45); the next is "a Grays

Inn wit" (63); the last is "a lady's eldest son" (69) looking to be instructed in the art of debauchery by these other "two worthies" (73). Yet while the narrator directs his haughty contempt at these rivals, Rochester's poem directs harsh irony at the narrator. Fundamentally, all four men are of a kind: arrogant oafs busily engaged in the prevailing male cult of sexual self-adoration. The ironic subtext of the narrator's outburst, then, is that he has been replaced by someone (or, in this instance, by a trio of stooges) of fundamentally his own select station in life whom the woman—for unknown reasons; women are frightening gaps in the male scheme of things in these works—finds more appealing, but whom he had always thought himself much superior.[16] Thus, in "Ramble" we see once more not only the target fop made ridiculous, but his lust abruptly negated within an intimidating climate of female sexual self-government. Indeed, by the middle of the composition the narrator who had begun the poem as the typically predatory sexual male starts to speak in the conventional (meaning male-imposed) voice of the long-suffering and passive female.

> But why am I, of all mankind,
> To so severe a fate designed?
> Ungrateful! Why this treachery
> To humble, fond, believing me?
> Who gave you privileges above
> The nice allowances of love?
>
>   *   *   *
>
> Nor ever thought it an abuse
> While you had pleasure for excuse.
> You that could make my heart away
> For noise and colours, and betray
> The secrets of my tender hours
> To such knight-errant paramours.
> When leaning on your faithless breast,
> Wrapped in security and rest,
> Soft kindness all my powers did move,
> And reason lay dissolved in love.
> 105–10, 123–32

In between these two sets of lines, he has railed against Corinna's "lewd cunt" (113) and sexual craving. Besides the obvious nonsense of the narrator's abhorrence over his mistress's animalistic sexual behavior while he is out looking to participate in animalistic sexual behavior himself, the menace of "your depraved appetite" (135), that is, insatiable female sexuality, enters the poem as a force no longer able to be squelched. Pivotal to the collapse of male desire in Rochester's poetry is not merely the faltering of male privilege via the frustration of male appetite, but the transposition of gender hegemony altogether.

The clearest statement of such an overthrow comes in "A Dialogue between Strephon and Daphne." There a thoroughly suave against-constancy argument by the man is derailed by the woman's sudden revelation to the "Silly swain" that she, too, has been "false in scorn of you" for some time (65–68). Daphne concludes her bombshell:

> By my tears, my heart's disguise,
> I thy love and thee despise.
> Womankind more joy discovers
> Making fools, than keeping lovers.

69–72

Literally, Strephon is left speechless. One does not sense an approval of female pleasure-seeking at the conclusion of the poem; rather, the panic at rebellion inhabits his silence.[17] Rochester's most remarkable poem challenging the hedonistic cult of Charles via inversion of gender role is his song of premature ejaculation aptly titled "The Imperfect Enjoyment." The piece shows that not just love, but equally lust is an unobtainable ideal in Rochester's poetry; as it does, male hegemony is revoked completely. Scholarship has placed "The Imperfect Enjoyment" within a minor commonplace of late seventeenth-century love lyric.[18] However, Rochester does not completely follow suit in this tradition. His poem's connection with it is at best attenuated; the thoughts animating his verse are far more rigorous and, in the end, vexing.[19] Where most poems of this genre delay and tease male satisfaction in order to accomplish their lighthearted and pornographic mission (and I use these adjectives well aware of their mutual exclusivity), early in Rochester's poem passion ignominiously overflows in the narrator before accomplishing coition.

> But whilst her busy hand would guide that part,
> Which should convey my soul up to her heart,
> In liquid raptures I dissolve all o'er,

> Melt into sperm, and spend at every pore:
> A touch from any part of her had done't,
> Her hand, her foot, her very look's a cunt.
>
> 13–18

Rather than pornographic, the mood of the piece changes at this moment to become one of aggression and intimidation. As the final couplet shows, the man is overwhelmed by his partner's sexuality; the ugliness of the word "cunt" strikes me as a kind of male verbal shield held up feebly against the female onslaught. Initially the predator, the narrator finds himself abruptly and unnervingly turned into prey and out of his sexual and emotional depth.

In the ensuing unsuccessful attempt to collect her "debt to pleasure" (24), the woman then initiates a terrifying inversion of sexual preeminence: she takes the role of the aggressor. Initially she chides him "in a kind murmuring noise" (19) for his misadventure, but when it becomes clear that he will not be able to deliver the sexual goods, she cries out, "'Is there then no more?'" (22). The rake has turned from victimizer into victim.

> But I, the most forlorn, lost man alive,
> To show my wished obedience vainly strive.
> I sigh, alas! and kiss, but cannot swive.
> Eager desires confound my first intent,
> Succeeding shame does more success prevent,
> And rage, at last, confirms me impotent.
>
> 25–30

The word "obedience" (despite his reaction to her demands being "wished obedience") marks the crucial transposition in their relationship. "Imperfect Enjoyment" is a poem not only of male sexual humiliation, but of outright sexual overthrow by the woman. The reaction of the narrator to his deposition is perhaps unique in Restoration lyric. Rather than a spiteful and unfounded denunciation of women, such as that concluding "Ramble," he engages in ardent scrutiny of himself. As a result, where pornography excites the phallus and sedates the brain, Rochester's obscene verse effects the converse: the narrator reverts to using what Woody Allen refers to in a movie as his second favorite organ. This rare introspection in the rake provokes, suggestively, vituperation against the driving force of Charles's brand of libertinism—the tarse.

> What oyster, cinder, beggar, common whore,
> Didst thou ere fail in all thy life before?
> When vice, disease and scandal lead the way,
> With what officious haste dost thou obey?
> Like a rude roaring hector, in the streets,
> That scuffles, cuffs, and ruffles all he meets.
>
> 50–55

In fact, in the language of the poem, the rake and his wretched member become one entity: "Trembling, confused, limber, dry, / A wishing, weak, unmoving lump I lie" (35–36). Verbatim in that word "I," men are pricks. Both are then made the objects of curse. Over the last third of the poem, the narrator reproaches himself for being a slave to lust while heaping malediction not upon the woman's genitalia, but upon his own offending appendage. The narrator calls his penis—and thus himself and, once more, by extension the narratee target fop as well—the "Worst part of me" (62) and "a common fucking-post" (63). A more overt element of sexuality-cum-polity finds its way into the poem as well. "Officius" or dutiful haste urges the narrator to obey the call of the libertine manifesto, and thus participate in the dominant rake culture of the day. Later, still railing at his pintle, the narrator declares:

> But if his king and country claim his aid,
> The rakehell villain shrinks, and hides his head:
> Even so thy brutal valour is displayed;
> Breaks every stew, does each small whore invade,
> But when great Love the onset does command,
> Base recreant to thy prince, thou darest not stand.
>
> 56–61

Such a characterization of the prick/libertine recalls Bulkeley's portrait in his letter to Rochester of men of mode who would rather fornicate than fight. Political manhood itself *as men like to define it* is under attack in this poem.

Finally, while under feminine government, the narrator commits two cardinal sins against the male libertine psyche. First, he laments the loss of "great Love" because of his profligate behavior; second, in a desperate act of self-hatred and lame contrition, he wishes his rivals better concupiscent fortune with his mistress (66–72). The narrator's concentration on emotion as well as his concern for the welfare of his partner impress me as two distinctly "feminine" traits according to the male stereotype of women. Rochester's poem recasts the narrator as a "woman" according to the sexist constructs of the era.[20] Thus, along with his atypical spate of soul-searching (no self-respecting playboy would waste his energy so), the narrator responds to the amorous advances of the now sexually superior woman in a routinely "womanish" way. Namely, he blames the victim, now her/himself. In this poem, the debauchee hits rock bottom according to his own social and sexual conventions: he becomes the self-degrading object of unwanted sexual pressure. Vicariously, then, the libertine reader is piqued into examining not only his own mindless profligacy, but more perturbingly the servile and paradoxical self-loathing that comes from *being* tyrannized—that is, the awful predicament into which he routinely places women. Via such gender bending and fulfilling the promise of its paradoxical title, "Imperfect Enjoyment" forces the sexual oppressor imaginatively to experience something of the crisis of the sexually oppressed.

Yet bending gender distinctions as well as creating other forms of linguistic chaos that fly in the face of literary convention, social custom, and rational order is commonplace in Rochester's writings. As we have seen, in many of Rochester's lyrics, the libertine status quo is questioned if not toppled. Gender bedlam of a much stranger order occurs in the sexual-political lament "Oh what damned aged do we live in." In that composition, more than change places, maleness and femaleness all but disappear as terms.

> Since fucking is not as 'twas wont
> The ladies have got a new trick:
> As an arsehole serves for a cunt,
> So a clitoris serves for a prick.
>
> 9–12

As in *Sodom* (discussed later), perversion, pandemonium, and politicality unite. Of course, linguistic assertion of chaos as superior to order finds best expression, though of a nonsexual nature, in Rochester's often praised "Upon Nothing." Over the first eighteen lines of that poem, one wonders if in fact the narrator discusses not so much the mysterious creation of the universe by God, but instead the linguistic creation of arbitrary order out of actual chaos by humans. Just as Locke worries about linguistic generalities (in the terms of this poem,

Something) fabricated from material particularities (i.e., Nothing), Rochester's poem describes how the "Form and Matter, Time and Place" of "Something" (7, 16) was concocted to "spoil thy peaceful realm and ruin all thy line" of "Primitive Nothing . . . the great united—what?" (5–6, 18). Like Locke, this poem asserts that Something, the "rebel light" that incongruously obscures the "reverend dusky face" of Nothing (15), is in fact only an assemblage of signs that do not belong to the real existence of things. After all, the creations of Something— a false order—are in the end "thy slaves" and will return to Nothing "where thy truth in private lies" (21, 24). Human taxonomy is not truth; original and ultimately unknowable anarchy is. In fact, I believe one way to clear up the confusion produced by the argument of the poem would be to substitute the word "Chaos" everywhere the word or concept "Nothing" appears or is meant. That way, instead of constantly stumbling over the disorientation of dealing with a negative expression as a positive entity, we would realize that the unmoved mover of the poem's cosmos is not God's Word but its antithesis— primordial cacophony. But then again, I believe the vernacular stupefaction generated by the use of the word "Nothing" is quite deliberate and a major component of how the poem relates to us.

Over the second half of "Upon Nothing," the narrator questions exactly how this delusional belief in the truth of Something operates in the world. As Thormählen points out when placing the poem into its historical context, the three most influential groups of truth-making men are denounced: churchmen and schoolmen briefly, politicians in some detail. She concludes that the work "is an extremely intelligent rebuttal of any and all claims of the human intellect to be able to guide mankind in any sort of direction at all, let alone a sound and consistent one."[21] For me, the specific intellectual function in question in the piece is the linguistic power play of instituting and enforcing truth. The stability of government depends on such an undertaking.

> Is or Is Not, the two great ends of fate,
> And true or false, the subject of debate
> That perfect or destroy the vast designs of State—
>
> When they have racked the politician's breast,
> Within thy bosom most securely rest,
> And when reduced to thee are least unsafe and blessed.

31–36

Actual truth and falsehood—not that created by politicians—
best resides with chaos, where humans cannot get at them.
Only there are they not dangerous to us. Enlightened *ignorance*
of what "Is or Is Not" is preferable to ignorant "enlightenment"
of what is compelled on us as true or false by the state (or by
the church and university). When we admit that truth is of a
particular, anarchic, and obscure nature rather than general,
orderly, and unmistakable, then it is "least unsafe and blessed"
because the potential for the abuse of power is removed. We
may have to fend with uncertainty, but better that than bond-
age under a tyranny of sham order and truth—that is, as
within Rochester's major satires, ruinous speculative reasoning. With still more dizzying wordplay, Rochester's poem
drives home this point by next asserting that the devotees of
Something are inept even at maintaining their own lies.

> But (Nothing) why does Something still permit
> That Sacred Monarchs should at Council sit
> With persons highly thought, at best for nothing fit,
>
> While weighty Something modestly abstains
> From Princes' coffers and from Statesmen's brains,
> And nothing there like stately nothing reigns?
>
> 37–42

Penurious and dissimulative monarchs, such as Charles, and
corrupt ministers, such as any number of Charles's advisors
and civil servants, might play at the manufacture and imposing of patriotic facades for king and country, but their own
schemes palpably misfire—such as the popularly perceived
misappropriation of funds for a phantom refurbishing of the
fleet that lead to the Medway disaster in 1667, to name but
one famous instance. Whether in this passage the noncapital-
ized uses of the word "nothing" denote specially chaos or the
ordinary condition of being naught—and the confusion well
can be intended—the upshot is the same: a fanciful rhetorical
question about why the entity Something puts up with incompetent supporters. According to the poem, not only is the truth
and order of Something groundless, it is not even particularly
well disguised or administered. The list of obvious examples
of chaos masquerading as order—to include "British Policy"
and "Kings' promises" (46, 50)—brings home perhaps this
most damaging point of all made by the poem: that we are
the willing dupes of such political, religious, and intellectual

nonsense. Rochester's poem recognizes that continual, fluttering flame in humans Nietzsche identifies as Vanity. Without
proposing pleasing alternative views, it prompts the contemporary reader to recognize vanity at work in his own life, too.

While overwhelmingly ignored by critics, Rochester's prose
tract *Doctor Bendo's Bill*, written as an advertisement for his
medical practice when masquerading as a physician in the city
of London, enacts this same critique of English society. More
than the jeu d'esprit for which the tract normally is taken, we
should read the bill primarily as a well-disguised satire on the
political elite of the 1670s.[22] What *Doctor Bendo's Bill constructs* before our eyes—as opposed to deconstructs as in the
case of "Upon Nothing"—is mock-truth. Namely, that such a
person as Alexander Bendo actually exists; that he has "spent
my time ever since I was fifteen years old to this my nine-and-
twentieth year" in France and Italy gathering medical secrets
(122); that currently he runs a clinic "at my lodgings in Tower
Street, next door to the sign of the Black Swan, at a goldsmith's
house" (123); and that he is open for business to cure a variety
of ills. As in so many of his other writings, Rochester plays
upon the intellectual and linguistic complexity of this narrative pose. In protesting that he is *not* a charlatan, Bendo in
essence credits Rochester with absolute expertise at *being* a
charlatan.

> All I shall say for myself on this score is this: if I appear to anyone
> like a counterfeit, even for the sake of that, chiefly, ought I to
> be construed a true man. Who is the counterfeit's example? His
> original; and that, which he employs his industry and pains to
> imitate and copy. Is it therefore my fault if the cheat, by his wits
> and endeavours, makes himself so like me, that consequently I
> cannot avoid resembling him? (119)

Similarly, when promoting his "knowledge of a great secret, to
cure barrenness" (121), Bendo playfully boasts of his creator's
prowess at swiving—or at least alludes to the rake's standard
pursuit of sexual conquest. Says Bendo/Rochester of his "great
secret," which in reality is for him to perform the sexual act
itself:

> I have made use of [this technique] for many years with great
> success, especially this last year, wherein I have cured one woman
> that had been married twenty years, and another that had been
> married one-and-twenty years, and two women that had been

three times married; as I can make appear by the testimonies of several persons in London, Westminster, and other places thereabouts. . . . Cures of this kind I have done signal, and many. (121)[23]

The locale of persons who will bear testimony to a rate of cure is significant: the city first, but then Whitehall and the town— "other places thereabouts." Just as John Dryden moves us down the Thames from Westminster to London in *Mac Flecknoe* as part of his satire against Shadwell, Rochester's tract (just as Pope would do later in *The Dunciad*) moves us back upstream to make a satiric point as well. If Charles and Rochester's cronies indeed ever read the advertisement, they might well have howled over the passages just quoted once appreciating the inside and aristocratic joke of them. According to the mythology that has grown around this bill, the king supposedly granted Rochester's return to court after the earl's prankishness among the cits was brought to his attention. But this is my basic point.

As a piece of writing, *Doctor Bendo's Bill* hinges on establishing a tension between those reading it who are in on the joke and those reading it who are not—between those who recognize it as mock-truth and those who are duped into accepting it as verifiable truth. We as in-the-know readers enjoy the bill *because* we know other, less informed readers are fooled by it. The mock-treatise creates and relies on a textual climate of double entendre—of the common sexual variety as in this example, but, more often, of a general nature as well. One other kind of double meaning is, at a fairly obvious level, classist: witty nobles scoff at gullible citizens. At a far less apparent level, however, commentary of a politically charged sort arises as well. If Charles and the social elite around him believed they had the last laugh over the affair, then they had fallen prey to Rochester's sophisticated satire. If one credulous reader's truth can be ridiculed by another as in fact mock-truth, then an even better reader can see that smug reader's world view as limited and pretentious in turn. The process of the joke can be repeated at least one more time (and possibly, as meta-laughter, endlessly?). Far more than making fun of merchants in the city, I believe Rochester's tract remarks scathingly on the court and the government of England centered at Whitehall and the houses of Parliament.

Emerging from a closer reading of *Doctor Bendo's Bill* is the exposure of the politician's regime of truth as *itself* mock-truth and tantemount to a mountebank's sham perpetrated to deceive the public.[24] Over the first half of Rochester's bill, the constant project is to equate the mountebank with the politician. At the outset of the tract, ostensibly referring to quack doctors, the narrator observes that London "has ever been infested with a numerous company of such, whose arrogant confidence, backed with their ignorance, has enabled them to impose upon the People" (118). When Bendo enumerates the fields of endeavor in which these cheats operate, however, it becomes apparent that the target of his comments is not bogus medical practitioners alone. Such frauds prey upon the simplicity of the population:

> in physic, chemical and Galenic; in astrology, physiognomy, palmistry, mathematics, alchemy, and even in government itself, the last of which I will not propose to discourse of, or meddle in at all, since it no way belongs to my trade or vocation, as the rest do; which—thanks to my God—I find much more safe, I think equally honest, and therefore more profitable. (ibid.)

Playing a subtle game, the advertisement expands the scope of Bendo's aspersions to include both mountebanks and politicians equally if not interchangeably. As a result, the scope of the satire expands: Rochester's bill supports now three distinct levels of understanding, of being in on the joke. The lowest order of course is that reader—generally, the citizen of London—who does not realize that Bendo is a farcical creation. The middle rank is that reader who does understand that Bendo is in fact the creature of the mad earl in yet another of his disguises; this insight calls for the relative sophistication of the town and court. The highest level of discernment (i.e., until another critic dismantles my reading) would be the reader who recognizes the political innuendo of the otherwise whimsical tract. Such recognition might only have come to Rochester's closest circle of friends, such as Henry Savile. In any event, the broad jest of clever deception foisted upon the unsuspecting citizen by *Doctor Bendo's Bill* is by comparison uninteresting when considered against the satiric trap set by the bill for that middle kind of reader—the west end patrician imagining that he or she is laughing at the east end clown. As we have seen in chapters 3 and 4, Rochester's major satires excel at manipulating various levels of awareness, of what might be termed *true wit* and *false wit*. Not only characters, but readers as well find themselves lost in linguistic mazes. Perhaps one mark of great satire is its ablility to arrange situations where a reader can laugh at the expense of someone laughing at the expense of someone else. Exposing would-be wits as in fact fools is the constant satiric avocation of Rochester's writings. In *Doctor Bendo's Bill*, the politically elite, in the end, find themselves the real butt of Rochester's prank.

Bendo's avowal that he "will not propose to discourse of, or meddle in at all" matters of government proves, predictably, to be less than genuine. After discoursing briefly on how artful error so often overwhelms plain truth (118–19)—this deft performance of mock-truth, for those in the know, serving as an excellent case in point—the good doctor offers specious argument for his own authenticity. As we have seen, this takes the form of contending that the counterfeit and the genuine article closely resemble each other. In citing exempla, Bendo names "the valiant, and the coward, the wealthy merchant and the bankrupt, the politician and the fool"; he says of these three pairs, "they are the same in many things, and differ but in one alone" (119). For the first, the point of real distinction is "courage." For the second, it is "real cash." For the third pairing, the politician and the fool, Bendo names no vital difference between them.

> Now for the politician; he is a grave, deliberating, close, prying man: pray, are there not grave, deliberating, close, prying fools? (119)

What's the difference here? Such hits against politicians might seem to be of an incidental and routine satiric ilk were it not for a digression by Bendo coming at the end of what has served in essence as a preamble for his advertisement. Before "I willingly submit myself" to the reader's experience in discerning between the learned doctor and the quack, Bendo pauses to "say something to the honour of the MOUNTEBANK, in case you discover me to be one" (119). The notion itself is amazing. A mountebank's honor is outrageous oxymoron—as well as a possible pun on Rochester's own social status. More audacious, Rochester's bill virtually admits its deception at this juncture. As it does, however, it ties the mountebank and the politician inextricably together—a move that I believe reverberates throughout the rest of the document. Asking us to reflect on the nature of the mountebank, Bendo says:

his is one then, who is fain to supply some higher authority he
pretends to with craft; he draws great companies to him by undertaking strange things, which can never be effected. The politician—by his example, no doubt—finding how the People are taken
with specious miraculous impossibilities, plays the same game;
protests, declares, promises I know not what things, which he is
sure can never be brought about. The People believe, are deluded,
and pleased; the expectation of a future good, which shall never
befall them, draws their eyes off a present evil. Thus *they* are kept
and established in subjection, peace, and obedience; *he* in great-
ness, wealth, and power. So you see the politician is, and must be,
a mountebank in State affairs; and the mountebank, no doubt, if
he thrives, is an arrant politician in physic. (120)

Both the mountebank and the politician are in the business of
manufacturing and profiting from the illusion of truth. They
formulate pleasing lies designed to deflect current unpleasant
reality, whether of the body politic or of the body corporeal.
The obvious and painful difference between them, though, is
that the quack conny-catches on a small scale, causing isolated
suffering. The politician, on the other hand, employs his rhetoric for the purpose of oppression and self-aggrandizement on
a national scale. Each produces mock-truth, just as does Rochester's bill through Bendo. Rochester's fabrication, however,
is an idle pastime. That of the mountebank and the politician
entails serious agendas of, in the case of the former, duplicitous
economic gain and, in the case of the latter, grave civic
consequence.

If, as Bendo concludes, a mountebank is "an arrant politician
in physic," then the rest of his bill is, in a sense, spoken in the
deceptive language of the politician. (The reverse is true as
well: politicians speak in the deceptive language of the mountebank.) After his digression, Bendo announces that "I will proceed faithfully to inform you what are the things in which I
pretend chiefly, at this time, to serve my country" (120). His
declaration is a beautifully loaded statement. For the rest of
the document we have before us not only mock-truth in the
form of a counterfeit doctor's advertisement, designed evidently to fool the Londoner in the street, but equally the mock-
promises of a pseudopolitician's speech, designed I believe to
satirize the grandees in Whitehall and Parliament. Probably
what Bendo names among his catalog of ailments treated and
services rendered in order "to serve my country" bears less
specific political significance than *how* he names them. Typi-

cally for Rochester's writings, Rochester's bill attacks more the general deceptive manner of the politician than, like Andrew Marvell, particular political acts of the day.

Bendo's first topic is "that *labes Britannica,* or the great English disease, the scurvy" (120). Of everything mentioned over the second half of the bill, this public ill brings with it the most political weight. Widespread scurvy aptly figures a malkept populace; such a condition naturally would result from, as Bendo asserted previously, a people held in subjugation and quiescence by politicians relishing power and wealth. Upon reflection, Bendo's guarantees successfully to treat the condition mimic a politician's promises. He will cure the disease

> with such ease to my patient that he shall not be sensible of the least inconvenience while I steal his distemper from him. I know there are many who treat this disease with mercury, antimony, spirits, and salt; being dangerous remedies; in which I shall meddle very little, and with great caution; but by more secure, gentle, and less fallible medicines, together with the observation of some few rules in diet, perfectly cure the patient . . . . And to say true, there are few distempers in this nation that are not, or at least proceed not originally from the scurvy; which, were it well rooted out, (as I make no question to do it from all those who shall come into my hands) there would not be heard of so many gouts, aches, dropsies, and consumptions; . . . but those who address themselves here, shall be informed by me of the nature of their distempers, and the grounds I proceed upon to their cure; so will all reasonable people be satisfied that I treat them with care, honesty, and understanding; for I am not of their opinion, who endeavour to render their vocations rather mysterious than useful and satisfactory. (120)

Not only does Rochester's bill perpetrate a medical hoax with these promises, but Bendo's words echo familiar devices of the politician. With smoke and mirrors, the mountebank-politician attests miracle cures without once mentioning how they will be accomplished or at what real cost to the patient. The tone is soothing; the content is obscure. Bendo engages in campaign rhetoric and doublespeak. Remedies are assured that bring no discomfort to the patient-citizen; these correctives are better, safer, easier, and more efficient than those offered by Bendo's competitors. What is more, by addressing this one affliction, many if not all collateral ailments will be alleviated as well. Bendo offers the English nation a nostrum.

As for personal ethos, Bendo vows to be open and honest about his methods of cure—once, that is, the patient-citizen has committed to his care. Equally, he promises to deal with clients fairly and respectfully—even though Bendo sells us snake oil at this point and, behind that, Rochester's prose makes monkeys of us. Finally, while keeping us entirely in the dark as to any specifics of his policy, Bendo professes that he is not like all those other doctors-politicians who make a living by keeping us in the dark. He makes a particular point, in fact, to distinguish himself from others who engage in the trade. In protesting his integrity, Bendo declares: "and, at least, he shall be secure with me from having experiments tried upon him; a privilege he can never hope to enjoy, either in the hands of the grand doctors of the court and town, or in those of the lesser quacks and mountebanks" (121). The phrase "the grand doctors of the court and town," I believe, is thick with amphiboly. While Bendo refers to west end physicians, Rochester's bill, recalling the digression wherein the mountebank and the politician are equated, insinuates that the English people suffer from quackery at the hands of their leaders of state. The blending of medical with political doubletalk is nearly seamless.

The remainder of *Doctor Bendo's Bill* equally can be read as a demonstration of bureaucratese. Fine lauguage covers up foul matters, as when venereal disease and abortion are cited:

> but I cure all suffocations in those parts producing fits of the mother, convulsions, nocturnal inquietudes, and other strange accidents not fit to be set down here; persuading young women very often that their hearts are like to break for love when, God knows, the distemper lies far enough from that place. (ibid.)

Vague claims of expertice and past success abound, as when Bendo vaunts his skills at astrological prediction:

> for I might say this of myself (did it not look like ostentations) that I have very seldom failed in any predictions, and often been very serviceable in my advice. How far I am capable in this way, I am sure is not fit to be delivered in print: those who have no opinion of the truth of this art, will not, I suppose, come to me about it; such as have, I make no question of giving them ample satisfaction. (122)

When discussing "rare secrets . . . for the help, conversation, and augmentation of beauty and comeliness" (ibid.), Bendo ventures into the arena of sexual politics:

> for when God had bestowed on man the power of strength and wisdom, and thereby rendered woman liable to the subjection of his absolute will, it seemed but requisite that she should be endowed likewise, in recompense, with some quality that might beget in him admiration of her, and so enforce his tenderness and love. (ibid.)

In offering women aids to improved complexion and teeth, treatment for bad-breath, and regimens to "take away from their fatness who have overmuch, and add flesh to those that want it" (123), Bendo seems to be an early perpetrator of what Naomi Wolfe has identified recently as the Beauty Myth.[25] In sum, *Doctor Bendo's Bill* shows as much linguistic complexity and political subtlety as any of Rochester's writings. With its three concentric levels of awareness, the piece resembles strikingly *Artemisa to Chloe*. In this instance of satiric observation of the powered class, however, the role of the absentee man of wit is played literally by the exiled Rochester himself. If, as tradition has it, Rochester were expelled from court in the first place for mistakenly handing Charles a satire upon the king, what wonderful irony it would be if Rochester actually was admitted back into Charles's good graces for writing a similar satire upon his government.

Finally, many of Rochester's writings excel as expositions of the arbitrary nature of truth as an instrument of political power. Rochester told Burnet that his notion of God was as "no more than a vast power, that had none of the Attributes of Goodness or Justice we ascribe to the Deity" and that morality was merely "a decent way of speaking"—that is, a convenient pretense.[26] For Rochester, then, the word of God is priestcraft, oppressive, and altogether human. In the terminology of "Upon Nothing," God is part of that unknowable expanse of chaos, of Nothing, while Burnet's Christian God is a construct of false order, of Something. Wherever these rival concepts cross paths in Rochester's works, I believe it is a political confrontation, for inevitably at stake is who will wield control over whom. As explored in chapter 4, a statement to this effect occurs in *Satire Against Mankind* when the narrator contends that, in this world, honesty is the worst policy (159–

63). If one does not participate in the power-word game, all
is lost.

> Nor can weak truth your reputation save,
> The knaves will all agree to call you knave.
> Wronged shall he live, insulted o'er, oppressed,
> Who dares be less a villain than the rest.

164–67

"Weak truth" perhaps signifies, as it seems to in "Upon Nothing," a realization of the deep obscurity and intricacy of existence, especially when measured against the facile human
notions of truth and order. Paradoxically, this more acute understanding of the nature of reality is, in the human social
order, a disadvantage. Power, esteem, wealth, and happiness
itself all hinge only upon "who's a knave of the first rate"
(173)—namely, who is the most adept at manipulating the
strings of truth and power for his own advantage. A recurring
individual illustration of this mode of knavery in Rochester's
works is Charles II. And once again, the element of sexuality
most often accompanies such castigation.

In spite of occasional efforts by critics to paint Charles as a
surrogate father to the younger nobleman, it seems that the
relationship between Rochester and his king was a rocky one.
While episodes of evident boon companionship figure prominently in the mythology of Charles's court wits, equally Rochester's dealings with Charles were laced with animosity.[27] The
poem "Verses for which he was Banished" (more widely known
as "A Satyr on Charles II") is an indispensable document for
understanding both this enmity and the political quality of
Rochester's works. That libel unites Rochester's entrapment
of the target fop specifically with Charles as the figurehead of
royalist libertinism; perhaps nowhere is the crucial connection
between sexuality and polity in Rochester's writings more
thoroughly established.[28] An integral part of the courtly ideology of Charles's reign was its particular attitude toward sex.
Sexual deportment at court brought with it political repercussions observed readily and frequently by Rochester (not to
mention by Marvell, Dryden, Butler, and many others as well).
In the poem, Charles is portrayed as the target fop ne plus
ultra; male passion is joined with unreason in the person of
the king. However, now unthinking appetite produces not only
derisible individual behavior, but deleterious collective behav-

ior as well in the form of bad government. Because he is a fool for lust, Charles is also an ineffectual monarch.

> Him no ambition moves to get renown,
> Like the French fool who wanders up and down
> Starving his soldiers, hazarding his crown.
> Peace is his aim, his gentleness is such,
> And love he loves, for he loves fucking much.
>
>   5–9

Approval of Charles in comparison with the tyrant Louis XIV dissipates the moment we understand that the ostensibly affirmative pursuits of peace, gentleness, and love mean for the English king only carnal gratification. Louis may place at risk his domain in an agitated quest for territorial acquisition, but, no better and in fact rather more ludicrously, Charles is guilty of similar civic folly in his coursing after women.[29]

Because Charles does not rule himself, he cannot effectively guide the country. According to the poem, the courtly pleasure cult installed and preserved by Charles is responsible for the nation's being adrift. Instead of the king, aphrodisia is in command.

> Nor are his high desires above his strength,
> His sceptre and his prick are of an equal length,
> And she that plays with one may play with t'other,
> And make him little wiser than his brother.
> The pricks of kings are like buffoons at Court:
> We let them rule because they make us sport.
>
>   10–15

The reference to Charles's pigheaded brother, James, might be taken as a routine denunciation of the king's counselors typical in political verse of the day. However, Rochester's poem goes beyond the bland fiction of relocating blame to the officials surrounding Charles. The king may be influenced by worthless fellows, but it is his own fault for leading with his penis. The couplet wherein the pricks of kings are likened to "buffoons at Court" carries the same allegation. Yet more than implicating Charles's ministers, that phrase certainly signals the Ballers as well—that merry gang, led by Rochester himself, with whom Charles enjoyed cavorting.[30] When the narrator declares in the voice of Charles (indicated by the use of the royal "we") that, "We let them rule because they make us sport," the king admits to being delinquent in his choice of company.[31] Thus Rochester's satire asserts intertextually that Charles is controlled by whomever titillates his imperial staff; equally, it demonstrates extra-textually that Charles, due to his intemperance, is oblivious to the fact that one of his eminent cohorts in self-gratification, Rochester, is also a merciless critic of his regime. Whether or not the king in fact was concerned greatly by his earl's libels, Charles emerges as a dunce in this poem—not unlike Pope's George I and II. At the same time, by characterizing the court wits as buffoons, the poem condemns the entire libertine-patrician ideal of Charles's reign. In the controlling metaphor of the couplet, courtiers are also pricks, mere joysticks to Charles. Once again, then, even the wits who might enjoy reading Rochester's libel against Charles are simultaneously victims of it.

Neither does the king escape the equation of profligate and prick. As we have witnessed already with the narrator of "Imperfect Enjoyment," Charles and his tarse grammatically become one and the same creature.

> He is the sauciest that e'er did swive,
> The proudest peremptoriest prick alive.
> Whate'er religion or his laws say on't,
> He'd break through all to come to any cunt.
> Restless he rolls about from whore to whore
> A merry monarch, scandalous and poor.
>
> 16–21

The "He" in the first line, which we naturally assume to mean Charles, suddenly becomes Charles's prick in the next line. From that point onward, the king and his royal member act as one roving, lawless agent of desire until the pintle is crowned with Charles's moniker, the "merry monarch," and both are described as scandalous and poor. Like the narrator and narratee in the obscene lyrics, Charles as King Prick is reduced to a common fucking post. Likewise, as in those same lyrics just discussed, the element of female sexual autonomy—more, actual political sway—figures prominently in "Verses for which he was Banished." Whether Charles's policies were influenced by his mistresses or not, that fear and perception certainly were strong during his reign, particularly with regard to his Catholic and French mistress, Louise de Kéroualle. The comment that she who plays with Charles's prick also plays with his scepter (11–12) was a serious political issue of the time.[32] In Rochester's poem, Charles is controlled by his penis, and his penis is controlled by women. Add to this misgiving the fact that Charles, at forty-three, is portrayed also as a roué in "my declining years" (23)—a sexual pun with grave political overtones given the fact that no legitimate heir was on the horizon; stubborn, belligerent, and openly Catholic James would inherit the throne. When coupling with his "dearest Carwell" (Kéroualle), Charles's "graceless bollocks hung an arse: / Nothing could serve his disobedient tarse" (22, 26–27). Even the popular protestant whore, Nell Gwynn, has difficulty rallying the royal staff (see 28–31).[33] The ultimate portrait of Charles is as a ludicrous target fop enfeebled both sexually and politically.

And yet, as the highest authority in English society, Charles is empowered with the capacity to frame truth. In Rochester's plays, the discrepancy between Charles's worthiness and his capability to perform such a task is explored attentively. If indeed *Sodom* is Rochester's work (whether he wrote the farce alone or as part of a clique), the character of King Bolloximian undeniably draws on Charles's reputation as an indolent sovereign more concerned with his own pursuit of pleasure than with the affairs of his kingdom and people.[34] At play's end, when Flux, the royal physician, warns the king that he must repeal the royal proclamation allowing buggery and return the realm to heterosexuality in order to avoid certain disaster, Bolloximian declares:

> Then must I go to the old whore, my wife?
> Why did the Gods, that gave me leave to be
> A king, not grant me immortality?
> To be a substitute for heaven at will—
> I scorn the gift—I'll reign and bugger still.
>
> 5.1.53–57

Not only is his response irresponsible stewardship, but in asserting his divine right Bolloximian also simultaneously admits that as king he has license to abuse that authority as he pleases. Just as with the portrait of Charles in "Verses for which he was Banished," what pleases Bolloximian is to base his political decisions upon the dictates of his penis. Leering at Pockenello, the king proclaims:

> Let heaven descend, and set the world on fire—
> We to some darker cavern will retire.
> There on thy buggered arse I will expire.
>
> 5.1.83–85

The play then ends in sexual and political apocalypse.[35] A more sober and extended investigation of Restoration truth as an artifice of Charles's power occurs, I believe, in Rochester's *Tragedy of Valentinian*. In Rochester's extensive reworking of Fletcher's play, many critics point to the republican leanings, the portraiture of Charles in the tyrant Valentinian, and the character of Maximus as a possible self-portrait.[36] What no one as yet has seen in *Valentinian* is its critique of the mechanics of power wherein the general politics of truth, as Foucault calls it, is clearly exposed for what it is—mere chicanery. More than republicanism, the play delivers nihilism of both a linguistic and a political nature.

Emperor Valentinian is the quintessence of Nietzschean vanity: his human cognition is applied only toward duplicity and terrible egoism. The most horrific sequence of the play is, provocatively, one of sexual politics. The libertine-potentate Valentinian has raped Lucina, a virtuous and noble woman of the Roman aristocracy, and he is unabashed for his behavior. When Lucina declares that "I'll cry for justice," he coolly replies, "Justice will never hear you. I am Justice" (4.3.4–5). When she rages that "The gods will find thee, / That's all my refuge now, for they are righteous. / Vengeance and horror circle thee" (4.3.12–14), initially (and typically within a rape culture) he blames the victim for attracting his lust: "curse that heavenly beauty, / And curse your being good, too" (4.3.28–29). As Lucina persists with her remonstrations, eventually Valentinian gets to the heart of the matter.

> Know I am far above the faults I do,
> And those I do I am able to forgive;
> And where your credit in the telling of it
> May be with gloss enough suspected, mine
> Is as my own command shall make it. Princes,
> Though they be sometimes subject to loose whispers,
> Yet wear they two-edged swords for open censures;
>
> *   *   *
>
> Nor can the gods be angry at this action,
> Who as they made me greatest, meant me happiest,
> Which I had never been without this pleasure.
> Consider and farewell.
>
>   4.3.83–89, 93–96

Laws and truth have no absolute, suprahuman source; instead, they are forms of constraint, mechanisms, techniques, procedures determined by the power elite of society—in this instance, by Valentinian. When the monstrosity of his words and of her situation fully impact Lucina, she concludes:

> Why then I see there is no god—but power,
> Nor virtue now alive that cares for us,
> But what is either lame or sensual.
> How had I been thus wretched else?
>
> 4.3.105–8

Such a recognition goes beyond protest of divine-right monarchy or even Charles's sensuous reign. It questions how any form of government can enjoy sanction other than that of a capricious and all-too human one.

If Lucina suffers from the machinations of power and thereby intuits the brutal realities of empire, her husband Maximus in the end comes to discern completely the awful falsity of truth. Fletcher's tragedy explores "the impasse into which believers in the divine right of kings found themselves when faced with an intolerable monarch,"[37] and Rochester's version makes much of the same issue, particularly in dialogue among Maximus, Aecius, and Pontius. However, after the rape of Lucina, Maximus experiences insights that eclipse that level of political discussion and extend into one more subtle still. When, like Lucina, he questions how the gods could have allowed such an atrocity to happen, Maximus does not stop at reprehension of absolute rule. He dismantles the doctrine of Providence itself.

> Had your eternal minds been bent to good,
> Could human happiness have proved so lame?
> Rapine, revenge, injustice, thirst of blood,
> Grief, anguish, horror, want, despair and shame,
> Had never found a being nor a name.
> 'Tis therefore less impiety to say,
> Evil with you has co-eternity,
> Than blindly taking it the other way,
> That merciful and of election free,
> You did create the mischiefs you foresee.
>
> 4.3.311–20

In this speech, Maximus may recapitulate the cruel state of human existence as described by Hobbes. More than that,

however, he exposes the political cover-up—that is to say,
God's eternal plan—designed to palliate those abominations
cataloged in lines 313–14. During the climactic confrontation
between Maximus and Valentinian, Maximus finally sees that
linguistic chaos in fact is in the ascendancy over *any* formation
of human government and order.

> Oh ye Gods!
> Is there no such thing as right or wrong,
> But force alone must swallow all possession?
> Then to what purpose in so long descents
> Were Roman laws observed or heaven obeyed?
> If still the great for ease or vice were formed,
> Why did our first king toil? Why was the plough
> Advanced to be the pillar of the State?
> Why was the lustful Tarquin with his house
> Expelled, but for the rape of bleeding Lucrece?
>
> 5.5.157–66

Law, truth, honor, justice, tradition, and history itself are all
meaningless, manipulable *signs* in the hands of "the great."
Not only do Maximus's allusions to *The Aeneid* function to negate the politically advantageous correlation between Au-
gustus and Valentinian/Charles, but the ideas expressed in his
speech raise extreme doubt over the nature of Virgil's (not to
mention much of Dryden's) project itself. The epic is less an
ideal than a ludicrous work of propaganda. Valentinian responds to Maximus's questions by saying, "I cannot bear thy
words. . . . Reason no more, thou troublest me with reason"
(5.5.167, 169). He also challenges his general by attempting to
play on Maximus's loyalty (via the example of Aecius) to king
and country: "How then darest thou. . . . / With impious arms
assault thy Emperor?" (5.5.192–93). At this point, however,
Maximus has thrown off faith and operates solely in the realm
of cognition. He has seen through the linguistic/cognitive
game. As a result, when Maximus decides to rebel against his
emperor, it is *not* as a morally superior subject overthrowing
a manifestly evil ruler. Divine right is *not* replaced by republicanism. Instead, Maximus rebels as a linguistic peer in the
fabrication of truth and thus as a coparticipant to Valentinian
in political chaos. He replies that he will enact revenge:

> Because I have more wit than honesty,
> More of thyself, more villainy than virtue,

More passion, more revenge, and more ambition
Than foolish honour and fantastic glory.

5.5.194–97

Whereas Aecius acted nobly and foolishly, believing in the Roman ideals as set forth in Virgil's epic, Maximus sees that such "fantastic glory" is a mug's game. Such "weak truth"—to recall the passage from *Satire Against Mankind*—leads to personal disaster in this world. Maximus has acquired too much wit (i.e., discernment) to follow Aecius's disastrous example of misguided honor and honesty that leads only to being oppressed. Instead, Maximus decides no longer to "be less a villain than the rest"; therefore, he will enter, however reluctantly, into the inescapable world of power-packed lies. That is the price of his new cognizance of the world. Where Valentinian was once the "knave of the first rate," now it will be Maximus. Rochester's tragedy does not furnish its Restoration audience with a republican hero; it forces contemporary onlookers to contemplate a man who has been forced tragically to internalize his oppressor. Is this not how *any* regime of truth operates in the world in order to maintain a hold on power? Like Maximus, if the narratee target fop were to fathom both the active duplicity and the passive gullibility requisite for his pledging himself to as well as patterning himself upon the conduct of his royal master, he too—like Rochester?—might unseat that intolerable civic lie.

6

Concluding Thoughts

I have a great goggle-eye to business.
　　　　　　—Rochester, in a letter to Henry Savile

IT is tempting to construct a personal-political relationship
between Rochester and Charles II based on a reading of Maximus and Valentinian. At this point in my study it is nearly
irresistible as well to offer routine lionization of the satirist
for mettle and acumen. Engaging in the dominant Epicurean
poetic of the day, Rochester turns the contingent epistemology
of the ruling class against itself. Rochester's writings push the
public negotiability of words to extremes, stretching with
them the interpretive competence of the target fop. If Rochester's firsthand readers read his works lazily and inadequately,
they fall victim to literary humiliation; they reveal themselves
as fools. If they read his writings carefully, however, they realize they are knaves. Moreover, the ultimate butt *and* source of
self-deluding folly *and* of self-serving knavery is the king himself in his libertine hegemonic practice. Thus, with masterful
satiric strokes, Rochester levels them all. Yet we must ask ourselves with regard to Rochester's erudite trap, humiliation or
realization toward what concrete purpose? Edward W. Said
urges critics to articulate "those voices dominated, displaced,
or silenced by the textuality of texts" and to find and expose
"things that otherwise lie hidden beneath piety, heedlessness,
or routine." He tells us that "criticism is worldly and in the
world so long as it opposes monocentrism . . . which licenses
a culture to cloak itself in the particular authority of certain
values over others."[1] Accordingly, should not Rochester's writings be commended for enacting just such a literate agenda
against the monocentrism of Charles's cultural order? Rochester's satiric critique of polity, sexuality, and society compel-

140

lingly deconstructs the dominant and oppressive elite of its day. The earl obviously deserves accolade—if not tenure—does he not?

Unfortunately, the matter is not so simple. While praise for an author's satiric heroism provides uplift in the final chapter of a book and is perhaps an industry standard for writing about the genre, I must tender something more complex and disturbing. If Rochester engages in a localized battle with the mechanics of power, in the end he seems to have accomplished little measurable success in that encounter. Without question his satire crosses swords (pens? words?) with the dominating legal entity of early modern kingship precisely at a time when new apparatuses of power incompatible with traditional views of monarchy were coming into being. As subjugated knowledge retrieved by Foucault's practice of effective history, Rochester's satire serves notably as a political window into how one well-situated English *subject*, not object, perceived kingly rule in its crucial moment of decline. However idiosyncratically brilliant, Rochester's works are an undeniable manifestation of the external visage of Restoration power. However, if by my study Rochester has been transformed from an historical object into an active subject resisting subjection, it must be concluded that he was not quite active enough in his resistance to the sovereign-subject relationship. To grasp the full politicality of Rochester's writings is to understand them as one instance from the period of how power installs itself and produces its real effects as a constitution of subjects. Constitutionally, Rochester seems limited to resisting Charles's regime of truth *in word only*. What we witness in Rochester's works is an uncanny degree of gnosis—of near-mystical knowledge and understanding of the collusion of language and power—accompanied by virtually no praxis—no practice, application, or use of that knowledge distinguished from theory. I speak of praxis at the level of measurable action in the world for the purpose of countering the forces of monocentrism in order to transform human communities into places where, as Paulo Freire calls it, humanization can occur.[2] This kind of opposition Rochester positively eschewed.

Rochester's attendance at the House of Lords, for example, was poor between 1667 and 1674.[3] While that improved after 1674, and while Wolseley credits Rochester with becoming more serious-minded late in his life by applying his wit "to publick Business" and informing himself "of the Wisdom of our Laws, and the excellent Constitution of the *English* Government,"[4] nonetheless Rochester seemed fundamentally incapable of surmounting his position of entitlement and immunity. Very true, the House of Lords functioned far more as an instrument of oppression and perpetuation of the status quo than as an institution of humanization (if that phrase is not itself an oxymoron). Rochester was unlikely to have changed the world much working within that political venue and so perhaps was wise to stay away. Still, as an agent for social change, one cannot withdraw completely from the palaces of power to contemplate moodily or giddily one's navel. The actions of Halifax and Marvell exemplify this notion. But in most respects withdraw is exactly what Rochester did.

In a letter of 1678, after complaining of downturns in his own political fortune, Savile suggests that his friend might have "your selfe talents for businesse." He urges Rochester to use them:

> yet you may find them in your owne flesh & blood, & doubtlesse there may some prudent embers lye hidden in y^r L^p if you would racke them up which in time might bee of use to your King and Country, I begg of y^r L^p to take this time of your leasure a little paines to examine yourselfe in this point.[5]

Did Rochester's best friend recognize in him an intensified grasp of polity and for that reason entreat the high-ranking nobleman to become involved in state affairs? If so, Rochester did not respond to Savile's summons. In his return letter, Rochester first wryly compares Savile to Falstaff, then lapses into facile *contemptus mundi:* "But most human affairs are carried on at the same nonsensical rate, which makes me . . . think it a fault to laugh at the monkey we have here when I compare his condition with mankind."[6] Here we perceive, perhaps, the lament and excuse of the materially comfortable intellectual who refuses to take action in the world because (in this instance) he can *afford* to regard human society as pointless. In his next letter, Savile perhaps offers mild reproof of the earl's reluctance to engage in politics, commenting that it undoubtedly is pleasant to withdraw to the country to gather "some philosophicall comfort out of Solomon or Seneca or any other who has treated de vanitate mundi."[7] Eventually, Rochester answers with an amusing description of a mock-Romance he should write "celebrating the memories of my most pocky friends, companions and mistresses." In that letter, Rochester comments with regard to himself what a miraculous thing it is "when a man half in the grave cannot leave off playing the fool and the buffoon."[8] During the summer of 1678, both Rochester and Savile were suffering from the medical downside of the libertine life-style. If Rochester consciously refuses to take responsible action in the world, he also seems aware of the fact of his own ludicrous paralysis.

One year later, in his most politically informed letter filled with news of the Scottish uprising and late developments in the Popish Plot, Rochester remarks to Savile in Paris: "Thus much to afford you a taste of my serious abilities and to let you know I have a great goggle-eye to business."[9] Evidently recalling Savile's earlier goad to activate him politically, Rochester seems ironically to concede here that he will ever be but an *observer* of business, not a player. His habitual reaction to affairs of state remained a combination of philosophical detachment, literary tomfoolery, and cynical self-reflection.[10] In *Satire Against Mankind*, the narrator admonishes that: "thoughts are given for action's government; / Where action ceases, thought's impertinent" (94–95); ironically, since he seems incapable of converting political thought into social action, Rochester himself is as desultory and buoyed up by useless bladders of philosophy—in his case *de vanitate mundi*—as the cleric satirized in that passage. If we do venture to draw parallels between Rochester and Maximus, remember that at the end of *Valentinian* Maximus does *not* kill the emperor himself; he lets the soldiers take that real action. Maximus then permits himself to be led off in a kind of stupor, mumbling about lost wives and friends, indifferent to whether the glory of empire or the punishment for rebellion is to follow. The scene makes for a very strange ending to the play. Are Rochester's satiric writings not a similarly odd hand-washing of the worldly business of politics?[11] In his writings has Rochester, or has Maximus in his existential musings, resisted his oppressor, namely Charles/Valentinian and the formidable libertine cult, or has he in fact internalized it? It seems to me that Rochester, like his tragic hero, risks only comprehending, voicing, and in a sense *reproducing* the dangerous fabrication of truth practiced by his master; he does little to end that oppressive linguistic and cognitive act. Resembling Maximus, Rochester builds no better society in his verse; he does nothing to unseat the *nature* of Charles/Valentinian's intolerable civic lies. Instead, he emulates their deception and will-to-power in his shrewd and brutal humiliation of the target fop. In a strange twist of their "resistance," does Rochester's verse in fact *con-tribute* to the maintenance of Charles's status quo? If so, rather than distancing Rochester from the social libertine he attacks, do his works paradoxically reduce the earl to the level of a half-libertine himself? Rochester deconstructs his culture se-lectively, conveniently, and only with pen and ink; he refuses to carry his iconoclasm into the realm of direct political ac-tion. On the contrary, at a surface level, Rochester lives quite the conventional life-style—albeit perhaps on the intense side—for an aristocrat of his day and station. Besides his li-bidinal and bibulous romps, he maintains estates, worries about coal shipments, is interested in the raising of carp, trains actresses, attends Oxford, duels, goes to war, enjoys a Grand Tour, keeps mistresses, argues with his wife and mother, pro-duces offspring, and frets over what the duchess of Portsmouth thinks about him. It would seem, then, that the regime of power that created Rochester is more or less content to allow him his literary challenges to its veracity. In the end, though invaluable windows into those mechanics of truth, Rochester's are ineffectual provocations; they seem to have posed no real threat to contemporary structures of power or to the rule of the dominant class.

This circumstance in turn raises concern, I believe, for the nature of satire itself. Instead of concrete action in the world against the palpable abuses of power they observe, Rochester's major satires, obscene lyrics, prose spoofs, and dramatic pieces become an intellectualized and elitist evasion of the hard issues of community. Instead of satiric heroism, Roches-ter engages in satiric cowardice in the form, finally, of political quietism. One legitimately wonders then if the genre of satire itself acts as the conscientious and socially committed literary form we like to theorize it is, or is it an elaborate mode for assuring ourselves that something is being accomplished in the world when in fact nothing of the sort is taking place? Is satire a means of action in the community or a means of witty literary gesture in that direction? Perhaps we fool ourselves badly when we write and read satire and then meditate upon its extreme social relevance. It strikes me that satire might be in many cases—in all cases?—the quintessence of gnosis removed from praxis: the sanctioned underbelly of propa-

ganda and encomium; the officially "radical" way to blow off
politically dangerous steam.

To relate these problems to our own positions as academics
and citizens at the end of the twentieth century, if criticism is
worldly and in the world so long as it *opposes* (active verb)
monocentrism, what have I accomplished by dismantling
Rochester's dismantling of Charles's libertine milieu? Like
Rochester, I can deconstruct, but I can't hide: metacritically,
someone always can come along after me to anatomize cleverly
my clever anatomization. But what does any of this do for
the people living in the run-down neighborhood nearest to my
tranquil, immaculately groundskept campus? I am forced to
ask myself an uncomfortable question. Am I a late-twentieth-
century American equivalent of the earl of Rochester? Lyons
remarks that Rochester is one of the "most accessible of the
major English poets."[12] He certainly has not always been.
What might be called the Rochester revival, culminating in
Vieth's edition of the complete poems in 1968, stems from basically the decade and a half before World War II and again from
the 1960s—arguably two eras of failed social revolution in the
United States and western Europe. His appeal among
twentieth-century academics might signal a real empathy between critic and text. No longer required to be appalled by
Rochester's obscenity or irreligious nature, scholars living
themselves in nonconformist ages were free to admire his irreverent panache. In the same way, could Rochester's new ac-
cessibility and continuing popularity be based on his being
so unexpectedly similar to liberal arts college professors and
students of this century—and especially of today? Charming,
witty, attractive, talented, chimeralike, sophisticated, irreverent, sexually charged, egalitarian, privileged, cynical, and
franchised and disenfranchised at once, Rochester offers something for everyone in current English major programs. Students find him bafflingly fun: he splashes the *f*-word across the
solemn pages of Literature and talks about hooking up in ways
even they have yet to conceptualize. As a teacher, I can entertain my young charges (a tough, MTV audience to amuse) with
his enlightened obscenities while imagining I introduce them
to something of the real world—albeit three centuries gone by.
However, are we, perhaps like he, in current political terms
mere limousine liberals? Are we only materially comfortable
radicals? Intellectual do-nothings? I imagine that many of us
worry about these questions from time to time.[13]

Hill comments that "Rochester's satires reveal a highly intelligent man seeing right through the shams of that glittering
world [of the Restoration court and aristocracy] to the hollow
compromise underneath."[14] No one can doubt that Rochester
came by his ostentatious contempt of regularity honestly. He
lived what the monocentrism of the powered class foisted upon
English society at large, and in his *writings* he rejected much
of it. Rather than call him "curiously apolitical," I think "curiously political" or even "politically curious" might be more on
the mark. No one and nothing *can* be apolitical. Our human
dependence on imperfect language and specious knowing pre-
cludes the possibility. Conceptually, Rochester fervently es-
poused the "sin" that he saw pitted against the "truth" of
people like Charles II and Gilbert Burnet. And who knows?
Had he lived longer perhaps he would have taken positive action against such false order and today we would name him
among others who resisted Stuart polity—Milton, Marvell,
Shaftesbury, and Locke. As it was, Rochester died a martyr
for that sin. To conclude my study, perhaps we can regard his
martyrdom—and hence his literary significance—in at least
two different ways.

Edward W. Said advises us not to regard criticism of a text
as being intrinsically secondary to that text. Criticism is not
inversely dated, that is, lessened in importance because of its
coming from a chronological time later than the text. Instead,
criticism represents a more recent manifestation of "the text's
social discursive presence in the world." Said contends:

> rather than being defined by the silent past, commanded by it to
> speak in the present, criticism, no less than any text, is the present
> in the course of its articulation, its struggles for definition.[15]

In the case of Rochester's texts and their politicality, a fair
treatment of those texts and their *ongoing* worldly circumstances, meaning subsequent critical contributions to their
discursive presence in the world, might suggest that, after
three hundred years of the modern era, not much has changed
politically. The external nature of the dominant culture, the
truth-makers of society, of course has altered since the reign
of Charles II. However, the internal workings of power remain
remarkably the same, particularly when it comes to the constitution of subjects. Understanding Rochester's works *and* our
criticism of them demonstrates, in a negative reading of the

earl's martyrdom, that intellectual dissidents in the West largely remain, like Rochester, political tigers on paper only. Many of us are excited by Rochester's incitement against the sovereign-subject relationship. We admire the sophistication of his deconstruction; we share the evident sincerity of his social critique. Yet since we, too, in our textual criticism of Rochester exercise critical skills divorced from coextensive critical acts, we participate as well in his fundamental pliancy, in his peculiar internalizing of the modern oppressor. Understanding and voicing disapproval of monocentrism, for us no less than for Rochester, is not enough. Theory without practice is politically inadequate, even asinine. That critics in the main mistakenly have characterized Rochester's writings *as* apolitical offers sad comment on our *own* lack of political savvy living under current avatars of truth and power. If we cannot recognize Rochester's unique and disturbing political compromise within a regime of truth, how can we hope to recognize—let alone act against—our own? More than embodying subjugated knowledge that provides an intriguing perspective on Stuart policy, Rochester's texts potentially teach us much about our own circumstance as subjects constituted and kept tractable by power. This lesson alone provides us with ample reason to pay close attention to his works.

But perhaps I am being too hard on the earl as well as too hard on ourselves as academics and as citizens. A second and more positive way of viewing Rochester's martyrdom for sin might be as follows. While apprehending the singular nature of Rochester's written political dissent *and* acknowledging the frankly limited nature of his political action in the world, we should understand as well that modern power typically allows its subjects very little real room for praxis. Massive armed confrontation or massive reeducation programs might broadly and swiftly reconstitute the state, but for the individual living within the regime of truth political options seem few. Such limitation is perhaps the true evil genius of the modern state. Its ideology and mechanics of power are so thoroughly naturalized and normalized as to be almost irresistible—and virtually unfightable. For the lone citizen, altering significantly a configuration of truth and power can seem to be a nearly impossible task—rather like changing the oil on a moving car. One supposes it can be done, but it would take an awful lot of work of a nature one suspects to be largely well beyond the individual's normal range of expertise. Hence the persistence of the status quo. Therefore, instead of damning Rochester as a limousine liberal, we should read and appreciate his writings as valiant works of linguistic demystification of the power structures around him—that is, as satires, lyrics, prose, and drama written in the face of nearly overwhelming intellectual and material opposition to their expression. After all, is not Rochester's dilemma also often our dilemma as teachers, critics, and members of the modern community? Moreover, we should acknowledge as well that such oppositional voices do indeed carry weight and make a difference in the real world. The state may not revolve overnight, but revolutionary ideas plant revolutionary seeds. To totalize Michel Foucault's conception of truth and power into an omnipresent, all-powerful state reduces his theories into simplistic notions of Big Brother. Because the modern state is more complex than that—perhaps infinitely complex—and because, as Rochester himself points out in "Upon Nothing," the modern state is by no means expertly run, the possibility for change probably exists. Just as the threat of increased dehumanization always looms over us, so too the possibility for increased humanization seems likely. Subversive writings such as Rochester's perhaps play a part in what might be the equally intricate mechanics of revolution. While obviously no Marxist, Rochester deserves to be read and studied both as expert testimony speaking to the need for greater insight into social reality as well as for more individual liberty during the early modern period. These two things alone surely make him pertinent reading for us. He also should be celebrated as someone with the courage at least to speak out—no matter how limited his concomitant political actions.

These are but two ways to regard Rochester's being a martyr for sin. No doubt other critics in future will voice other readings about what his writings accomplish. And in that worldly circumstance exists what I take to be Rochester's real strength and importance as a writer: that after more than three hundred years his works still have us arguing, thinking, and puzzling over our essential and existential place in the world. Rochester's works don't answer questions; they raise them. In our attempts to find responses, we have the opportunity to glimpse the complex nature of human being.

Notes

Chapter 1. Current Theory

1. The question of Rochester's canon is by no means settled. D. M. Vieth admirably lays the groundwork for attributing poems to Rochester in both his 1963 study *Attribution in Restoration Poetry: A Study of Rochester's Poems of 1680* (New Haven and London: Yale University Press) and in his 1968 edition of Rochester's "complete" poems (Vieth, *The Complete Poems of John Wilmot, Earl of Rochester* [New Haven and London: Yale University Press]). In his 1984 old-spelling edition of Rochester's poems, Keith Walker largely follows Vieth's editorial lead, performing invaluable work in collating manuscript variants as he does (Walker, *The Poems of John Wilmot Earl of Rochester* [Oxford: Oxford University Press, 1984]). However, in editing the poems and plays of Rochester, Paddy Lyons now has proposed some twenty new poems be added to those we might reasonably view as Rochester's, offering over one hundred pieces. While acknowledging the importance of Vieth's attributions, Lyons feels as well that many of Vieth's decisions to exclude poems were based on personal assumptions about Rochester's style rather than on all of the evidence available for inclusion (see Lyons, *Rochester: Complete Poems and Plays* [London and Rutland, Vt.: J. M. Dent and Charles E. Tuttle, 1993], xx). Realizing that all of these editions are sound, I have chosen to use Lyons's collection when quoting Rochester's works. Parenthetically in my study, his poems are cited by line number, his prose by page number, and his plays by act, scene, and line numbers.

2. Edward W. Said, *The World, the Text, and the Critic* (Cambridge: Harvard University Press, 1983), 35.

3. See, for example, Jeremy Treglown who asserts that Rochester "despised politics except as a source of gossip, and took little part in them although he had become a member of the House of Lords unconventionally early" (Treglown, *The Letters of John Wilmot, Earl of Rochester* [Oxford: Basil Blackwell, 1980], 30). Similarly, Basil Greenslade, while acknowledging Rochester's close experience of the court and the government, believes his satire "is not in any important sense a product of political understanding or engagement" (Greenslade, "Affairs of State," in *Spirit of Wit: Reconsiderations of Rochester*, ed. J. Treglown [Oxford: Basil Blackwell, 1982], 106). Paul Hammond goes even farther, maintaining that Rochester lacked any serious view of politics and, indeed, may have been so deficient in his regard for human institutions that we cannot take him for an artist at all (Hammond, "Was Rochester an Artist?" *Cambridge Quarterly* 12 (1983): 56–66). More recently, Dustin Griffin, a remarkably perceptive reader of Rochester, has termed the court wits "curiously apolitical" (Griffin, "Rochester and the 'Holiday

Writers,'" in *Rochester and Court Poetry*, eds. D. M. Vieth and D. Griffin [Los Angeles: William Andrews Clark Memorial Library, 1988], 38).

4. For details regarding Rochester's status at court, see J. H. Wilson (*The Court Wits of the Restoration: An Introduction* [Princeton: Princeton University Press, 1948], 47–53) and Vieth (*Complete Poems*, xvii–xxiv). Both note the fact that as a member of the nobility Rochester was raised in the tradition that the duty of an English gentleman was to govern the masses. Vieth comments: "In an age when the English aristocracy was still politically, socially, and culturally supreme, Rochester was socially and culturally potent" (xvii). While Christopher Hill characterizes Rochester as an "alienated aristocrat," that is, as a courtier with no real political function but rather as something of a court jester for Charles, he nonetheless also associates Rochester with Buckingham and the Whig leaders during the later 1670s (Hill, *The Collected Essays of Christopher Hill: Writing and Revolution in 17th Century England*, vol. 1 [Amherst: University of Massachusetts Press, 1985], 301, 307). In a sense, by virtue of his very person, Rochester could not avoid being political to some degree. See, for example, a series of letters from Buckingham asking Rochester to intercede with Charles on his behalf—"to loose noe time in making use of the Kings good nature and kindnes to mee"—and how, as a consequence of Rochester's intervention, certain "noble friends at cowrt" resolved "to ly most abominably of your Lordship and mee" (Treglown, *Letters*, 145–54).

5. Hill, *Collected Essays*, 298. Equally, however, a clever argument could be made for Rochester's being something of an aristocratic Trimmer in the mold of George Savile, the marquess of Halifax. During the late 1670s, simultaneous with supporting Whig initiatives in Parliament and helping to spring Buckingham from the Tower, Rochester regularly accompanied Charles to Newmarket to bet on the horses (see Vieth, *Complete Poems*, xxxi–xxxii). Rochester and Halifax's younger brother, Henry Savile—a courtier and diplomat himself—of course were great friends and correspondents. Rochester might be seen as well sharing key political views with Halifax. For example, at the close of "Verses for which he was Banished" (discussed in chapter 5), Rochester damns all monarchs. Louis XIV is "the hector of France," a despot; Charles is "the cully of Britain," a mere dupe to sensual pleasure (33). The contrast between these two examples of monarchical style may be telling. Louis serves as an example of too much authority in a monarch, while Charles stands for too lax and merciful a king. In "The Character of a Trimmer," Halifax names the extremes "of unbounded power and the extravagance of liberty not enough restrained" as both needing to be avoided (*Halifax: Complete Works*, ed. J. P. Kenyon [Harmondsworth, England: Penguin, 1969], 102). Perhaps Rochester's poem similarly calls for something in between. Halifax also warns against a king shrinking "into the head of a party" (99). Possibly Rochester saw this happening to Charles as the events of the Popish Plot unfolded and as the issues of the Exclusion Crisis began to form. Halifax asserts as well the Trimmer's passion for liberty (62), and that while the Trimmer favors the king naturally, neither can he betray liberty in the face of "the imperious dictates of unlimited authority" (99). Again, perhaps we may speculate that something like this attitude toward kingship motivated Rochester's attitude toward Charles. Even though Rochester did lean toward the Whig faction prior to his death, he seems more anti-Charles than antimonarchy. Thus, while he certainly did not share the

political agenda of Marvell, Rochester may have held to something like an aristocratic and privileged version of that agenda.

6. For an excellent overview of the history of Rochester studies, see Marianne Thormählen's introduction to *Rochester: The Poems in Context* (Cambridge: Cambridge University Press, 1993). This book is the most recent full-length study of Rochester's poetry. Thormählen's approach is to situate the poems in their historical context. She asserts: "Rochester's poetry repays efforts to contemplate it in the light of Restoration events, developments and personalities in the fields of national and international politics, religion, philosophy and social life." Thormählen contends that, far from being apolitical, in many of Rochester's satires, "history is transmuted into poetry" (2). I could hardly agree more with her, and I would like to acknowledge here the importance of Thormählen's study to my own reading of Rochester's works. Another recent work dealing extensively with Rochester is Warren Chernaik's *Sexual Freedom in Restoration Literature* (Cambridge: Cambridge University Press, 1995.) While Chernaik with regard to Rochester's verse nicely examines "the implicit political dimension in the sexual ideology of libertinism" (19), his focus is on "the problems which arise when ideas originally developed in a political context by such authors as Hobbes and Locke are applied to the domestic sphere, and in particular to the conduct of sexual relationships inside and outside the constraints of marriage" (18). Thus, his reading of Rochester's verse is markedly biographical and psychoanalytical in nature, and his primarily concern is with sexual politics. By contrast, in my study I hope to carry out something of the reverse: I hope to extend Rochester's own sexual politics into the realm of Foucauldian realpolitik. My primary concern, then, is not with sexual politics but with political sexuality (see chapter 5).

7. Michel Foucault, *Power/Knowledge: Selected Interviews and Other Writings 1972–1977*, ed. C. Gordon (New York: Pantheon, 1977), 116, 118.

8. Foucault tells us:

> Truth is a thing of this world: it is produced only by virtue of multiple forms of constraint. And it induces regular effects of power. Each society has its régime of truth, its "general politics" of truth: that is, the types of discourse which it accepts and makes function as true; the mechanisms and instances which enable one to distinguish true and false statements, the means by which each is sanctioned; the techniques and procedures accorded value in the acquisition of truth; the status of those who are charged with saying what counts as true. (Foucault, *Power*, 131)

In his work *Mythologies* (trans. A. Lavers [New York: Hill and Wang, 1972]), Roland Barthes proposes prior to Foucault perhaps an effective semiotic means by which to read through such formulations of truth and power—what Barthes terms *myth* (see particularly 109ff.).

9. Foucault, *Power*, 93.

10. Ibid., 98, 119.

11. Says Foucault: "Humanity does not gradually progress from combat to combat until it arrives at universal reciprocity, where the rule of law finally replaces warfare; humanity installs each of its violences in a system of rules and thus proceeds from domination to domination" (Foucault, *Language, Counter-Memory, Practice: Selected Essays and Interviews*, ed. D. F. Bouchard [Ithaca: Cornell University Press, 1977], 151; see also Foucault, *Power*, 90–91, 123).

12. "On Truth and Falsity in Their Ultramoral Sense," in Friedrich Nietzsche, *The Complete Works of Friedrich Nietzsche*, ed. O. Levy, vol. 2 (New York: Russell, 1964), 175.

13. Similarities between certain ideas expressed by Nietzsche and by those found in Rochester's satires are often striking. With regard to the human intellect, Nietzsche asserts that "haughtiness connected with cognition and sensation, spreading blinding fogs before the eyes and over the senses of men, deceives itself therefore as to the value of existence owing to the fact that it bears within itself the most flattering evaluation of cognition" (Nietzsche, "Truth and Falsity," 174). He also insists that humans "are deeply immersed in illusions and dream fancies; their eyes glance only over the surface of things and see 'forms'; their sensation nowhere leads to truth, but contents itself with receiving stimuli and, so to say, with playing hide-and-seek on the back of things" (175). For Nietzsche as for Rochester (see the analysis of his major satires in chapters 3 and 4), intellect itself is dissimulation: we are arch-deceivers who deceive even ourselves—and those who dissimulate best are deemed most intelligent. Human existence therefore is a tournament of nescience and narcissism.

14. Christopher Norris, *Deconstruction: Theory and Practice* (London and New York: Methuen, 1982), 89; see chapter 5.

15. In *An Essay Concerning Human Understanding* (1690), John Locke worries about bogus axioms of the general and the universal as well. In book 3, chapter 3, "Of General Terms," he writes: "To return to general words, it is plain by what has been said, that general and universal belong not to the real existence of things, but are the inventions and creatures of the understanding, made by it for its own use, and concern only signs, whether words or ideas. Words are general, as has been said, when used for signs of general ideas, and so are applicable indifferently to many particular things: and ideas are general, when they are set up as the representatives of many particular things; but universality belongs not to things themselves, which are all of them particular in their existence; even those words and ideas which in their signification are general" (Locke, *The Works of John Locke*, vol. 2 [Darmstadt, Germany: Scientia Verlag Aalen, 1963], 172). Reality is thus chaotic and individual; order and universality are products of human thought and, essentially, convenience when faced with the overwhelming task of naming the world. Nietzsche extends this observation to its full potential, characterizing post-Socratic Western humanity as guilty both of deluding itself and of anthropomorphizing nature in seeking after idealism and system where none in fact exist. Both art and science are examples of such false order to Nietzsche.

16. Dustin Griffin, for example, characterizes Rochester as a libertine and skeptic who rejected orthodoxy but who nonetheless ultimately was disappointed with a life of the passions; therefore, he unsuccessfully sought for rest, quiet, and certainty (Griffin, *Satires Against Man: The Poems of Rochester* [Berkeley and Los Angeles: University of California Press, 1973], 17, 20). David Farley-Hills asserts that Rochester "attempts to create an order with the aid of laughter that he can impose on the disorderliness of experience," and that it was "this search for orderliness that produced the great satires" (Farley-Hills, *The Benevolence of Laughter: Comic Poetry of the Commonwealth and Restoration* [London: Macmillan, 1974], 133). While the former statement accurately reflects a general spirit of Rochester's writings, perhaps it

confuses an intellectual and textual stance with that of a more emotional and personal nature. With regard to the latter statement, where Farley-Hills sees a search for order via benevolent laughter on Rochester's part, I see quite the opposite emerging in Rochester's writings: an imposition of disorder on the reader, often via the instrument of malevolent laughter. Rochester's most recent editor remarks: "Rochester is a poet of unbelief, of intelligent and vigorous doubt, of tensions that resist easy resolutions, and his poems have a tendency to put their own apparent assumptions into question" (Lyons, *Complete Poems and Plays*, xii). Similarly, Thormählen observes: "Rochester's verse shows us a mind which constantly demands that the body supply evidence of true worth. Despite its yearning for fixity, for the moment when the senses provide complete and immutable satisfaction, that mind has the strength to refuse to be taken in by tainted ware. . . . I think that Rochester's mind was the most interesting thing about him, and that the way in which that mind tackled great existential issues in a particularly turbulent historical period was the most interesting thing about it" (Thormählen, *Poems in Context*, 5). Certainly other critics have recognized such qualities in Rochester as well, for example, Barbara Everett in her fine essay "The Sense of Nothing" (in *Spirit of Wit: Reconsiderations of Rochester*, ed. J. Treglown [Oxford: Basil Blackwell, 1982], 1–41).

17. Paul De Man, "Semiology and Rhetoric," in *Allegories or Reading: Figural Language in Rousseau, Nietzsche, Rilke, and Proust* (New York and London: Yale University Press, 1979), 10, 17.

18. Barthes, "The Death of the Author," in *Image-Music-Text*, trans. S. Heath (New York: Hill and Wang, 1977), 145–46.

19. Asserts Barthes: "writing ceaselessly posits meaning ceaselessly to evaporate it, carrying out a systematic exemption of meaning. In precisely this way literature, . . . by refusing to assign a 'secret', an ultimate meaning, to the text (and to the world-as-text), liberates what may be called an antitheological activity, an activity that is truly revolutionary since to refuse to fix meaning is, in the end, to refuse God and his hypostases—reason, science, law" (Ibid., 147).

20. Again, I am not the first to notice such characteristics in Rochester's writing. For example, Anne Righter (later Barton), reading *Doctor Bendo's Bill*, points out that soon the "language breaks down. . . . Truth and falsehood, reason itself, begin to run round in circles" (Righter, "John Wilmot, Earl of Rochester," in *John Wilmot, Earl of Rochester: Critical Essays*, ed. D. M. Vieth [New York and London: Garland, 1988], 3). Similarly, John Sitter has argued that Rochester works to deprive readers of specific interpretive certainties, conducting a kind of linguistic guerrilla warfare (Sitter, "Rochester's Reader and the Problem of Satiric Audience," *Papers on Language and Literature* 12 (1976): 285–98). Generally, Griffin holds the same view of Rochester's poetry (*Satires*), and Vieth makes a similar point about two of Rochester's longer satires ("Towards an Anti-Aristotelian Poetic: Rochester's *Satyr Against Mankind* and *Artemisia to Chloe*, With Notes on Swift's *Tale of a Tub* and *Gulliver's Travels*," *Language and Style* 5 [1972]: 123–45).

21. Said, *World*, 45–49.

22. See also Barthes, "Death of the Author," 145–48.

23. This is not to suggest that Rochester's texts cannot speak to us today. They can, but necessarily in a different way than they spoke to Rochester's contemporaries. That conversation is considered in chapter 6.

24. As De Man explains: "The interpretation of the sign is not, for Peirce, a meaning but another sign; it is a reading, not a decodage, and this reading has, in its turn, to be interpreted into another sign, and so on *ad infinitum*" (De Man, "Semiology and Rhetoric," 9).

25. Chernaik, *Sexual Freedom*, 52.

26. Said, *World*, 35.

27. Terry Eagleton, *Literary Theory: An Introduction* (Oxford: Basil Blackwell, 1983), 145; see 144–50.

28. Elsewhere I have discussed the delicate and puzzling problem of attempting to segregate the synchronic from the diachronic in satire with regard to a work's social location as compared to its traditional literary influences (Kirk Combe, "The New Voice of Political Dissent: The Transition from Complaint to Satire," in *Theorizing Satire: Essays in Literary Criticism*, eds. B. A. Connery and K. Combe [New York: St. Martin's, 1995], 73–94). When trying to generalize satire into a clearly recognizable structure and genre, critics often ignore the historical moment of individual works. However, any strictly local reading of a satire equally overlooks a very tangible and powerful satiric heritage within which most satirists consciously write—especially before 1800. In that essay as well as here in my study of Rochester I adopt an acute awareness of the ambiguity that exists between the synchronic and the diachronic, the particular and the general, the parole and the langue of satiric expression. If a line indeed separates these things, it is a blurry one which, upon reflection, disrupts any simplistic reading of a text.

29. At the end of the twentieth century, in a (if we must) post-postmodern world, acting *within* undecidability has become our task and our challenge as scholars and, to become philosophical for a moment, as people. We can no longer be naive users of language, but neither can we give up on language—as if such a thing even were possible. Language *makes* our world and the kinds of oppression or justice that exist in it. Hence it is best to take care with how we understand *and* use our language. As linguistic creatures, humans are doomed to perpetual discussion—to the constant creation and revision of necessarily imperfect readings of the world in an unending and perhaps impossible—but *not* useless—struggle to comprehend the world. Applying signified to signifier represents, I believe, the big adventure not only of critical practice but of all human endeavor. Therefore fixing—or, really, venturing—a reading is not heinous; it is inevitable. What often can become heinous, however, is the attempt to concretize readings into truths. Striving to *end* conversation is the real crime, not close reading.

30. I use the term *political* in my study in a (perhaps now predictably) dualistic way. At certain points it clearly refers to the immediate, synchronic civil affairs of Restoration England during Rochester's lifetime. At other points it signals the broader, more diachronic conception of political as "describing the whole of human relations in their real, social structure, in their power of making the world" (Barthes, *Mythologies*, 143) or in "the way we organize our social life together, and the power-relations which this involves" (Eagleton, *Literary Theory*, 194). However, accompanying either specific use of the word (political immediate or broad) is, in a shadowy manner, its companion meaning (political broad or immediate) as well.

31. Foucault, *Power*, 82.

32. Ibid., 83. Foucault defines the term *genealogy* as "the union of erudite

knowledge and local memories which allows us to establish a historical knowledge of struggles and to make use of this knowledge tactically today" (ibid.). He regards genealogy as an attempt to emancipate historical knowledges from the coercion of unitary, scientific discourses. Says Foucault: "If we were to characterise [this project] in two terms, then 'archaeology' would be the appropriate methodology of this analysis of local discursivities, and 'genealogy' would be the tactics whereby, on the basis of the descriptions of these local discursivities, the subjected knowledges which were thus released would be brought into play" (85).

33. Ibid., 81. For Foucault's ideas on effective history, see Foucault, *Language*, 153–57. On the difference between effective history and traditional history Foucault states: "We want historians to confirm our belief that the present rests upon profound intentions and immutable necessities. But the true historical sense confirms our existence among countless lost events, without a landmark or a point of reference" (*Language*, 155). Many of Foucault's views are based upon Nietzsche's conception of history where there is only "the iron hand of necessity shaking the dice-box of chance" (quoted in ibid.).

34. Foucault, *Power*, 82.

35. Ibid., 97.

36. Foucault asserts: "It is in response to the demands of royal power, for its profit and to serve as its instrument or justification, that the juridical edifice of our own society has been developed. Right in the West is the King's right" (ibid., 94).

37. Ibid., 95; see 94–96.

38. Ibid., 104; see 103–8; 124–25.

39. See in particular Brian A. Connery and Kirk Combe, "Theorizing Satire: A Retrospective and Introduction," in *Theorizing Satire: Essays in Literary Criticism* (New York: St. Martin's, 1995), 1–15.

Chapter 2. Contemporary Idiom

1. Dustin Griffin, "Rochester and the 'Holiday Writers,'" in *Rochester and Court Poetry*, eds. D. M. Vieth and D. Griffin (Los Angeles: William Andrews Clark Memorial Library, 1988), 37.

2. The idea of *libertinism* in the seventeenth and eighteenth centuries is a broad and problematic one. In his essay considering the difficulties of defining the term, James G. Turner finds that while the concept of libertinism is central to any discussion of "some combination of irreligion and sexual rampancy" during the period, equally its specific precepts are nebulous. Contemporary usage varies as much as current scholarly assessments (Turner, "The Properties of Libertinism," *Eighteenth Century Life* 9, no. 3 [May 1985]: 75; see 75–80). Turner locates not "a single entity with different facets, but . . . three distinct movements of thought or clusters of attitudes" to which the word refers; these are "religious ('spiritual') libertinism, philosophical libertinism (the combination of antireligious skepticism and scientific materialism. . . .), and sexual libertinism" (79). In my analysis of Rochester's writings, all three kinds of libertinism come into play. The English libertine cult that held Charles II as its focal point generally partook of the ongoing libertine movement on the continent, particularly in France.

Not only had this European movement given rise to eroticism in general and to prose pornography specifically, but more importantly the freethinking associated with it carried religious, political, social, scientific, and literary ramifications as well. Rochester's writings are concerned with these social and intellectual aspects of libertinism as much and probably much more than the movement's obscene and libidinal fixations. Writing about the comedy of Etherege, Dale Underwood characterizes the English libertine as a skeptic and an Epicurean, an advocate of freedom and pleasure, as one who rebels against marriage and the conventions of courtly love, and who tends to scorn the institutions of family, church, and state (Underwood, *Etherege and the Seventeenth-Century Comedy of Manners* [New Haven: Yale University Press, 1957], 10–40). Underlying that scorn of conventional institutions, however, Turner sees not anarchy but aristocratic privilege as a motivating force. He likens libertine rebelliousness to "a kind of dramatic testing procedure, like a child's testing of the boundaries of parental tolerance" (Turner, "Properties," 81). For whatever reason, asserts Turner, libertines tend to feel *above* the law, not *against* the law as it applies to everyone else (see 80–81). Thus questions of radicalness or conservatism are basic to my discussion of the participants in Charles's Anglo-libertine circle. For other accounts of libertinism in England, see as well Marianne Thormählen, *Rochester: The Poems in Context* (Cambridge: Cambridge University Press, 1993), 198–201; David Foxon, *Libertine Literature in England, 1660–1745* (New Hyde, N.Y.: University Books, 1966), 48–51; Angeline Goreau, "'Last Night's Rambles': Restoration Literature and the War Between the Sexes," in *The Sexual Dimension in Literature*, ed. A. Bold (London and Totowa, N.J.: Vision and Barnes & Noble, 1982), 49–56; and Warren Chernaik, *Sexual Freedom in Restoration Literature* (Cambridge: Cambridge University Press, 1995), 1–51, 80–84. For the French libertine movement of this period, see, among many other works, studies by Antoine Adam, *Histoire de la littérature française au dix-septième siècle*, 5 vols. (Paris: Del Duca, 1962); Adam, *Les Libertins au dix-septième siècle* (Paris: Buchet/Chastel, 1964); Adam, *Théophile de Viau et la libre pensée française en 1620* (Paris: Droz, 1935); Joan DeJean, *Libertine Strategies: Freedom and the Novel in Seventeenth-Century France* (Columbus: Ohio State University Press, 1981); Lise Leibacher-Ouvrard, "Metaphore, Ideologie et Utopies Libertines au Temps de Louis XIV," *Papers on French Seventeenth Century Literature* 16, no. 31 (1989): 431–44; Leibacher-Ouvrard, "Sexe, Simulacre et 'Libertinage Honnete': La Satyre Sotadique (1658/1678) de Nicolas Chorier," *Romanic Review* 83, no. 3 (May 1992): 267–80; René Pintard, *Le libertinage érudit dans la première moitié du XVIIᵉ siècle* (Genève-Paris: Slatkine, 1983); and J. S. Spink, *French Free Thought from Gassendi to Voltaire* (London: Athlone, 1960).

3. See also Reba Wilcoxon, "Rochester's Sexual Politics," in *John Wilmot, Earl of Rochester: Critical Essays*, ed. D. M. Vieth (New York and London: Garland, 1988), 116; and Chernaik, *Sexual Freedom*, 4–5, 18. In the following analysis of Rochester's writing, there might be a temptation to regard the earl as something of a protofeminist. Wilcoxon does as much (particularly in "Sexual Politics"), and both Sarah Wintle ("Libertinism and Sexual Politics," in *Spirit of Wit: Reconsiderations of Rochester*, ed. J. Treglown [Oxford: Basil Blackwell, 1982], 133–65) and Felicity Nussbaum (*The Brink of All We Hate: English Satires on Women, 1660–1750* [Lexington: University Press of Kentucky, 1984]) explore that possibility as well. However, the urge to label

Rochester *himself* as nonsexist should be avoided. I believe Rochester is sexist; he comes from sexist circumstances. His motive in setting lewd poetical ambuscades for his brothers was not to elevate women, but rather to deride men. By definition, the obscene offends not only modesty and decency, but, in the older usage of the word, our sense of taste and refinement as well. In writing smutty lyrics, Rochester automatically subverts both standards. Not only is Rochester openly sexist, he is candidly obscene. However, unlike his sexism, he sometimes employs his obscenity for a purpose other than that normally proposed. Rochester not only upends the decency of the dominant Christian tradition, but he sabotages the bawdiness of the empowered libertine subculture. What greater act for a satirist than to please no one? Thus his obscenity is more than naughty words evoking lurid images: it serves as a powerful rhetorical device used for cultural criticism. With regard to his sexual politics, however, he offers no radical alteration of the status quo. Thormählen remarks of Rochester's works: "It is interesting to note the high frequency of 'power language' in the love poems. . . . There is much talk of vanquishing, submission and tyranny. Is there any evidence that Rochester 'rejects enslavement of either of the sexes', as Reba Wilcoxon claims ["Sexual Politics," 137], and that—consciously or not—he regarded sexual equality as an ideal?" (Thormählen, *Poems in Context*, 123; see also 123–26).

4. Timothy Raylor, *Cavaliers, Clubs, and Literary Culture: Sir John Mennes, James Smith, and the Order of the Fancy* (Newark: University of Delaware Press; London and Toronto: Associated University Presses, 1994), 152; see chapters 6–9.

5. Angeline Goreau characterizes this new royalist libertinism after 1660 as "an atmosphere in which promiscuity, systematic frivolity, and extravagance were adhered to as a social norm almost as dogmatically as the more severe of the Puritan party had adhered to godliness" (Goreau "'Last Night's Rambles,'" 49). A letter from Henry Bulkeley to Rochester in 1676 captures the spirit of the society of modish gentleman I propose. Bulkeley complains that

> ye Fop is the only fine Gentlman of the Times, & a committee of those able Statesmen assemble dayly to talke of nothing but fighting & fucking at Locketts, & will never be reconciled to men who speake sense & Reason at ye Beare or Coven garden. It is thay are the hopeful spriggs of ye Nation whose knowledge lyes in their light Periwiggs & trimed shoes, who herd wth one another not because thay love y^{em}selves, but understand noe body else, whose Honour, Honesty & Freindship is like the consent of Hounds, who knowe not why thay runn together, but y^t thay hunt ye same sent, fellowes that woud make ye World believe they are not afraid of dying, & yet are out of heart if the Wind disorders their Hair or ruffles their Cravatts. . . . These are Men I'me sure soe inconsiderable that thay are fitter to provoke ones spleen y^{en} his rage, but that I doen't know how this damn'd Allay is preferred before ye true Ore, & ye Genius y^t Governs now seems to stand at arms length wth men of sense & Vnderstanding, but embraces ye dull Image & ye formal Coxcomb. (*The Letters of John Wilmot, Earl of Rochester*, ed. J. Treglown [Oxford: Basil Blackwell, 1980], 125–26)

Rochester's verse cuts through rivalries between mobs of gentlemen, however. While sometimes applicable to factious infighting among the fashionable power elite, Rochester's writings potentially target Bulkeley as fop as much as those Bulkeley here condemns as formal Coxcombs. Potentially,

Rochester's works skewer *everyone* within this privileged social stratum—to include their author.

6. Rochester enjoyed making monkeys out of those less well-positioned and poetically endowed than himself. His well-known portrait (after Jacob Huysmans) posed with a literary simian and any number of the satires and lampoons suggest as much. Chernaik comments on how many of Rochester's obscene poems "set out to embarrass or trap the reader by bringing out into the open what normally is kept discreetly concealed" (Chernaik, *Sexual Freedom*, 8). I suggest that the nature of Rochester's unanticipated poetic exposé often goes well beyond merely sexual matters and into issues intellectual and political.

7. "On Truth and Falsity in Their Ultramoral Sense," in Friedrich Nietzsche, *The Complete Works of Friedrich Nietzsche*, ed. O. Levy, vol. 2 (New York: Russell, 1964), 180.

8. Thormählen, *Poems in Context*, 305.

9. John Aubrey, *Aubrey's Brief Lives*, ed. O. L. Dick (London: Secker and Warburg, 1950), 321.

10. David Farley-Hills, ed., *Rochester: The Critical Heritage* (New York: Barnes & Noble, 1972), 37; hereafter cited parenthetically in the text as *Heritage*.

11. Joseph Spence, *Observations, Anecdotes, and Characters of Books and Men Collected From Conversation*, ed. J. M. Osborn, vol. 1 (Oxford: Clarendon Press, 1966), 201–2.

12. Turner, "Properties," 76.

13. Ibid., 81.

14. See Raylor, *Cavaliers*, chapters 12–13.

15. See ibid., 116–17, 136–37.

16. Jacques Derrida, "Structure, Sign and Play in the Discourse of the Human Sciences," in *Writing and Difference*, trans. A. Bass (Chicago: University of Chicago Press, 1978), 292.

17. Ibid., 279.

18. For example, in 1676 Rochester writes to Savile: "They who would be great in our little government seem as ridiculous to me as school-boys who with much endeavour and some danger climb a crab-tree, venturing their necks for fruit which solid pigs would disdain if they were not starving" (Treglown, *Letters*, 119). In 1679, during the Popish Plot, Rochester observes: "The general heads under which this whole island may be considered are spies, beggars and rebels. The transpositions and mixtures of these make an agreeable variety: busy fools and cautious knaves are bred out of them and set off wonderfully, though of this latter sort we have fewer now than ever, hypocrisy being the only vice in decay amongst us. Few men here dissemble their being rascals and no woman disowns being a whore" (232).

19. Ibid., 67, 93, 166, 230.

20. As with Marvell, criticism of bad ministers and courtiers surrounding the king flimsily masks criticism of Charles himself. Perhaps the politically minded Marvell praises Rochester for this same opposition to oppression noted by Wolseley when the MP speaks of the earl as "the only man in England that had the true veine of Satyre" (Aubrey, *Brief Lives*, 196). In 1711, Defoe speaks of Marvell and Rochester in the same breath as those "whose Wit made the Court odious to the People, beyond what had been possible if the Press had been open" (Farley-Hills, *Heritage*, 186). For commentary on

Defoe's admiration of what he perceived as Rochester's radical politics, see Christopher Hill, *The Collected Essays of Christopher Hill: Writing and Revolution in 17th Century England*, vol. 1 (Amherst: University of Massachusetts Press, 1985), 308, 311, as well as John Mc Veagh, "Rochester and Defoe: A Study in Influence," *Studies in English Literature, 1500–1900* 14 (summer 1974): 327–41.

21. John Oldham, *The Poems of John Oldham*, eds. H. F. Brooks and R. Selden (Oxford: Clarendon Press, 1986); see also *Heritage* 8.

22. Aphra Behn, *The Works of Aphra Behn*, ed. M. Summers, vol. 6 (New York: Benjamin Blom, 1967), 369.

23. Treglown, *Letters*, 88.

24. Dryden in fact soon would receive the lambasting he seems to fear from Rochester in the form of *An Allusion to Horace*. See my article "'But loads of Sh— almost choked the way': Shadwell, Dryden, Rochester, and the Summer of 1676," *Texas Studies in Literature and Language* 37, no. 2 (summer 1995): 127–64.

25. George deF. Lord, ed., *Poems on Affairs of State: Augustan Satirical Verse, 1660–1714*, vol. 1 (New Haven and London: Yale University Press, 1963–1975), 412.

26. J. E. Spingarn, ed., *Critical Essays of the Seventeenth Century*, vol. 2 (Oxford: Clarendon Press, 1908–9), 288.

27. R. W. F. Kroll, *The Material Word: Literate Culture in the Restoration and Early Eighteenth Century* (Baltimore and London: Johns Hopkins, 1991), 7–8; for the remainder of the present chapter, page citations of Kroll's study will appear parenthetically in the text.

28. Turner notes that minimalist views of libertinism often exclude Epicureanism from a definition of the libertine milieu. He also points out, however, that "for many contemporary witnesses, sympathizers and critics alike, these [Epicurean traits] were qualities definitive of the libertine" (Turner, "Properties," 77). In his call for a maximalist conception of libertinism, Turner believes that religious and moral systems must be included in our considerations of the libertine phenomenon (80).

29. Ibid., 83, 84.

CHAPTER 3. NARRATIVE ANGST

1. For D. M. Vieth, these are *Timon* (April, May, or early June 1674), *Tunbridge Wells* (spring 1674), *A Satyr against Reason and Mankind* (before 23 March 1675–76), *A Letter from Artemisia in the Town to Chloe in the Country* (? 1675), and *An Allusion to Horace, the Tenth Satyr of the First Book* (winter of 1675–76). See Vieth, *The Complete Poems of John Wilmot, Earl of Rochester* (New Haven and London: Yale University Press, 1968).

2. See also Kirk Combe, "The New Voice of Political Dissent: The Transition from Complaint to Satire," in *Theorizing Satire: Essays in Literary Criticism*, eds. B. A. Connery and K. Combe (New York: St. Martin's, 1995), 73–94.

3. In "Discourse Concerning Satire," John Dryden calls Juvenal the severe and relentless pursuer of "Tragical Vices, to which Men are hurri'd by their unruly Passions and exorbitant Desires," while by comparison "Folly was the proper Quarry of *Horace*, and not Vice." Horace pursues "Blindsides and Follies" instead of indignantly attacking vice as does Juvenal; he

"laughs to shame, all Follies, and insinuates Virtue, rather by familiar Examples, than by the severity of Precepts" (Dryden, *The Works of John Dryden*, eds. E. N. Hooker and H. T. Swedenberg Jr., vol. 4 [Berkeley: University of California Press, 1956–], 62–63). Similarly, John Dennis finds Horace to be essentially a comic poet and Juvenal a tragic one (Dennis, *Critical Works*, ed. N. Hooker, vol. 2 [Baltimore: Johns Hopkins, 1943], 218–19). Following critical suit, Thomas Brown sees English satire as having derived its "Force" from Horace's "Gentleman-like Learning" and its "Virtues" from Juvenal's "Vigorous Morals" (Brown, *The Works of Mr. Thomas Brown, in Prose and Verse; Serious, Moral, and Comical*, vol. 1 [London, 1707], 33). Recent scholarship quibbles with many errors of detail in this early criticism (e.g., Niall Rudd, "Dryden on Horace and Juvenal," *University of Toronto Quarterly* 32 [1963]: 155–69); nonetheless, twentieth-century scholars of both Latin and English satire concur with the seventeenth-century omnibus judgments of Horace as light (both delicate in tone and sanguine in attitude) and Juvenal as dark (overpowering and grim). Thus Horace epitomizes satire written in a low, conversational style, Juvenal that written in a high, declamatory style (see, e.g., Rudd, "Dryden," 160–61). For similar assessments in English satiric criticism, see Raman Selden, *English Verse Satire 1590–1765* (London: Allen & Unwin, 1978), 27–34; Alvin Kernan, *The Cankered Muse* (New Haven: Yale University Press, 1959), 28–30; P. K. Elkin, *The Augustan Defence of Satire* (Oxford: Clarendon Press, 1973), chapter 8 "Smiling versus Savage Satire"; and Gilbert Highet, *The Anatomy of Satire* (Princeton: Princeton University Press, 1962), 235ff. Examples could be multiplied.

4. Selden, *English Verse Satire*, 89, 100.

5. As Thomas Brown complained of past critiques of Horace: "They have commented upon him like Grammarians, not Philosophers; as if *Horace* had writ meerly to have his Language understood, and rather to divert, than instruct" (Brown, *Works*, 27). With regard to satire, even Dryden in "Discourse" admits reluctantly that instruction takes precedence over delight. He writes: "They who will not grant me, that Pleasure is one of the Ends of Poetry, but that it is only a means of compassing the only end, which is Instruction; must yet allow that without the means of Pleasure, the Instruction is but a bare and dry Philosophy, a crude preparation of Morals, which we may have from *Aristotle* and *Epictetus*, with more profit than from any Poet" (88).

6. To be fair, Selden does warn us not to attach the facile labels of an English Horace to Pope and an English Juvenal to Swift (Selden, *English Verse Satire*, 128); their satires are far more complex in expression than that. The critic who has done most to dispute the concept of a wholesale shift in English letters to Horatian satire after 1660, however, is Howard D. Weinbrot (see *Eighteenth-Century Satire: Essays on Text and Context from Dryden to Peter Pindar* [Cambridge: Cambridge University Press, 1988], 30–33). Weinbrot observes that if the French paradigm for satire during the seventeenth century became primarily the satiric model of "Horace with generous dollops of Juvenalian anger and Persian solemnity added as required," in England during the later seventeenth and early eighteenth centuries that formula was the reverse (Weinbrot, *Alexander Pope and the Traditions of Formal Verse Satire* [Princeton: Princeton University Press, 1982], 82).

7. Dryden notes that "*Horace* is teaching us in every Line, and is perpetually Moral" (Dryden, *Works*, 62). Similarly, Brown remarks on readers unable

to accept Horace's remedial satire: "those who do not endeavour to correct themselves by so beautiful a Model, are just like sick Men, who having a Book full of Recepts, proper to their Distempers, content themselves to read 'em, without comprehending them, or so much as knowing the Advantage of them" (*Works*, 28). For a good example of Horace's remedial inclination, see Satire 1.1, especially the good humor at lines 102–7 where Horace's narrator engages an interlocutor defending the practice of avarice. For a particularly fine example of the intimate, ironic, and commonsensical intonations of Horace's *vir bonus*, see the opening fifteen lines of Satire 2.6.

  8. Dryden, *Works*, 63–64.

  9. See, for example, John Oldham's views expressed in the Advertisement to *Some New Pieces* (1681) on the appropriateness of the irate man as a narrative voice for satire. Responding to criticisms of harsh cadence and rough versification in his earlier satires, Oldham remarks

> I confess, I did not so much mind the Cadence, as the Sense and expressiveness of my words, and therefore chose not those, which were best dispos'd to placing themselves in Rhyme, but rather the most keen and tuant, as being the suitablest to my Argument. And certainly no one that pretends to distinguish the several Colours of Poetry, would expect that *Juvenal*, when he is lashing of Vice and Villany, should flow so smoothly as *Ovid*, or *Tibullus*, when they are describing Amours and Gallantries, and have nothing to disturb and ruffle the evenness of their Stile." (Oldham, *The Poems of John Oldham*, eds. H. F. Brooks and R. Selden [Oxford: Clarendon Press, 1986], 89)

Though in a minority position stylistically by the early 1680s, Oldham aptly describes the rigor and savagery of satiric standpoints taken by Hall, Marston, and Cleveland before him and pursued, albeit in more civil metric fashion, by Pope, Swift, and Johnson after him.

  10. Translations of Juvenal are by Peter Green, *Juvenal: The Sixteen Satires* (New York: Penguin, 1974).

  11. Juvenal's satiric expression in fact compares favorably with Derrida's original use for deconstruction. For Derrida, deconstruction is ultimately a political practice where an attempt is made to dismantle the logic by which a particular system of thought—such as a political structure or a social institution—maintains its force (Terry Eagleton, *Literary Theory: An Introduction* [Oxford: Basil Blackwell, 1983], 148). Within the casuistic realm of individual action, Juvenalian satire has a similar disruptive aim.

  12. William Soames and John Dryden, trans., *The Art of Poetry, Written in French by The Sieur* de Boileau, *Made* English (London, 1683), 385–86.

  13. For a full account of the neo-Epicurean movement in English literate society during the second half of the seventeenth century, see R. W. F. Kroll, *The Material Word: Literate Culture in the Restoration and Early Eighteenth Century* (Baltimore and London: Johns Hopkins, 1991), chapters 3–5. See also Warren Chernaik's first chapter, which discusses the confluence of Hobbesian, Epicurean, and libertine thought during the Restoration (Chernaik, *Sexual Freedom in Restoration Literature* [Cambridge: Cambridge University Press, 1995]). Democritus was also fashionable during the Elizabethan and Jacobean vogue for melancholy. Elizabethan satirists invoke his name, and Burton, in his *Anatomy of Melancholy*, writes as "Democritus Junior." In the eighteenth century, the Laughing Philosopher is not

forgotten by satirists. Burton was one of Dr. Johnson's favorite authors, for example.

14. See D. M. Vieth, *Attribution in Restoration Poetry: A Study of Rochester's Poems of 1680* (New Haven and London: Yale University Press, 1963), 293–94.

15. Although Lyons in his edition gives this satire the title *After Boileau*, to avoid confusion I will use the more critically familiar title of *Timon*. All quotations from Rochester's poems are from Lyons's edition and will be cited parenthetically in the text by line number.

16. Marianne Thormählen, *Rochester: The Poems in Context* (Cambridge: Cambridge University Press, 1993), 284; see also 266–74.

17. See ibid., 279–80.

18. During the summer of 1994, the National Portrait Gallery in London presented a special exhibit entitled "Portraits in Disguise." Among its paintings was the portrait of Rochester copied after that by Jacob Husymans that shows the earl not only holding a wreath of laurels over the head of a monkey while it tears pages from a book, but doing so while he is dressed in the tunic of a Roman aristocrat (thus the portrait in disguise). The exhibitors noted that in donning this costume, Rochester wears a symbol of authority, knowledge, and power. It occurs to me that one possible meaning of Rochester's lark in this painting is slander of Dryden and, perhaps, adverse comment on the literary taste of Charles as well. In his costume of classical authority, Rochester wryly impersonates the king; as Charles, Rochester then ironically awards the post of poet laureate to a chattering and fawning ape—from Rochester's point of view not an inaccurate description of Dryden during the early 1670s. At that point in his career, Dryden had produced marginal comedies, obsequious celebrations of Charles's regime, and caterwauling heroic drama. At every turn, the laureate—similar to the posture of the monkey in the painting—seemed pathetically to try to court popular and royal favor in literary matters.

19. See Thormählen, *Poems in Context*, 281–82.

20. See Ronald Hutton, *Charles the Second: King of England, Scotland, and Ireland* (Oxford: Oxford University Press, 1989), 279–80.

21. In looking for a way to identify Huff and Kickum with actual pro-French and thus staunchly royalist advisors, as well as Dingboy and Halfwit (Buckingham?) with anti-French and perhaps Parliament-leaning advisors, I hoped a key to the puzzle might be found in the dramatic preferences expressed by each of the four in the poem. Unfortunately, this idea did not pan out. Huff likes Settle, while Halfwit prefers Orrery—a crossing of political lines right there. While true Whig and Tory factions had yet to form when *Timon* was written, and thus room might exist for imaginative critical explication still, it strikes me that there is no good basis for conjecturing political identifications as a result of the passages on contemporary drama.

22. For an account of Charles's actions during the war, see chapter 11, "Charles's Second Dutch War, 1672–1674," of Hutton's biography, *Charles the Second*. I am indebted to Hutton especially, but also to David Ogg, for my details of English political affairs as they relate to *Timon* (see Ogg, *England in the Reign of Charles II*, 1934 [Oxford: Oxford University Press, 1984]).

23. Hutton, *Charles the Second*, 313.

24. Ibid., 315.

25. Ibid., 318.

26. Quoted in ibid.

27. See the alleged impromptu made by Rochester on Charles's court, titled by Lyons "Here's Monmouth the Witty," as well as the quatrain entitled "On the King" that by legend began as a quip. Supposedly, both were originally spoken to Charles's face by Rochester. The latter slur asserts that none can rely on a promise made by the king; equally, Charles "never said a foolish thing, / Nor ever did a wise one." Story has it that Charles spontaneously replied that was because his words were his own, while his actions were those of his ministers. The provocative "Verses for which he was Banished" is discussed in detail in chapter 5.

28. Thormählen, *Poems in Context*, 279.

29. Anthony à Wood informs us that Charles's court not only debauched the young Rochester but "made him a perfect *Hobbist*," meaning probably atheist (David Farley-Hills, *Rochester: The Critical Heritage* [New York: Barnes & Noble, 1972], 170).

30. Thormählen reviews various critical views of both Timon as a character and Timon as a representation of Rochester (see Thormählen, *Poems in Context*, 276–79). With regard to the second issue, while it is certainly intriguing to associate the creation with its author and such a reading cannot be entirely denied, I agree with Thormählen that the characteristics given Timon "are typical of the inner circle of Court Wits" (278). More than a specific person, Timon is a type—specifically what I have termed at the beginning of chapter 2 as the target fop.

31. For Boileau's satires, I work from the edition by A. Cahen, *Boileau-Despréaux: Satires* (Paris: Librairie E. Droz, 1932). For a dutiful English translation of Boileau, see Hayward Porter, *The Satires of Boileau Despréaux* (Glasgow: James MacLehose and Sons, 1904). Citations to Boileau's satires appear parenthetically in the text.

32. Harold Love, "Rochester and the Traditions of Satire," in *Restoration Literature: Critical Approaches*, ed. H. Love (London: Methuen, 1972), 153, 162.

33. Thormählen notes that from start to finish the speaker in *Tunbridge Wells* "is a disgusted listener as well as a nauseated observer" (Thormählen, *Poems in Context*, 242).

34. Thormählen demonstrates how the satire is filled with leading contemporary issues of politics, religion, and social order (see ibid., 241–65). She concludes: "A study of the historical context of *Tunbridge Wells* helps a present-day reader develop a greater awareness of the ironical dimensions that Rochester's contemporaries recognized and enjoyed." The poem "energetically dissects foolish pretentiousness in Restoration society" (264–65).

35. Ibid., 242.

36. See also Timothy Raylor, *Cavaliers, Clubs, and Literary Culture: Sir John Mennes, James Smith, and the Order of the Fancy* (Newark: University of Delaware Press; London and Toronto: Associated University Presses, 1994), chapters 1–2.

37. Although Lyons removes these final four lines from *Tunbridge Wells*, offering them only in a list of possibly authentic variants, I tend to think they belong in Rochester's poem, and so will use them in my argument.

Chapter 4. Linguistic Iconoclasm

1. Joan DeJean points out that virtually all of the libertine writings of seventeenth-century France were "characterized by an underlying spirit of

questioning" (DeJean, *Libertine Strategies: Freedom and the Novel in Seventeenth-Century France* [Columbus: Ohio State University Press, 1981], 24; see chapter 1). With regard to *Satire Against Mankind*, Marianne Thormählen asserts the certainty of influence and relationship between Rochester's satire and the libertinage tradition in France (see Thormählen, *Rochester: The Poems in Context* [Cambridge: Cambridge University Press, 1993],198–201). She comments: "There can be no doubt that Rochester was familiar with this French tradition of decrying reason" (201).

2. In two long chapters, Thormählen demonstrates extensively how Rochester's satire "constitutes a digest of religious and philosophical notions in the seventeenth century as well as of people and events in Restoration society" (Thormählen, *Poems in Context*, 162). Emphasizing the social relevance of the piece, she asserts that the satire "places the reader right in the storm centre of the late seventeenth century. In little more than two hundred lines, it brings a painfully chaotic period to life, a time when scholasticism was slowly forced to yield to the new science, when Parliament asserted its power over the Sovereign without having to resort to decapitation, and when Anglicanism secured its supremacy in the religious life of the nation" (239).

3. The dual nature of Rochester's attack—that is, half of the satire deals with reason and half with "mankind"—has long been recognized. See T. H. Fujimura, "Rochester's 'Satyr Against Mankind': An Analysis," *Studies in Philology* 55 (1958): 576–90; and D. M. Vieth, "Towards an Anti-Aristotelian Poetic: Rochester's *Satyr Against Mankind* and *Artemisia to Chloe*, With Notes on Swift's *Tale of a Tub* and *Gulliver's Travels*," *Language and Style* 5 (1972): 125–27. Structurally, the dividing line comes at line 110 of the poem.

4. See also Thormählen, *Poems in Context*, 193–94.

5. Ibid., 171.

6. Just as Bacon, Hobbes, and Butler in their writings took on the Aristotelian Schoolmen, Rochester responds to the Latitudinarians in his satire. As a theological circle, the Cambridge Platonists envisioned God as pure reason. Nathanael Culverwell wrote in *A Discourse of the Light of Nature* (1652) that "To blaspheme reason is to reproach Heaven itself, and to dishonour the God of reason, to question the beauty of his image." Benjamin Whichcote added to this in his *Aphorisms* (section 76), "To go against Reason is to go against God." A poem such as *Satire Against Mankind* (also titled *A Satire Against Reason and Mankind* in some manuscript sources) obviously is designed to upset such concepts of God. For detailed discussions of the conflict between Rochester and these churchmen, see Dustin Griffin, *Satires Against Man: The Poems of Rochester* (Berkeley and Los Angeles: University of California Press, 1973), chapter 4; and Thormählen, *Poems in Context*, 167–74.

7. Thormählen, *Poems in Context*, 172–73.

8. See, for example, Ronald Berman, "Rochester and the Defeat of the Senses," *Kenyon Review* 26 (1964): 354–68.

9. See Thormählen, *Poems in Context*, 193–94, 201.

10. See ibid., 174–84.

11. Thormählen notes: "Rochester's most famous long poem directs its satirical thrusts at much the same targets as *Upon Nothing:* the pride, vanity, folly and treachery of men, especially those who would govern and influence others" (ibid., 190). "Upon Nothing" is discussed in chapter 5 as one of Rochester's shorter political poems.

12. For this reading of John Locke's *Two Treatises of Government*, see Ste-

ven N. Zwicker, *Lines of Authority: Politics and English Literary Culture, 1649–1689* (Ithaca and London: Cornell University Press, 1993), chapter 5.

13. While such an occurrence does nothing to bolster a political reading of the narrator's right reason, neither does it serve to cancel that reading. On this point Thormählen and I disagree. She sees hedonism at the heart of the narrator's perceptual doctrine; she interprets right reason to be a practice where "the only acceptable rational activity consists in finding ways to enhance one's physical pleasures and to satisfy one's appetites, unhampered by any intervening considerations" (Thormählen, *Poems in Context*, 202). This quest to satisfy bodily appetites is a distinctly apolitical pursuit: "There is nothing to suggest that this process might be affected by other people pursuing the same aim for themselves. . . . The passage is thus a libertine's credo" (217). Nevertheless, Thormählen also believes that the brashness of the lines on right reason are a calculated stance designed to "incite disagreement even in the most docile reader" (218). Even if not intentionally political in nature, the narrator's right reason serves as a goad to the contemporary reader to reexamine orthodoxy. In a sense, then, either Thormählen's or my view of the politicality of right reason ultimately points to one prominent rhetorical consequence of the satire being that of calling the status quo into question. That expression of doubt in itself constitutes a political act.

14. See Griffin, *Satires*, 167, 202.

15. See also Thormählen, *Poems in Context*, 223.

16. See also Warren Chernaik, *Sexual Freedom in Restoration Literature* (Cambridge: Cambridge University Press, 1995), 24.

17. See also Thormählen, *Poems in Context*, 223–24.

18. At the heart of Samuel Butler's miscellany satire is the same notion of reason as a double-edged sword, capable of harming as well as helping humanity. In his *Observations*, Butler writes that human thinking must stay within proper limits: "The understanding of Man hath a Sphaere of Activity, beyond which if it be forc'd, it become's unactive, as it do's vigorous by being confin'd." Overstepping these boundaries is both fruitless and destructive: "Opinion of Knowledg ha's ever beene one of the Chiefest Causes of Ignorance, for most men know less then they might, by attempting to know more then they can" (Samuel Butler, *Samuel Butler: Prose Observations*, ed. H. De Quehen [Oxford: Clarendon Press, 1979], 10). This idea repeatedly finds expression in satires such as *Satyr Upon the Imperfection and Abuse of Human Learning*, *The Elephant in the Moon*, and *Satyr Upon the Weakness and Misery of Man* (which, as the title indicates, bears a striking resemblance to Rochester's *Satire Against Mankind*).

19. The question remains whether or not the final portion of *Satire Against Mankind* (lines 174–221 of Vieth's version of the poem) is by Rochester at all. Lyons prints the piece as it was often presented during the Restoration era, that is, as a separate poem entitled *Addition*, but he leaves authorship an open question (see 263–64). It has been argued compellingly that the addition itself is an apology or postscript appended by Rochester in reply to a sermon preached before the king (24 February 1675) by the Reverend Edward Stillingfleet, Charles's chaplain-in-ordinary since 1667. In that sermon the author of *Satire Against Mankind* is accused of atheism and blasphemy. See also the following: K. F. Paulson, "The Reverend Edward Stillingfleet and the 'Epilogue' to Rochester's *A Satyr against Reason and Mankind*," *Philological Quarterly* 50 (1971): 657–63; Vieth, *Attribution in Res-*

toration Poetry: A Study of Rochester's Poems *of 1680* (New Haven and London: Yale University Press, 1963), 370–75; Bror Danielsson and D. M. Vieth, eds., *The Gyldenstolpe Manuscript Miscellany of Poems by John Wilmot, Earl of Rochester, and other Restoration Authors* (Stockholm: Almqvist & Wiksell, 1967); and David Trotter, "Wanton Expressions," in *Spirit of Wit: Reconsiderations of Rochester,* ed. J. Treglown (Oxford: Basil Blackwell, 1982), 111–32. If the polemic of the satire were shaped so acutely by these local circumstances, Rochester's duel with the Latitudinarians reads even less well as universalized satire. I accept the *Addition* as part of Rochester's poem. As a conclusion to the satire, even if added subsequently, it performs useful rhetorical functions for the piece as a whole. Primarily, it brings the arguments of the narrator to a sharper close than in the first 173 lines of the satire. The piece ties together argumentative loose strings and reestablishes the dialectic with the adversarius. In what amount to mock-exempla, the ironic descriptions of the good politician and clergyman serve to illustrate the narrator's portrait of ignorant and vicious human nature. The lines also make a special point of locating the debate at court, where the outcome of the controversy would be most real and important. At its very end, by circling back to the striking opening figure of *Satire Against Mankind,* the superiority of beasts, the addition gives the satire as well an equally contentious closing idea. If Rochester does append this part of the composition later and in response to attacks on his satire, the lines nonetheless maintain the integrity and augment the premise of the original satire on reason.

20. Thormählen, *Poems in Context,* 226.

21. Andrew Marvell, *The Poems and Letters of Andrew Marvell,* ed. H. M. Margoliouth, rev. P. Legouis and E. E. Duncan-Jones, 3d ed., 2 vols. (Oxford: Clarendon Press, 1971); quotations from Marvell's poems are cited parenthetically in the text by line number.

22. For a discussion of the controversy, see Thormählen, *Poems in Context,* 228–35.

23. See ibid., 231–33.

24. This formula for self-deception is Friedrich Nietzsche's assertion as well in "On Truth and Falsity in Their Ultramoral Sense." In that essay, he describes humans fundamentally as arch-deceivers who want and need themselves to be deceived: "The intellect, as a means for the preservation of the individual, develops its chief power in dissimulation" (Friedrich Nietzsche, *The Complete Works of Friedrich Nietzsche,* ed. O. Levy, vol. 2 [New York: Russell & Russell, 1964], 174; see also chapter 1, note 13). Arrogantly, we construct order and system where none exist. Those who dissemble best are considered most intelligent.

25. Ronald Hutton, *Charles the Second: King of England, Scotland, and Ireland* (Oxford: Oxford University Press, 1989), 358.

26. Thormählen, *Poems in Context,* 104, 110, 111.

27. Ibid., 112.

28. Ibid., 115, 118; see her whole argument, 114–18.

29. See Thormählen's "pleasing speculation," ibid., 134–35.

30. See note 3 of chapter 2. See also chapter 5. In her chapter on *Artemisa,* Thormählen hedges somewhat on the issue of Rochester's sexism. Asserting at one point that "I have found nothing to suggest that Rochester was in any way interested in, let alone committed to, the notion of sexual equality" (123), when it comes to her contention that we read Artemisa without narra-

tive compromise, she attempts to palliate damaging evidence for Rochester's "dully conventional view of writing women" (135).

31. I can understand how diachronically, that is, from our current point of view, certain aspects of Rochester's writings and even certain information that we know about his life might lead us to regard him at times in a positive sexual-political light. Quite possibly in some ways Rochester was less sexist than the run-of-the-mill aristocratic, in-crowd libertine of Charles's entourage—which, of course, is not saying a lot. True, Rochester attacks unthinking libertinism in many of his works, and in some of his letters he expresses a tender regard for his wife and children. Such statements can bolster feminist readings. However, since sexism and patriarchy are such a profound part of the power structure Rochester takes on, it is to be expected, I think, that what might be called residual or incidental feminist notions might be available to us to read into his writing and his life. Synchronically, I find scant evidence of Rochester's fundamental regard for women being very much more than disappointingly, if not disturbingly, conventional. Neither do I think it a contradiction for Rochester to be fundamentally sexist himself yet at the same time debunk the phallogocentrism of his brother libertines. I would argue that this circumstance merely demonstrates the depth of his sexism as well as his blindness to the naturalized sexism of his culture— problems we still face today. Rochester's concern is *primarily* with belittling his brothers, not with also liberating his sisters in any active way. As I will discuss in my final chapter, Rochester is not quite *that* political, nor is he political enough to live up to, perhaps, some of our standards for enlightened politicality today. Equally, to imagine that, in some kind of black-or-white formula, Rochester must either be completely feminist or completely sexist dangerously oversimplifies the complexities of gender politics. As a man and as a, I hope, feminist, I uncover all too frequently in my own attitudes and behaviors vestiges of deeply rooted sexist assumptions and habits. And I'm *not* living at the court of Charles II. Rochester's feminism, if it exists at all, is weak. Similarly, because Rochester potentially disabuses a reader from the self-serving constructs of Restoration upper class ideology, do not imagine him a Marxist before his time, either.

32. See, for example, James E. Gill, "The Fragmented Self in Three of Rochester's Poems," *Modern Language Quarterly* 49, no. 1 (March 1988): 19–37.

33. For a similar reading of the structure and import of *Artemisa*, developed as part of a different argument, see J. Douglas Canfield, *Word as Bond in English Literature from the Middle Ages to the Restoration* (Philadelphia: University of Pennsylvania Press, 1989), 171–73.

34. See also Thormählen, *Poems in Context*, 140.

35. Thormählen notes: "Despite this difference with regard to the targets of their respective attacks, the *Satyr* speaker and Artemiza both castigate the offenses of their respective sex against Nature, contending that those offenses are foolish human fabrications which bring nothing but unhappiness on their misguided creators" (ibid., 108).

36. See, for instance, Vieth, *Attribution* 293; and David Farley-Hills, *Rochester's Poetry* (London: Bell & Hyman, 1978), 206.

37. See David Hume, *A Treatise of Human Nature*, ed. L. A. Selby-Biggs (Oxford: Oxford University Press, 1978), 67–68.

38. One need only think of Wycherley's dance of cuckolds at the end of

The Country Wife (first performed and published in 1675, when Vieth dates the writing of *Artemisa*) to confirm this contemporary literary depiction of town society.

39. Another interpretation of Rochester's portrait with a monkey occurs at this point (see also note 18 of chapter 3). Perhaps the book-destroying simian represents the target fop, Rochester's reader. To exercise reception theory, a book is only as good as its reader. In the painting, the attentive beast seems to be doing its best at exegesis. Perhaps the bay leaves above the head of the monkey signal that the ape-reader is the true poet in this relationship: what Rochester's verse *means* to his readers is limited to their powers of comprehension. The earl wears a detached, almost-ironic, almost-accusing expression on his face that seems to say *ecce homo*. I believe Rochester enjoyed making monkeys of his readers in at least two ways: first, with the patrician social critique of his verse; second, by setting sophisticated linguistic traps in which to catch his naive and wanton male-as-brute readership (see chapter 5).

40. Thormählen, *Poems in Context*, 112; see 112–14.

41. Remarks Michel Foucault:

Here I believe one's point of reference should not be to the great model of language (*langue*) and signs, but to that of war and battle. The history which bears and determines us has the form of a war rather than that of a language: relations of power, not relations of meaning. History has no "meaning", though this is not to say that it is absurd or incoherent. On the contrary, it is intelligible and should be susceptible of analysis down to the smallest detail—but this in accordance with the intelligibility of struggles, of strategies and tactics. Neither the dialectic, as logic of contradictions, nor semiotics, as the structure of communication, can account for the intrinsic intelligibility of conflicts. "Dialectic" is a way of evading the always open and hazardous reality of conflict by reducing it to a Hegelian skeleton, and "semiology" is a way of avoiding its violent, bloody and lethal character by reducing it to the calm Platonic form of language and dialogue." (Foucault, *Power/Knowledge: Selected Interviews and Other Writings 1972–1977*, ed. C. Gordon [New York: Pantheon, 1977], 114–15)

42. See also Thormählen, *Poems in Context*, 114.

43. Hutton, *Charles the Second*, 458.

44. Universally, critics recognize the pervading negativism underlying the dramatic luster of Rochester's verse. Howard D. Weinbrot, for example, calls *Artemisa* "an apocalyptic satire that proclaims the triumph of Hell" (Weinbrot, "The Swelling Volume: The Apocalyptic Satire of Rochester's *Letter From Artemisia In the Town to Chloe In the Country*," *Studies in the Literary Imagination* 5, no. 2 [October 1972]: 37).

45. See also Thormählen, *Poems in Context*, 140.

CHAPTER 5. POLITICAL SEXUALITY

1. For these series of quotes, see Dustin Griffin, "Rochester and the 'Holiday Writers,'" in *Rochester and Court Poetry*, eds. D. M. Vieth and D. Griffin (Los Angeles: William Andrews Clark Memorial Library, 1988), 55; Samuel Rogal, "The Earl of Rochester: 'Why Am I No Poet of the Times?'" *College Language Association Journal* 32, no. 1 (1988): 92–93; Thomas Pasch, "Con-

centricity, Christian Myth, and the Self-Incriminating Narrator in Rochester's *A Ramble in St. James's Park*," in *John Wilmot, Earl of Rochester: Critical Essays*, ed. D. M. Vieth (New York and London: Garland, 1988): 149; Sarah Wintle, "Libertinism and Sexual Politics," in *Spirit of Wit: Reconsiderations of Rochester*, ed. J. Treglown (Oxford: Basil Blackwell, 1982), 148; and Felicity Nussbaum, *The Brink of All We Hate: English Satires on Women, 1660–1750* (Lexington: University Press of Kentucky, 1984). Specifically, Nussbaum believes that Rochester does not produce standard antifeminist satire or linguistic violence against women, as one might expect, but in fact acknowledges the potency of women and the impotence of men in order to achieve the authority of wit. See her chapter "'That Lost Thing, Love': Women and Impotence in Rochester's Poetry." For other estimations of Rochester's verse reversing reader expectations, see also Reba Wilcoxon, "Mirrors of Men's Fears: The Court Satires on Women," *Restoration* 3 (fall 1979): 45–51; Carole Fabricant, "Rochester's World of Imperfect Enjoyment," *Journal of English and Germanic Philology* 73 (1974): 338–50; Marianne Thormählen, *Rochester: The Poems in Context* (Cambridge: Cambridge University Press, 1993), 1; and Warren Chernaik, *Sexual Freedom in Restoration Literature* (Cambridge: Cambridge University Press, 1995), 8.

2. Thormählen comments: "It is not surprising that Kate Millett's term 'sexual politics' has been applied to Rochester's poems. From the youthful pastoral efforts to the lampoons of the late 1670s, his love poetry is forever concerned with power-structured relationships, men and women controlling, influencing and dominating one another" (Thormählen, *Poems in Context*, 122–23).

3. Steven N. Zwicker, *Lines of Authority: Politics and English Literary Culture: 1649–1689* (Ithaca and London: Cornell University Press, 1993), 97.

4. Ibid., 3–7.

5. In 1681, for example, Dryden opens *Absalom and Achitophel*, the most imposing discussion of Stuart policy of the century, with a strenuous if not daring effort to defuse the matter of the king's lechery. See also Howard D. Weinbrot's reading of the poem as respectful criticism of the king by his poet laureate; "'Natures Holy Bands' in *Absalom and Achitophel*: Fathers and Sons, Satire and Change" in *Eighteenth-Century Satire: Essays on Text and Context from Dryden to Peter Pindar* (Cambridge: Cambridge University Press, 1988). See notes 11 and 29 as well.

6. Zwicker's chapter 4, "The Politics of Pleasure: *Annus Mirabilis*, *The Last Instructions*, *Paradise Lost*," is especially relevant to my reading of Rochester's works as political productions. However, while Zwicker terms Rochester's satires as "scurrilous and brilliant," he nonetheless implies that they were part of accepted courtly culture in that they "found a forgiving audience in the king" (Zwicker, *Lines of Authority*, 92). Zwicker includes no Rochester compositions in his study for detailed political examination. I believe that Charles might have been forgiving of Rochester's satiric efforts not because they were politically toothless, but because he and others of courtly society might not fully have appreciated their real political bite. Besides, if stories are true that Rochester was banished for, while drunk, mistakenly handing Charles the wrong sheaf of libels, perhaps the king was not so forgiving nor so ignorant of the civic implications behind Rochester's writings as we think. Also, I will not attempt to supply exhaustive evidence from Rochester's canon of the political functions I have named. Thormählen has

placed Rochester's poems admirably and thoroughly into their local context. Rather, I will investigate closely a few specific works and refer to others as need be. I do want to make clear, however, that I believe these traits to be nearly universal in his poems and plays.

7. Claude Rawson points out, correctly I think, that the hyperbole of Rochester's obscenity prevents his works from being merely pornographic; in this regard the works are similar to the satire of Rabelais (Rawson, *Satire and Sentiment 1660–1830* [Cambridge: Cambridge University Press, 1994], 5.) With the exception of "Signior Dildo," Thormählen calls "Fair Cloris" the "only poem in the Rochester canon where obscenity is wholly amusing" (Thormählen, *Poems in Context*, 52). Uncharacteristically, I think she has overlooked the darker implications of the song.

8. For a brief summary of seventeenth-century attitudes toward rape, see Thormählen, *Poems in Context*, 52–55. Basically, the male perspective considered rape an impossibility; women who said "no" in fact meant "yes." See also Angeline Goreau, "'Last Night's Rambles': Restoration Literature and the War Between the Sexes," in *The Sexual Dimension in Literature*, ed. A. Bold (London and Totowa, N.J.: Vision and Barnes & Noble, 1982).

9. Other reasons for making Cloris a tender of pigs rather than the more conventional sheep have been suggested. Ken Robinson identifies the prototype of Rochester's Cloris as the pig-woman in the satire of Semonides of Amorgos; see Robinson, "Rochester and Semonides," *Notes and Queries* 224 (December 1979): 521–22. Robert Holton points out that during the seventeenth century pigs became a symbol for rustic boorishness—was the pun intended?—and therefore something rejected by polite society; see Holton, "Sexuality and Social Hierarchy in Sidney and Rochester," *Mosaic* 24, no. 1 (winter 1991): 63–64.

10. In Tonson's 1691 edition of Rochester's poems, the final stanza of "Fair Cloris" was expunged, thus converting evidently unacceptable female masturbation to perfectly acceptable rape (see Paddy Lyons, *Complete Poems and Plays* [London and Rutland: J. M. Dent and Charles E. Tuttle, 1993], viii). This fact lends support to the view that Rochester's poems can supply their reader with what he does *not* necessarily want to hear.

11. Besides Marvell's satire now to be discussed, see as well Samuel Butler's *Satyr Upon the Licentious Age of Charles 2D*, and John Oldham's *Satyr III: Loyola's Will* of his *Satyrs upon the Jesuits*, and John Dryden's *Absalom and Achitophel* (particularly as read by Weinbrot; see note 5 and also note 29). In all of these pieces, lechery equals bad polity. More than satiric bromide, such an equation held particular and significant civil import during the reign of the Merry Monarch. Sex was politicized when Charles sat on the English throne.

12. For other examples of political sexuality in *Last Instructions*, see Andrew Marvell's portraits of Henry Jermyn, earl of St. Albans (29–34); the duchess of York (49–78); and Charles's current mistress, Barbara Villiers, then lady of Castlemaine (79–96). See also Zwicker, *Lines of Authority*, 107ff. In the case of Castlemaine, more than just depicting her as an aging and sexually voracious woman, Marvell virtually charges the lady with bestiality when, through imagery alone, the footman with whom she copulates turns into a horse.

13. Zwicker, *Lines of Authority*, 117.

14. See also J. Douglas Canfield, *Word as Bond in English Literature from*

the Middle Ages to the Restoration (Philadelphia: University of Pennsylvania Press, 1989), 167–68.

15. Critics who equate narrators, such as the vulgar-mouthed speaker of "Ramble," with self-portraits, do their best to think the worst of Rochester by offering amateur psychoanalyses of him (e.g., Johannes Prinz, *John Wilmot Earl of Rochester: His Life and Writings* [Leipzig: Mayer & Mueller, 1927], 155–56; and Vivian De Sola Pinto, *Enthusiast in Wit: A Portrait of John Wilmot, Earl of Rochester 1647–1680* [Lincoln: University of Nebraska Press, 1962], passim). Not only do such interpretations permit too much of the earl's biography to cloud the analysis, but they underestimate his intelligence and craft as a poet (e.g., David Farley-Hills, *The Benevolence of Laughter: Comic Poetry of the Commonwealth and Restoration* [London: Macmillan, 1974], 148–51).

16. Thormählen views the three young blades as social climbers looking to profit from their liaison with Corinna by virtue of her intimacy with the narrator. Town gallants seek to copy the ways and even to procure the position of the court wit (Thormählen, *Poems in Context*, 97–99). I would place all four men, nonetheless, in the category of Rochester's target fop (see my definition for this Restoration social type, in chapter 2). For a useful, brief reading of this poem that in many ways agrees with mine, see also Canfield, *Word as Bond*, 169.

17. Nussbaum (*Brink*), Wilcoxon ("Sexual Politics," 118–19), and Canfield (*Word as Bond*, 170–71) also find strong elements of female sexual autonomy in Rochester's poems. For an account of how Restoration libertine culture found female promiscuity intolerable, see Goreau ("'Last Night's Rambles,'" 66–67). For another poem by Rochester with a strongly antimale speaker, see his "Fragment of a Satire on Men."

18. See R. E. Quaintance, "French Sources of the Restoration 'Imperfect Enjoyment' Poem" *Philological Quarterly* 42 (April 1963): 190–99 as well as J. H. O'Neill, "An Unpublished 'Imperfect Enjoyment' Poem," *Papers on Language and Literature* 13 (spring 1977): 197–202.

19. Thormählen notes that Rochester's contribution "is the only poem in which the inability to restore erection immediately after premature ejaculation results in furious imprecations" (Thormählen, *Poems in Context*, 94). See also Canfield, *Word as Bond*, 170. For an example of the amiable sort of imperfect enjoyment poem, see John Adlard, ed., *The Fruit of that Forbidden Tree: Restoration Poems, Songs and Jests on the Subject of Sensual Love* (Cheadle: Carcanet Press, 1975), 73–74.

20. Thormählen comments that the second half of the poem "codifies the impossibility of giving sexual satisfaction where emotion comes into play, at least in the speaker's case" (Thormählen, *Poems in Context*, 94). The narrator's normal libertine sexual ability is thus canceled by love, something more spiritual than mere lust and something normally identified as womanly. Goreau informs us that "Libertine philosophy held that love was merely an illusion—an elaborate myth to cover what was really no more than sexual desire pressing to be satisfied" and was generally mocked by wits of the day (Goreau, "'Last Night's Rambles,'" 53; see also 53–56; see as well Thormählen, *Poems in Context*, 122). Thus, Rochester's narrator is behaving very badly in this poem according to the conventions of his rake's fraternity.

21. Thormählen, *Poems in Context*, 161; for the historical circumstances of the poem, see 141–61. In more limited praise of "Upon Nothing," Dustin

Griffin similarly finds that over the first half of the poem "Rochester demonstrates wittily that nothing is *something*," while over the second half "the corresponding thesis that what the world values as 'something'—the rewards of virtue and faith, the glories of learning and statecraft, the strength of human vows and bonds—is in fact nothing" (Griffin, *Satires Against Man: The Poems of Rochester* [Berkeley and Los Angeles: University of California Press, 1973], 277–78).

22. For a brief account of the textual history of the bill as well as of the incident itself where, as tradition has it, Rochester played the mountebank during one of his exiles from court, see Lyons, *Complete Poems and Plays*, 311–12. For an interesting if not inventive account of Rochester's performance as Bendo, mainly via Thomas Alcock's 1687 account of the episode, see Jeremy Lamb's nonscholarly biography of Rochester, *So Idle a Rogue: The Life and Death of Lord Rochester* (London: Allison & Busby, 1993), 178–82. Without saying why or to what degree, Lamb calls *Doctor Bendo's Bill* "a work of some literary importance" (179).

23. Compare this same cure for barrenness, although this time applied by rustics, in *Tunbridge Wells*, 121–55. The conceit was a common one and generally intended as a celebration of men of wit as cuckold-makers, whether their rival male was a citizen, a booby gentry, or a pretentious aristocrat.

24. Thormählen remarks as well that Bendo "goes out of his way to be rude to politicians" (Thormählen, *Poems in Context*, 154), and that the bill serves as a "brief, cool exposition on the treachery and greed of this race of men" (155).

25. Naomi Wolfe, *The Beauty Myth: How Images of Beauty are Used Against Women* (New York: Doubleday, 1991).

26. Farley-Hills, ed., *Rochester: The Critical Heritage* (New York: Barnes & Noble, 1972), 53; hereafter cited in this chapter as *Heritage*.

27. In his *History of the Reign of King Charles II*, Burnet says of Rochester: "The King loved his company for the diversion it afforded, better than his person: And there was no love lost between them" (Farley-Hills, *Heritage*, 93). Jeremy Treglown notes the extreme intimacy with the king that Rochester's duties as Gentleman of the Bedchamber would have afforded him (Treglown, *The Letters of John Wilmot, Earl of Rochester* [Oxford: Basil Blackwell, 1980], 19; hereafter cited in this chapter as *Letters*). Perhaps such familiarity bred contempt. In 1676, Rochester comments to Savile in a letter: "Kings and princes are only as incomprehensible as what they pretend to represent, but apparently as frail as those they govern" (Treglown, *Letters*, 117).

28. Goreau describes the cult of loyal Tory libertines that revolved around Charles both as a social and as a political force (Goreau, "'Last Night's Rambles,'" 50). Holton lucidly addresses the crux of the alliance between sexuality and polity in Rochester's texts when he writes:

> Rochester *was* writing about sexual libertinism and promiscuity, but also about politics because the very categories he makes use of are inevitably involved in the political sphere. Sexual imagery reflects a great deal about fundamental value structures in society and should not be merely deciphered and discarded. It is not so much a matter of showing that sexual terms can be translated into social or political ones, but that the terms of each discourse are inextricably connected: as the poetry indicates in its constantly shifting metaphoric ground, the sexual is always already political. (Holton, "Sexuality," 48)

As mentioned earlier, see also Zwicker, *Lines of Authority*, chapter 4.

29. D. M. Vieth notes that the ambition of Louis and the passivity of Charles may be more than political abstractions of the two monarchs. Rochester's characterizations could be based on the recently concluded Treaty of Westminster (9 February 1673/74), whereby Charles managed to withdraw from the Third Dutch War (Vieth, *The Complete Poems of John Wilmot, Earl of Rochester* [New Haven and London: Yale University Press, 1968], 60). Thormählen thoroughly situates Rochester's poem in its current political context (Thormählen, *Poems in Context*, 295–303). The composition is not just an amusing and obscene court libel; it participates in the concretions of political satire as well. Charles's conduct has real consequences for England. Notably, in *defending* Charles politically, John Dryden does not hesitate in *Absalom and Achitophel* to open with a very similar reference to the king's sexual escapades. Whether Dryden's use of Charles's renowned voluptuosity is a calculated risk designed to negate Monmouth's recent claims of legitimacy or, as Weinbrot has argued, a respectful admonition for Charles to amend his ways (see also notes 5 and 11), what is important to note is not *how* Dryden manipulates Charles's political sexuality but *that* he feels compelled to. In the end, Dryden employs Charles's sex life for Tory propaganda just as Andrew Marvell uses it for what would become more or less Whiggish pursuits. Again, Rochester's verse is by no means unique in its consolidation of sex and politics during the Restoration era.

30. Ronald Hutton points out that one of the political strengths of Charles was "his ability to divide his ministers from his playthings" (Hutton, *Charles the Second: King of England, Scotland, and Ireland* [Oxford: Clarendon Press, 1989], 451). Despite popular conception to the contrary, the king kept business and pleasure distinct. Along with Charles's mistresses, Rochester fell into this latter category of royal plaything. In both *Timon* (9–12) and *Satire Against Mankind* (35–42), men of wit are compared to whores: both are creatures of pleasure to be enjoyed then discarded by fools. Even if Rochester was not a party to the political business of court, nevertheless he observed the process of Charles's government at close quarters and passed judgment on it. As discussed in chapter 4, Rochester's satire tends to characterize the reign of Charles as an elaborate sham or masquerade.

31. Alternatively, line 15 could be read to mean that "We" the people— or, more exactly, we the power elite of the kingdom—permit "them" the "pricks of kings"—that is, kings who are driven by their pricks—to rule because of the fun and privilege afforded to us by such a situation. Either reading, and I believe both are available to us, results in the same picture of Charles and his court as dissolute.

32. See Hutton, *Charles the Second*, 451; see also Harold Weber, "Carolinean Sexuality and the Restoration Stage: Reconstructing the Royal Phallus in *Sodom*," in *Cultural Readings of Restoration and Eighteenth-Century English Theater*, eds. J. D. Canfield and D. C. Payne (Athens and London: University of Georgia Press, 1995), 69–73.

33. For another diatribe against Charles where sexual and political misadventure converge, see "Dialogue (When to the King I bid good-morrow)." There poor Nell still labors to arouse Charles, Kéroualle still performs less than satisfactory coitus with her monarch, and the English people fret over their king's dalliance with the French Catholic faction at court. Other compositions possibly by Rochester where sexual and political license and incom-

petence all join together are "Oh what damned aged do we live in" and "A new Ballad to the Tune of Chevy Chase."

34. J. W. Johnson concludes that "From his own day to ours, evidence has been clear that nobody else was as likely to have written *Sodom* as Rochester was" (Johnson, "Did Lord Rochester Write *Sodom?" The Papers of the Bibliographical Society of America* 81 [June 1987]: 120). He also asserts that "Bolloximian, the satyr-figure representing Charles II, is a commentary on insatiable womanizing and sexual boredom arising from jaded appetites and decreased prowess" (135) and goes on to identify various other characters in the play with Charles's queen, ministers, and mistresses (136). For another reading of *Sodom* as political satire on Charles, see Richard Elias, "Political Satire in *Sodom," Studies in English Literature, 1500–1900* 18 (summer 1978): 423–38. Lyons questions a strict comparison to Charles's court, and wonders instead if the play is not designed to explore the political issues of dynasty (Lyons, *Complete Poems and Plays,* xv–xvi). Chernaik sees in both *Sodom* and *Valentinian* issues of sexuality and polity converging (Chernaik, *Sexual Freedom,* 60–61). He writes: "The blind battering ram of the penis, ruled by the animal instinct of self-gratification, is equivalent to the insatiable demands of royal power, claiming sovereign sway over private property, freedom of conscience, law, public safety, even life itself" (Chernaik, *Sexual Freedom,* 60). For an excellent recent study of *Sodom,* see Weber, who believes that in the play "political and sexual anxiety join to create a powerful vision of the male desire for self-sufficiency and transcendence" (Weber, "Carolinean Sexuality," 69). The overt sexuality of the play, however, has served "to obfuscate its far more dangerous political implications" (Weber, "Carolinean Sexuality," 73).

35. See also Weber, "Carolinean Sexuality," 76, 82–83.

36. For example, see Lyons, *Complete Poems and Plays,* xvi; Griffin, *Satires,* 288–90; J. H. Wilson, "Satiric Elements in Rochester's *Valentinian," Philological Quarterly* 16 (January 1937): 41–48; and Larry Carver, "Rochester's *Valentinian," Restoration and 18th Century Theatre Research* 4, no. 1 (summer 1989): 25, 31, 34. For a dissenting view of *Valentinian* as a play that "emphasizes the theme of divinely sanctioned loyalty even to a thoroughly corrupt king," see Canfield, "Royalism's Last Dramatic Stand: English Political Tragedy, 1679–89," *Studies in Philology* 82 (spring 1985): 251, 250–53. In his preface to the play, Wolseley comments how much better suited was Rochester over Fletcher to render the details of court life and intrigue since "my Lord's constant living at Court, and the Conversation of Persons of Quality, to which from his greenest Youth both his Birth and his Choice had accustom'd him, gave him some great Advantages above this so much and so justly applauded Author [i.e. Fletcher]" (Farley-Hills, *Heritage,* 138). Carver details Rochester's extensive changes made to Fletcher's 1614 play (Carver, "Rochester's *Valentinian,"* 25). Passages I quote all come from these revised sections of the tragedy.

37. Christopher Hill, *The Collected Essays of Christopher Hill: Writing and Revolution in 17th Century England,* vol. 1 (Amherst: University of Massachusetts Press, 1985), 13–14.

CHAPTER 6. CONCLUDING THOUGHTS

1. Edward W. Said, *The World, the Text, and the Critic* (Cambridge: Harvard University Press, 1983), 53.

2. See especially chapter 1 of Paulo Freire, *Pedagogy of the Oppressed* (New York: Continuum, 1990).

3. J. H. Wilson, *The Court Wits of the Restoration: An Introduction* (Princeton: Princeton University Press, 1948), 64; D. M. Vieth, ed., *The Complete Poems of John Wilmot, Earl of Rochester* (New Haven and London: Yale University Press, 1968), xxiii.

4. David Farley-Hills, ed., *Rochester: The Critical Heritage* (New York: Barnes & Noble, 1972), 141.

5. Jeremy Treglown, ed., *The Letters of John Wilmot, Earl of Rochester* (Oxford: Basil Blackwell, 1980), 192.

6. Ibid., 193–94.

7. Ibid., 195.

8. Ibid., 201–2.

9. Ibid., 226.

10. In the spring of 1676, in a letter from the country to Savile in London, Rochester shows this same seriocomic attitude toward government. He writes: "Only I would be glad to know if the parliament be like to sit any time, for the peers of England being grown of late years very considerable in the Government, I would make one at the session. Livy and sickness has a little inclined me to policy. When I come to town I make no question but to change that folly for some less, whether wine or women I know not, according as my constitution serves me" (ibid., 117).

11. Warren Chernaik observes as well in Rochester's works the tendency to demystify Charles's social and political dominion without, however, "a shadow of a suggestion of possible action" against that government (Cherniak, *Sexual Freedom in Restoration Literature* [Cambridge: Cambridge University Press, 1995], 58). Withdrawal rather than reform mark Rochester's political expression (see 58–59).

12. Paddy Lyons, ed., *Complete Poems and Plays* (London and Rutland: J. M. Dent and Charles E. Tuttle, 1993) vii.

13. In my own teaching at a small, private, liberal arts college, I attempt to help what I see as overprivileged, oppressed children of the middle and upper classes understand that by internalizing their oppressor—in our case, the dominant American culture—they become increasingly dehumanized themselves: fools and buffoons as Rochester called the result of his own disengagement from the world. As my students (just as I did at their age) over the first eighteen-odd years of their lives buy into the prevailing monocentrism of the day, the world takes on for them a sparse, unrealistic order— elementally a mythological quality—increasingly divorced from the rich, messy chaos and complexity of human history and existence. In the classroom I try to engineer experiences that demonstrate the danger of this situation to them intellectually as well as the social irresponsibility it necessarily engenders. Outside the classroom, my courses also often require activity in the form of community activism that compliments such theoretical pursuits. However, as well-trained children of consumer society, most students are not much interested to hear nor motivated to encounter a new version of reality. It is easier and safer—indeed, educationally traditional— for them to endure lectures and complain of boredom instead. I suspect as well the degree to which administrators genuinely want students questioning our social status quo. Freire speaks of the difficulty educators in the United States experience when trying to enact active, problem-posing

pedagogy (see especially Freire, *Pedagogy* chapter 2). Due to commonplace assumptions of the fundamentally apolitical nature of the educational process, teachers and students alike in America routinely fail to read the political world. Eerily echoing Rochester's *Satire Against Mankind*, Freire notes a tendency for people in highly modernized societies such as the United States to "carry with them a long capitalistic historical experience that sustains a general theme of human existence always evolving from fear" (Freire and Donald Macedo, *Literacy: Reading the Word and the World* [South Hadley, Mass.: Bergin & Garvey, 1987], 129; see especially chapter 6). In particular, he cites the fear of being denied tenure as a potent motivating force serving to domesticate college educators. Once granted tenure, those same educators naturally tend to remain within the fold of the pedagogical status quo. What Freire terms *radical teachers*, as a result, rarely are found in U.S. higher education.

14. Christopher Hill, *The Collected Essays of Christopher Hill: Writing and Revolution in 17th Century England*, vol. 1 (Amherst: University of Massachusetts Press, 1985), 311.

15. Said, *World*, 51.

Select Bibliography

Adam, Antoine. *Histoire de la littérature française au dix-septième siècle.* 5 vols. Paris: Del Duca, 1962.

———. *Les Libertins au dix-septième siècle.* Paris: Buchet/Chastel, 1964.

———. *Théophile de Viau et la libre pensée française en 1620.* Paris: Droz, 1935.

Adlard, John, ed. *The Fruit of that Forbidden Tree: Restoration Poems, Songs and Jests on the Subject of Sensual Love.* Cheadle: Carcanet Press, 1975.

Aubrey, John. *Aubrey's Brief Lives.* Edited by O. L. Dick. London: Secker and Warburg, 1950.

Barthes, Roland. "The Death of the Author." In *Image-Music-Text,* translated by S. Heath. New York: Hill and Wang, 1977.

———. *Mythologies.* Translated by A. Lavers. New York: Hill and Wang, 1972.

Behn, Aphra. *The Works of Aphra Behn.* Vol. 6. Edited by M. Summers. 1915. Reprint, New York: Benjamin Blom, 1967.

Berman, Ronald. "Rochester and the Defeat of the Senses." *Kenyon Review* 26 (1964): 354–68.

Boileau-Despréaux, Nicolas. *Boileau-Despréaux: Satires.* Edited by A. Cahen. Paris: Librairie E. Droz, 1932.

———. *Oeuvres de Boileau.* Edited by G. Mongrédien. Paris: Librairie Garnier Freres, 1943.

Brown, Thomas. *The Works of Mr. Thomas Brown, in Prose and Verse; Serious, Moral, and Comical.* Vol. 1. London, 1707.

Butler, Samuel. *Samuel Butler: Prose Observations.* Edited by H. De Quehen. Oxford: Clarendon Press, 1979.

Canfield, J. Douglas. "Royalism's Last Dramatic Stand: English Political Tragedy, 1679–89." *Studies in Philology* 82 (spring 1985): 234–63.

———. *Word as Bond in English Literature from the Middle Ages to the Restoration.* Philadelphia: University of Pennsylvania Press, 1989.

Carver, Larry. "Rochester's *Valentinian.*" *Restoration and 18th Century Theatre Research* 4, no. 1 (summer 1989): 25–38.

Chernaik, Warren. *Sexual Freedom in Restoration Literature.* Cambridge: Cambridge University Press, 1995.

Combe, Kirk. "'But loads of Sh—almost choked the way': Shadwell, Dryden, Rochester, and the Summer of 1676." *Texas Studies in Literature and Language* 37, no. 2 (summer 1995): 127–64.

———. "The New Voice of Political Dissent: The Transition from Complaint to Satire." In *Theorizing Satire: Essays in Literary Criticism,* edited by B. A. Connery and K. Combe. New York: St. Martin's, 1995.

Connery, Brian A., and Kirk Combe. "Theorizing Satire: A Retrospective and

Introduction." In *Theorizing Satire: Essays in Literary Criticism*, edited by B. A. Connery and K. Combe. New York: St. Martin's, 1995.

Danielsson, Bror, and D. M. Vieth, eds. *The Gyldenstolpe Manuscript Miscellany of Poems by John Wilmot, Earl of Rochester, and other Restoration Authors*. Stockholm Studies in English 17. Stockholm: Almqvist & Wiksell, 1967.

DeJean, Joan. *Libertine Strategies: Freedom and the Novel in Seventeenth-Century France*. Columbus: Ohio State University Press, 1981.

De Man, Paul. "Semiology and Rhetoric." In *Allegories of Reading: Figural Language in Rousseau, Nietzsche, Rilke, and Proust*. New York and London: Yale University Press, 1979.

Dennis, John. *Critical Works*. Edited by N. Hooker. Vol. 2. Baltimore: Johns Hopkins: 1943.

Derrida, Jacques. "Structure, Sign and Play in the Discourse of the Human Sciences." In *Writing and Difference*, translated by A. Bass. Chicago: University of Chicago Press, 1978.

Dryden, John. *The Works of John Dryden*. Edited by E. N. Hooker and H. T. Swedenberg Jr. Vol. 4. Berkeley and Los Angeles: University of California Press, 1956–.

Eagleton, Terry. *Literary Theory: An Introduction*. Oxford: Basil Blackwell, 1983.

Elias, Richard. "Political Satire in *Sodom*." *Studies in English Literature, 1500–1900* 18 (summer 1978): 423–38.

Elkin, P. K. *The Augustan Defence of Satire*. Oxford: Clarendon Press, 1973.

Everett, Barbara. "The Sense of Nothing." In *Spirit of Wit: Reconsiderations of Rochester*, edited by J. Treglown. Oxford: Basil Blackwell, 1982.

Fabricant, Carole. "Rochester's World of Imperfect Enjoyment." *Journal of English and Germanic Philology* 73 (1974): 338–50.

Farley-Hills, David. *The Benevolence of Laughter: Comic Poetry of the Commonwealth and Restoration*. London: Macmillan, 1974.

———, ed. *Rochester: The Critical Heritage*. New York: Barnes & Noble, 1972.

———. *Rochester's Poetry*. London: Bell & Hyman, 1978.

Foucault, Michel. *Language, Counter-Memory, Practice: Selected Essays and Interviews*. Edited by D. F. Bouchard. Ithaca: Cornell University Press, 1977.

———. *Power/Knowledge: Selected Interviews and Other Writings 1972–1977*. Edited by C. Gordon. New York: Pantheon, 1977.

Foxon, David. *Libertine Literature in England, 1660–1745*. New Hyde, N.Y.: University Books, 1966.

Freire, Paulo. *Pedagogy of the Oppressed*. New York: Continuum, 1990.

Freire, Paulo, and Donald Macedo. *Literacy: Reading the Word and the World*. South Hadley, Mass.: Bergin & Garvey, 1987.

Fujimura, T. H. "Rochester's 'Satyr Against Mankind': An Analysis." *Studies in Philology* 55 (1958): 576–90.

Gill, James E. "The Fragmented Self in Three of Rochester's Poems." *Modern Language Quarterly* 49, no. 1 (March 1988): 19–37.

Goreau, Angeline. "'Last Night's Rambles': Restoration Literature and the

War Between the Sexes." In *The Sexual Dimension in Literature*, edited by A. Bold. London and Totowa, N.J.: Vision and Barnes & Noble, 1982.

Greenslade, Basil. "Affairs of State." In *Spirit of Wit: Reconsiderations of Rochester*, edited by J. Treglown. Oxford: Basil Blackwell, 1982.

Griffin, Dustin. "Rochester and the 'Holiday Writers.'" In *Rochester and Court Poetry*, edited by D. M. Vieth and D. Griffin. Los Angeles: William Andrews Clark Memorial Library, 1988.

———. *Satires Against Man: The Poems of Rochester*. Berkeley and Los Angeles: University of California Press, 1973.

Hammond, Paul. "Was Rochester an Artist?" *Cambridge Quarterly* 12 (1983): 56–66.

Highet, Gilbert. *The Anatomy of Satire*. Princeton: Princeton University Press, 1962.

Hill, Christopher. *The Collected Essays of Christopher Hill: Writing and Revolution in 17th Century England*. Vol. 1. Amherst: University of Massachusetts Press, 1985.

Holton, Robert. "Sexuality and Social Hierarchy in Sidney and Rochester." *Mosaic* 24, no. 1 (winter 1991): 47–65.

Horace. *Horace: Satires and Epistles. Persius: Satires*. Translated by N. Rudd. New York: Penguin, 1979.

Hume, David. *A Treatise of Human Nature*. Edited by L. A. Selby-Biggs. 2d ed. Oxford: Oxford University Press, 1978.

Hutton, Ronald. *Charles the Second: King of England, Scotland, and Ireland*. Oxford: Clarendon Press, 1989.

Johnson, J. W. "Did Lord Rochester Write *Sodom*?" *The Papers of the Bibliographical Society of America* 81 (June 1987): 119–53.

Juvenal. *Juvenal: The Sixteen Satires*. Translated by Peter Green. New York: Penguin, 1974.

Kernan, Alvin. *The Cankered Muse*. New Haven: Yale University Press, 1959.

Kroll, R. W. F. *The Material Word: Literate Culture in the Restoration and Early Eighteenth Century*. Baltimore and London: Johns Hopkins, 1991.

Lamb, Jeremy. *So Idle a Rogue: The Life and Death of Lord Rochester*. London: Allison & Busby, 1993.

Leibacher-Ouvrard, Lise. "Metaphore, Ideologie et Utopies Libertines au Temps de Louis XIV." *Papers on French Seventeenth Century Literature* 16, no. 31 (1989): 431–44.

———. "Sexe, Simulacre et 'Libertinage Honnete': La Satyre Sotadique (1658/1678) de Nicolas Chorier." *Romanic Review* 83, no. 3 (May 1992): 267–80.

Locke, John. *The Works of John Locke*. Vol. 2. London, 1823. Reprint, Darmstadt, Germany: Scientia Verlag Aalen, 1963.

Lord, George deF., ed. *Poems on Affairs of State: Augustan Satirical Verse, 1660–1714*. Vol. 1. New Haven and London: Yale University Press, 1963–1975.

Love, Harold. "Rochester and the Traditions of Satire." In *Restoration Literature: Critical Approaches*, edited by H. Love. London: Methuen, 1972.

Lyons, Paddy, ed. *Rochester: Complete Poems and Plays*. Everyman's Library. London and Rutland, Vt.: J. M. Dent and Charles E. Tuttle, 1993.

Marvell, Andrew. *The Poems and Letters of Andrew Marvell.* Edited by H. M. Margoliouth, revised by P. Legouis and E. E. Duncan-Jones. 3d ed. 2 vols. Oxford: Clarendon Press, 1971.

Mc Veagh, John. "Rochester and Defoe: A Study in Influence." *Studies in English Literature, 1500–1900* 14 (summer 1974): 327–41.

Nietzsche, Friedrich. "On Truth and Falsity in Their Ultramoral Sense." In *The Complete Works of Friedrich Nietzsche,* edited by O. Levy. Vol. 2. 1909–24. Reprint, New York: Russell & Russell, 1964.

Norris, Christopher. *Deconstruction: Theory and Practice.* London and New York: Methuen, 1982.

Nussbaum, Felicity. *The Brink of All We Hate: English Satires on Women, 1660–1750.* Lexington: University Press of Kentucky, 1984.

Ogg, David. *England in the Reign of Charles II.* 1934. Reprint, Oxford: Oxford University Press, 1984.

Oldham, John. *The Poems of John Oldham.* Edited by H. F. Brooks and R. Selden. Oxford: Clarendon Press, 1986.

O'Neill, J. H. "An Unpublished 'Imperfect Enjoyment' Poem." *Papers on Language and Literature* 13 (spring 1977): 197–202.

Pasch, Thomas. "Concentricity, Christian Myth, and the Self-Incriminating Narrator in Rochester's *A Ramble in St. James's Park.*" In *John Wilmot, Earl of Rochester: Critical Essays,* edited by D. M. Vieth. New York and London: Garland, 1988.

Paulson, K. F. "The Reverend Edward Stillingfleet and the 'Epilogue' to Rochester's *A Satyr against Reason and Mankind.*" *Philological Quarterly* 50 (1971): 657–63.

Pintard, René. *Le libertinage érudit dans la première moitié du XVIIe siècle.* Genève-Paris: Slatkine, 1983.

Pinto, Vivian De Sola. *Enthusiast in Wit: A Portrait of John Wilmot, Earl of Rochester 1647–1680.* Lincoln: University of Nebraska Press, 1962.

Porter, Hayward, trans. *The Satires of Boileau Despréaux.* Glasgow: James MacLehose and Sons, 1904.

Prinz, Johannes. *John Wilmot Earl of Rochester: His Life and Writings.* Leipzig: Mayer & Mueller, 1927.

Quaintance, R. E. "French Sources of the Restoration 'Imperfect Enjoyment' Poem." *Philological Quarterly* 42 (April 1963): 190–99.

Rawson, Claude. *Satire and Sentiment 1660–1830.* Cambridge: Cambridge University Press, 1994.

Raylor, Timothy. *Cavaliers, Clubs, and Literary Culture: Sir John Mennes, James Smith, and the Order of the Fancy.* Newark: University of Delaware Press; London and Toronto: Associated University Presses, 1994.

Righter, Anne. "John Wilmot, Earl of Rochester." In *John Wilmot, Earl of Rochester: Critical Essays,* edited by D. M. Vieth. New York and London: Garland, 1988.

Robinson, Ken. "Rochester and Semonides." *Notes and Queries* 224 (December 1979): 521–22.

Rogal, Samuel. "The Earl of Rochester: 'Why Am I No Poet of the Times?'" *College Language Association Journal* 32, no. 1 (1988): 91–102.

Rudd, Niall. "Dryden on Horace and Juvenal." *University of Toronto Quarterly* 32 (1963): 155–69.

Said, Edward W. *The World, the Text, and the Critic.* Cambridge: Harvard University Press, 1983.

Saussure, Ferdinand De. *Course in General Linguistics.* Edited by C. Bally et al. Translated by R. Harris. La Salle, Ill.: Open Court, 1986.

Savile, George (Marquess of Halifax). *Halifax: Complete Works.* Edited by J. P. Kenyon. Harmondsworth, England: Penguin, 1969.

Selden, Raman. *English Verse Satire 1590–1765.* London: Allen & Unwin, 1978.

Sitter, John. "Rochester's Reader and the Problem of Satiric Audience." *Papers on Language and Literature* 12 (1976): 285–98.

Soames, William, and John Dryden, trans. *The Art of Poetry, Written in* French *by The Sieur* de Boileau, *Made* English. London, 1683. Ms. Wood 320 (4). Bodleian Library, Oxford.

Spence, Joseph. *Observations, Anecdotes, and Characters of Books and Men Collected from Conversation.* Edited by J. M. Osborn. Vol. 1. Oxford: Clarendon Press, 1966.

Spingarn, J. E., ed. *Critical Essays of the Seventeenth Century.* Vol. 2. Oxford: Clarendon Press, 1908–9.

Spink, J. S. *French Free Thought from Gassendi to Voltaire.* London: Athlone, 1960.

Thormählen, Marianne. *Rochester: The Poems in Context.* Cambridge: Cambridge University Press, 1993.

Treglown, Jeremy, ed. *The Letters of John Wilmot, Earl of Rochester.* Oxford: Basil Blackwell, 1980.

Trotter, David. "Wanton Expressions." In *Spirit of Wit: Reconsiderations of Rochester,* edited by J. Treglown. Oxford: Basil Blackwell, 1982.

Turner, James G. "The Properties of Libertinism." *Eighteenth Century Life* 9, no. 3 (May 1985): 75–87.

Underwood, Dale. *Etherege and the Seventeenth-Century Comedy of Manners.* New Haven: Yale University Press, 1957.

Vieth, D. M. *Attribution in Restoration Poetry: A Study of Rochester's* Poems *of 1680.* New Haven and London: Yale University Press, 1963.

———, ed. *The Complete Poems of John Wilmot, Earl of Rochester.* New Haven and London: Yale University Press, 1968.

———. "Towards an Anti-Aristotelian Poetic: Rochester's *Satyr Against Mankind* and *Artemisia to Chloe,* With Notes on Swift's *Tale of a Tub* and *Gulliver's Travels." Language and Style* 5 (1972): 123–45.

Walker, Keith, ed. *The Poems of John Wilmot Earl of Rochester.* Oxford: Oxford University Press, 1984.

Weber, Harold. "Carolinean Sexuality and the Restoration Stage: Reconstructing the Royal Phallus in *Sodom.*" In *Cultural Readings of Restoration and Eighteenth-Century English Theater,* edited by J. D. Canfield and D. C. Payne. Athens and London: University of Georgia Press, 1995.

Weinbrot, Howard D. *Alexander Pope and the Traditions of Formal Verse Satire.* Princeton: Princeton University Press, 1982.

————. *Eighteenth-Century Satire: Essays on Text and Context from Dryden to Peter Pindar*. Cambridge: Cambridge University Press, 1988.

————. "The Swelling Volume: The Apocalyptic Satire of Rochester's *Letter From Artemisia In The Town To Chloe In The Country*." *Studies in the Literary Imagination* 5, no. 2 (October 1972): 19–37.

Wilcoxon, Reba. "Mirrors of Men's Fears: The Court Satires on Women." *Restoration* 3 (fall 1979): 45–51.

————. "Rochester's Sexual Politics." In *John Wilmot, Earl of Rochester: Critical Essays*, edited by D. M. Vieth. New York and London: Garland, 1988.

Wilson, J. H. *The Court Wits of the Restoration: An Introduction*. Princeton: Princeton University Press, 1948.

————. "Satiric Elements in Rochester's *Valentinian*." *Philological Quarterly* 16 (January 1937): 41–48.

Wintle, Sarah. "Libertinism and Sexual Politics." In *Spirit of Wit: Reconsiderations of Rochester*, edited by J. Treglown. Oxford: Basil Blackwell, 1982.

Wolfe, Naomi. *The Beauty Myth: How Images of Beauty Are Used Against Women*. New York: Doubleday, 1991.

Zwicker, Steven N. *Lines of Authority: Politics and English Literary Culture, 1649–1689*. Ithaca and London: Cornell University Press, 1993.

Index